Name: _____

Address: _____

Email: _____

Phone: _____

LOG PERIOD   START: _____   END: _____

TRAINING

for

MORTALS

A RUNNER'S

LOGBOOK

AND

SOURCE OF

INSPIRATION

John "The Penguin" Bingham

and

Coach Jenny Hadfield

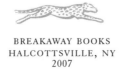

BREAKAWAY BOOKS
HALCOTTSVILLE, NY
2007

Training for Mortals: A Runner's Logbook and Source of Inspiration
Copyright 2007 by John Bingham and Jenny Hadfield

Photos courtesy of Getty Images and Runphoto.com

ISBN: 978-1-891369-69-8
Library of Congress Control Number: 2007922681

Published by:
Breakaway Books
P.O. Box 24
Halcottsville, NY 12438
www.breakawaybooks.com

Visit the Penguin's website:
www.johnbingham.com

Visit Jenny Hadfield's sites:
wwwjennyhadfield.com
www.ChicagoEnduranceSports.com

INTRODUCTION

Training for Mortals is a must-have in the complete runner's library and the perfect companion to every runner's training schedule. Just like their bestselling book *Marathoning for Mortals* and *Running for Mortals, Training for Mortals* combines John Bingham's trademark humor and motivation with Coach Jenny Hadfield's detailed training advice and common-sense training tips. This inspirational husband-and-wife team can help you achieve your goals. This logbook is dedicated to athletes of all ages, shapes, and sizes who have taken on the challenge of changing their lives with their own two feet.

Training for Mortals contains detailed log entry pages, monthly essays from John Bingham's classic "Penguin Chronicles" column in *Runner's World,* and new words of wisdom from John and Coach Jenny Hadfield. Together they give tips to instruct and inspire runners every day.

This logbook is written by you, for you, and is ultimately your own book about you. With each entry you are writing your own athletic biography.

The log helps you track your progress, exercise sessions and food choices. It is a comprehensive tool that guides you in establishing realistic goals, planning and tracking your training and celebrating your progress. Week by week, the log will motivate you to get in your workouts, encourage smart training and guide you to make healthier food choices.

Training for Mortals also includes a special place to **record your race experiences,** a **Pace Chart** to check your pace and a way to monitor your intensity with the **i-Rate**™ system.

The i-Rate™ scale helps you rank the effort of each of your workouts. The goal of the i-Rate™ scale is to help you learn to discriminate among your daily workouts. We've given you some general guidelines to help get you started, but in time you will develop your own, highly personal, i-Rate™ scale.

Keeping a log is very personal. There are plenty of places to **track lots of information about your training and fuel.** The key is to record the information you think is important. The best way to improve your training is to monitor your progress and plan realistic workouts and goals. A well-documented log will keep you honest and allow you keep checks and balances of your fitness and fuel activity.

Training for Mortals guides you in monitoring **distance, time, heart rate, and perceived exertion, weight, sleep hours, weather and mood.** All of these have a direct role in helping or hurting your performance. Keeping track of this information will motivate you to modify behaviors and notice trends. More importantly, logging will guide you to making healthy choices and optimal training and racing strategies.

There is room to plan your daily workouts with **"Today's Goal"** and maintain focus on short-term goals with the **"Goals for the Week"** section.

To you, the reader, welcome. We're glad you're here, and whatever your starting date is, and what ever your athletic goals are, we hope that the next twelve months are the most exciting, satisfying, and productive year you've ever had.

—John "The Penguin" Bingham and Coach Jenny Hadfield

NOTE: This log book is undated, so you can use it in any year. You can start anytime and anywhere you like. Following each of the essays are four weeks, each spanning a Monday to a Sunday, of log pages. To catch up periodically with the real-world calendar, after every third month we throw in a fifth week (and a bonus *six* weeks after the last essay) so you have a total of fifty-three weeks for the year.

WHY KEEP TRACK?

Monitoring your workouts provides a great source of motivation. It feels rewarding to log your activity after a workout especially after major accomplishments like races, personal records or new distances. It is a place to keep a personal journal of your activity. A safe place to celebrate YOU!

HOW TO USE THE LOG

Training for Mortals is easy to use. In just a few steps you will be on your way to planning and tracking your journey.

1. Just in case, complete the personal information and date in the front of the log.

2. Familiarize yourself with the entire log. There is lots of motivational and useful information like the Pace Chart, a place to set short and long term goals and a place to keep track of your races! Check it out and use it as a training tool.

3. Open to the first week and notice the information that can be tracked. Begin to complete the information that is important to you.

4. Keep track of mileage totals for the week and year-to-date. Be cautious to train smart. It can be tempting to fill the log and make it look impressive. Stick to a realistic and smart training regimen.

BEFORE YOU BEGIN TO TRAIN

Regardless of the shape you're in before you start an exercise regimen it is advisable to note advice from the American College of Sports Medicine:

At or above the age of 35 years of age, it is necessary for individuals to have a medical examination and a maximal exercise test before beginning a vigorous exercise program.

At any age, the information gathered from an exercise test may be useful to establish an effective and safe exercise prescription. Maximal testing done for men at age 40 or above or women age 50 or older, even when no symptoms or risk factors are present, should be performed with physician supervision.

WHY DO I NEED TO MONITOR INTENSITY?

There is one rule that applies to all athletes of all levels at all times. Simply put: EFFORT IS EQUAL, PACE IS PERSONAL. What that means is that at a given level of effort, whatever that is, your pace, my pace, and the pace of a world-class athlete will be different. You'd think that this would be easy to grasp, but it is one of the *most* misunderstood aspects of training. You don't go faster by just trying harder. You get faster by training your body to move faster at the same level of effort. This is true for you, the elite athlete, and me.

Learning to measure your level of effort is key to short term and long-term improvement. If you don't find a way to know how hard your working at a given pace, you'll never be able to tell if your training is doing you any good. There are two ways to measure effort. The most precise is by wearing a heart rate monitor. These monitors will provide instant and accurate feedback and are invaluable if you understand how to use them and what the data means. The second way is to monitor your perceived effort, or what we call the i-Rate Scale™.

Using the i-Rate Scale™ is easy to learn and it guides you in learning how to listen to your body. Familiarize yourself with the 1-10 scale. Then assign a numeric value or adjective that best defines what it feels like during your workouts.

Listen to your breathing: are you gasping for air? If so, you would label that a 10 on the i-Rate Scale™, and would want to slow down. Are you able to sing a song? Then you might label this a 3-4 and may need to pick it up a little. Use the "talk test" as a guide. If you can hold a conversation you are in the "aerobic" (with oxygen) zone between 5-7. If you are unable to talk you are most likely at or beyond your anaerobic (without oxygen) threshold and in the 8-9 zone. If you are ready to just slug anybody that says anything to you this is the "bite me" zone or otherwise known as a 10 on the i-Rate Scale™.

Focus on how your body feels and how hard or easy you are working.

Use the i-Rate™ for every workout. Learn to feel your effort. Even if you have no idea at first, write something down. Make a guess if you have to. But monitor your effort. In time, you'll get better.

i-RATE™ SCALE

0 At rest.
1
2 Very, very, easy. Almost moving backwards.
3
4 Easy effort. Can sing the entire "Star Spangled Banner."
5
6 Moderate effort. Can Sing "Row, Row, Row Your Boat" but with breaths in between.
7
8 Comfortably hard effort.
9
10 Very, very heavy. Almost maximum effort

The key to maintaining an active and healthy lifestyle involves both exercise and nutrition. If one or both are out of balance, your wheel won't roll efficiently. For this reason is the Fuel Log was incorporated. It provides a guide for eating a well balanced diet and monitoring daily food choices.

On a daily basis, simply check off servings of water, veggies, fruits, grains and protein. It subtly reminds you to limit your intake of fat, empty carbohydrates and alcohol. Use the Fuel Log to balance your diet, lose weight or improve your performance by including high nutrient foods.

WHAT IS A SERVING SIZE?

Water: 8 ounces Recommended Daily Servings: 6-8

Fruits: Recommended Daily Servings: 2-4
Serving is 1 medium apple, orange, or banana. 3/4 cup juice: 1/2 cup diced fruit, 1/4 cup dried fruit.

Veggies: Recommended Daily Servings: 3-5
1 cup raw, leafy vegetables; 1/2 cup chopped raw or cooked veggies; or 3/4 cup vegetable juice

Whole Grains: Recommended Daily Servings: 6-11
1 slice bread; 1/2 bun;bagel or English muffin; 1 ounce dry ready to eat cereal; 1/2 cup cooked cereal, rice or pasta.

Protein: Recommended Daily Servings: 6 oz.
Cooked lean beef, pork, lamb, veal, poultry or fish the size of deck of cards; 1/2 cup cooked beans, 1 egg, 2 tbs. peanut butter, 4 ounces tofu (2 ounces extra firm) 1/4cup nuts or seeds = 1 ounce of meat.

Limit your consumption of high fat foods and "empty" carbohydrates like fries, chips and pie. The nutrient value is very low and the caloric value very high. Fatty foods dramatically increase your calorie intake with very little quantity of food. You are paying for a Cadillac but driving a Pinto. Fill up on high quality foods like fruits, veggies and lean meats.

Limit your consumption of alcoholic beverages. This is an easy way to reduce your caloric intake during the week. Alcohol provides *no* nutrient value and it helps you keep those extra pounds you want to lose. Often tracking your intake will allow you to look at how much and how often you are consuming. From there you can modify your consumption and track your results.

WHERE DO YOU SEE YOURSELF ONE YEAR FROM NOW?

Setting realistic goals is the foundation of a healthy and successful exercise program. Whether you are training to complete and marathon or aiming for a regular exercise regimen the first step is to develop your game plan. Focus on what you want long term, one or more years from now. And then work back and set several short-term goals to get you there. Setting shorter, more digestible goals gives your program focus, purpose and reward.

Set them so you can reach them, that is, realistic for where you are now and where you can go. If you are a new runner or walker and want to compete in a race, the race is the long-term goal while getting in twelve workouts in one month is a short-term goal. If you are trying to improve your performance in a marathon, the marathon is the long-term goal, while completing several "practice" races along the way is a good short-term goal strategy. Goals are important, they will guide and motivate your journey and make it meaningful.

Think about what you want to achieve. It doesn't have to be going to the moon. It could be as simple as getting in shape. But define the goal and be specific so you can qualify it and know if you are there. (i.e. To get in shape by the end of the year and complete my first half marathon.) Here's a sample:

My Long Term Plan (goals):
1) Run-walk the Chicago Distance Classic 20K on August 3.
2) Lose 20 pounds slowly and healthfully by monitoring my food choices, eating balanced meals and controlling portions.

How I am going to get there — Short-term goals:
1) Develop a buddy system with John and train three times per week.
2) Sign up for and participate in the Shamrock Shuffle 8K March 23.
3) Monitor and track my fuel choices every day. One day at a time I will consume the minimum recommended servings of water, fruits, and veggies.
4) I will limit my sweets or sugar consumption to three treats per week.
5) I will not eat after 8 P.M. every night.

PLAN YOUR PATH TO REACHING YOUR LONG-TERM GOALS:

_____

_____

_____

_____

_____

_____

_____

How will you get there? Write down a few specific checkpoints (short-term goals) to reach along the way.

_____

_____

_____

_____

_____

_____

_____

_____

_____

NOTES TO MYSELF

THIS IS A GREAT PLACE TO WRITE DOWN NOTES ON
TRAINING, RACING, AND LIVING.

TOP TEN TIPS

1. Size matters, at least when in comes to shoes.
I'd worn size 8 1/2 shoes since I was 17 years old. So at age
42, when I went to buy my first pair of running shoes, I
bought—you guessed it—size 8 1/2. I didn't even bother to
try them on, I was so sure they would fit. And they did fit.
Sorta. I thought that running shoes should hug my feet,
make my toes feel "snug," and be laced up so tight that they
nearly cut off my circulation. I didn't lose all of my toenails
before I figured it out, but almost. **Buy shoes that fit, without even looking at the size on the manufacturer's
label.**

2. Clothes make the man.
I thought that I could just dig out some of my old T-shirts
and sweatpants and start running. I thought that all the
technical "stuff" that real runners wear was only for the fast
runners. I was wrong. The reason why those runners wear
technical clothing is the same reason that I finally did.
Performance. Fabrics that wick moisture are cooler in the
summer and warmer in the winter. **You don't have to carry
the weight of your own perspiration on your favorite
cotton T-shirt anymore.**

3. Three steps forward, two steps back.
I thought that I would continue to get better and better. I
thought my progress would be linear. For a while, it worked
that way, although considering where I started that should-
n't be a surprise. For several months I got faster with nearly every run. Then the progress suddenly stopped. **Long
term improvement is a constant cycle of getting faster,
hitting a plateau, slipping backwards, regrouping, and
then getting faster again.**

4. Talk is cheap.

When I first started, I spent more time planning my runs than actually running. I also spent a lot of time talking about running, and not nearly enough time running. I thought that knowing about running was the same as being able to run. I thought that being able to using a phrase like anaerobic threshold in a sentence was as good as experiencing it. **Once you start training more and talking less, your running improves.**

5. Garbage in, garbage out.

I had no idea how food worked once it was inside my body. I understood how it made me feel when I ate it, but knew nothing about how food functions. I didn't understand the correlation between what I was asking my body to process and what I was asking my body to perform. As I began to view food as fuel rather than as comfort or recreation, I discovered that the foods I wanted and the foods I needed were almost always the same. **That doesn't mean you can't give in to an occasional craving, but don't ignore the effect that food has on your performance.**

6. Sometimes, less is more.

I never considered myself the sharpest knife in the drawer. I knew there were people smarter, better educated, and more talented that I in my profession. But I also knew that I had the capacity to outwork anybody I had ever met. I took that attitude into my running. When I read that one day of speed work was good, I thought that three days would be better. If everyone else increased their mileage by 10% per week, then I'd increase mine by 20%. **Improvement comes at the point of balance between effort and recovery.**

7. There are no secrets.

I was sure that there were hidden 'truths' about running that would make me faster sooner. I read everything I could find, trying to uncover those hidden truths. After a while I discovered that most of what I needed to learn I was going to have to find out on my own, with my own two feet. Training for a long distance race is sometimes a frustrating process of trial and error. **If there are any secrets, you are going to have to find them on the roads, not in books.**

8. My body, my self.

In the early stages I waited for the magic transformation of my body into the body of a runner. I expected my legs to get longer and leaner, my muscles to become tight and sinewy, and all my joints to work exactly like they were supposed to. There may be less of it now, but it is still basically the same body I had when I started running. **It turns out that you have to learn how to train with the body you have.**

9. Being a runner is a process, not a destination.

I was convinced that I could get into shape and stay there. I thought that once I had achieved a certain speed or distance, I could relax and enjoy the view. But, there is always something new to learn, some new distance to try, or some new pace to struggle toward. **Running is a constant process of assessing and evaluating where you've been, where you are, and where you want to be.**

10. Races are celebrations.

I've always been a big motorsports fan. I've attended hundreds of races. They were battlegrounds. But runners are different. Once I overcame my fear, I raced nearly every weekend. I couldn't wait to line up with friends and find out what their best was on that day, and to show them MY best at the same time. **Despite the competition between individuals, there is still an overwhelming sense of shared achievement at races.**

RACE CELEBRATION!

Make memories. Whether you reach your goal or come in a little short, there is always something to learn from every experience. Use these pages to log your race progress. Some day you'll look back at your log, realize your accomplishments, and revel in just how far you've come.

Race or event: _____
Date:_____
Notes:_____
_____
_____

Race or event: _____
Date:_____
Notes:_____
_____
_____

Race or event: _____
Date:_____
Notes:_____
_____
_____

Race or event: _____
Date:_____
Notes:_____
_____
_____

Race or event: _____

Date:_____

Notes:_____

_____

_____

Race or event: _____

Date:_____

Notes:_____

_____

_____

Race or event: _____

Date:_____

Notes:_____

_____

_____

Race or event: _____

Date:_____

Notes:_____

_____

_____

Race or event: _____

Date:_____

Notes:_____

_____

_____

Race or event: _____

Date:_____

Notes:_____

_____

_____

Race or event: _____
Date:_____
Notes:_____
_____
_____

Race or event: _____
Date:_____
Notes:_____
_____
_____

Race or event: _____
Date:_____
Notes:_____
_____
_____

Race or event: _____
Date:_____
Notes:_____
_____
_____

Race or event: _____
Date:_____
Notes:_____
_____
_____

Race or event: _____
Date:_____
Notes:_____
_____
_____

PACE CHART

PACE (minutes per mile)	5K (3.107 miles)	5 Miles	10K (6.214 miles)	10 Miles	1/2 Marathon (13.109 miles)	15 Miles	20 Miles	Marathon (26.219 miles)
6:00	18:39	30:00	37:17	1:00:00	1:18:39	1:30:00	2:00:00	2:37:19
6:30	20:12	32:30	40:23	1:05:00	1:25:13	1:37:30	2:10:00	2:50:25
7:00	21:45	35:00	43:30	1:10:00	1:31:46	1:45:00	2:20:00	3:03:32
7:30	23:18	37:30	46:36	1:15:00	1:38:19	1:52:30	2:30:00	3:16:39
8:00	24:51	40:00	49:43	1:20:00	1:44:52	2:00:00	2:40:00	3:29:45
8:30	26:25	42:30	52:49	1:25:00	1:51:26	2:07:30	2:50:00	3:42:52
9:00	27:58	45:00	55:56	1:30:00	1:57:59	2:15:00	3:00:00	3:55:58
9:30	29:31	47:30	59:02	1:35:00	2:04:32	2:22:30	3:10:00	4:09:05
10:00	31:04	50:00	1:02:08	1:40:00	2:11:05	2:30:00	3:20:00	4:22:11
10:30	32:37	52:30	1:05:15	1:45:00	2:17:39	2:37:30	3:30:00	4:35:18
11:00	34:11	55:00	1:08:21	1:50:00	2:24:12	2:45:00	3:40:00	4:48:25
11:30	35:44	57:30	1:11:28	1:55:00	2:30:45	2:52:30	3:50:00	5:01:31
12:00	37:17	1:00:00	1:14:34	2:00:00	2:37:18	3:00:00	4:00:00	5:15:37
12:30	38:50	1:02:30	1:17:41	2:05:00	2:43:52	3:07:30	4:10:00	5:27:44
13:00	40:23	1:05:00	1:20:47	2:10:00	2:50:25	3:15:00	4:20:00	5:40:51
13:30	41:57	1:07:30	1:23:53	2:15:00	2:56:58	3:22:30	4:30:00	5:53:57
14:00	43:30	1:10:00	1:27:00	2:20:00	3:03:32	3:30:00	4:40:00	6:07:04
14:30	45:03	1:12:30	1:30:06	2:25:00	3:10:05	3:37:30	4:50:00	6:20:10
15:00	46:36	1:15:00	1:33:13	2:30:00	3:16:38	3:45:00	5:00:00	6:33:17
15:30	48:09	1:17:30	1:36:18	2:35:00	3:23:03	3:52:30	5:10:00	6:46:24
16:00	49:43	1:20:00	1:39:26	2:40:00	3:29:45	4:00:00	5:20:00	6:59:31
16:30	51:16	1:22:30	1:42:33	2:45:00	3:36:18	4:07:30	5:30:00	7:12:38
17:00	52:50	1:25:00	1:45:39	2:50:00	3:42:52	4:15:00	5:40:00	7:25:44
17:30	54:23	1:27:30	1:48:46	2:55:00	3:49:25	4:22:30	5:50:00	7:38:51
18:00	55:56	1:30:00	1:51:52	3:00:00	3:55:58	4:30:00	6:00:00	7:51:57
18:30	57:29	1:32:30	1:54:59	3:05:00	4:02:32	4:37:30	6:10:00	8:05:03
19:00	59:03	1:35:00	1:58:05	3:10:00	4:09:05	4:45:00	6:20:00	8:18:10
19:30	1:00:36	1:37:30	2:01:12	3:15:00	4:15:38	4:52:30	6:30:00	8:31:16
20:00	1:02:09	1:40:00	2:04:18	3:20:00	4:22:11	5:00:00	6:40:00	8:44:23

ARE WE THERE YET?

I've always liked traveling by car. And, I've always subjected my family to my terminal wanderlust. On many occasions my then young son would moan from the back seat, "Are we there yet?"

My response was always. "Yep, we're here." He would sit up eagerly and look out the window. Then, in a disappointed voice, he would say, "Aw, Pop, this isn't where we're going," to which I would reply, "But this is where we are!" He was not a happy traveler.

Every time I started a journey of fitness and better health, including the "diet du jour," the first thing I did was choose a destination. I'd decide that when I had lost ten or twenty pounds (or eventually fifty or sixty), I'd be thin. So every day I'd stand at the scale and ask myself if I was there yet. Of course, the answer was always no.

Oh, I'd get closer; for a day or two. I'd lose a few pounds, put a couple back on, then loose a few more. I'd get stuck in a cycle of three steps forward, two steps back. Each time I went back, it was harder to move forward.

When I found running, I decided that when I could run three miles I'd be a runner. I was convinced that three miles was as far as any rational person would want to run. Most days, I *still* think it's as far as any rational person wants to run.

So I'd run, and not make it to three miles. Day after day I failed to reach my arbitrary destination. Day after day I accumulated evidence that I was *not* a runner. Every run convinced me that I was not a runner. I wasn't there yet.

What I didn't know then about running was what I *did* know about traveling. Postponing the joy of the journey until you reach your destination is the *worst* possible plan. Waiting to celebrate until you've gotten to where you want to go means missing all the wonderful places you pass along the way.

In my ignorance and enthusiasm to reach my running goals, I took every possible shortcut. I was sure there was a magic carpet that would transport me to my destination. It never occurred to me that I'd have to get there one step at a time.

Every new runner knows the game I played. If running three days a week is good, running six days a week must be *twice* as good. If running fast one day a week improves your running efficiency, running fast *every* day must be better still. When such ignorance collides with enthusiasm, the result is almost always injury.

The truth didn't reveal itself to me the first time I was injured. Probably not the second or third time either. But eventually, as weeks of recovery replaced weeks of training, I began to understand. Every run is a gift. Every run is a chance to be where you want to be.

With that one thought, my running changed. I stopped deferring the joy I was feeling. I stopped accumulating days of failure. I started looking at each run, at each time I moved my body, as an opportunity to learn, to see and experience what was in front of me at that moment.

The results of that change are not merely philosophical, but practical as well. Recently, while traveling, I found myself running in Burlington, Colorado. It was Wednesday morning, the day I normally do some faster interval work.

But on this Wednesday I found myself in the middle of acres and acres of sunflowers, neck-deep in a sea of yellow in the bright morning sun. I knew the speed work would have to wait. On this day, my gift to myself was to run surrounded by thousands of smiling yellow faces.

I'm still not there yet. I know that. On the days when I struggle to find a pace or a distance that suits me, I know that I'm not there yet. But I am where I am. And I can tell you that it's better than anywhere else I've ever been.

Waddle on, friends.

MONDAY / Date:

Today's goal:

Training notes:

FUEL LOG

WATER: 6-8 x 8 OZ.	FRUITS: 2-4	VEGGIES: 3-5	WHOLE GRAIN SERVINGS: 6-11	PROTEIN: 4-6 OZ.	LIMIT FAT?	ALCOHOLIC BEVERAGES?	LIMIT "EMPTY" CARBS?
☐☐☐☐ ☐☐☐☐	☐☐ ☐☐	☐☐ ☐☐	☐☐☐ ☐☐☐ ☐☐	☐☐☐ ☐☐☐	Y N	Y N	Y N

WEATHER: SUN WIND RAIN CLOUDY SNOW TEMP:_____

Distance:
Time:
Heart Rate:
i-Rate (1-10)
X-Training:
Sleep Hours:
Weight:
Mood: ☺ 😐 ☹ Other

TUESDAY / Date:

Today's goal:

Training notes:

FUEL LOG

WATER: 6-8 x 8 OZ.	FRUITS: 2-4	VEGGIES: 3-5	WHOLE GRAIN SERVINGS: 6-11	PROTEIN: 4-6 OZ.	LIMIT FAT?	ALCOHOLIC BEVERAGES?	LIMIT "EMPTY" CARBS?
☐☐☐☐ ☐☐☐☐	☐☐ ☐☐	☐☐ ☐☐	☐☐☐ ☐☐☐ ☐☐	☐☐☐ ☐☐☐	Y N	Y N	Y N

WEATHER: SUN WIND RAIN CLOUDY SNOW TEMP:_____

Distance:
Time:
Heart Rate:
i-Rate (1-10)
X-Training:
Sleep Hours:
Weight:
Mood: ☺ 😐 ☹ Other

WEDNESDAY / Date:

Today's goal:

Training notes:

FUEL LOG

WATER: 6-8 x 8 OZ.	FRUITS: 2-4	VEGGIES: 3-5	WHOLE GRAIN SERVINGS: 6-11	PROTEIN: 4-6 OZ.	LIMIT FAT?	ALCOHOLIC BEVERAGES?	LIMIT "EMPTY" CARBS?
☐☐☐☐ ☐☐☐☐	☐☐ ☐☐	☐☐ ☐☐	☐☐☐ ☐☐☐ ☐☐	☐☐☐ ☐☐☐	Y N	Y N	Y N

WEATHER: SUN WIND RAIN CLOUDY SNOW TEMP:_____

Distance:
Time:
Heart Rate:
i-Rate (1-10)
X-Training:
Sleep Hours:
Weight:
Mood: ☺ 😐 ☹ Other

THURSDAY / Date:

Today's goal:

Training notes:

FUEL LOG

WATER: 6-8 x 8 OZ.	FRUITS: 2-4	VEGGIES: 3-5	WHOLE GRAIN SERVINGS: 6-11	PROTEIN: 4-6 OZ.	LIMIT FAT?	ALCOHOLIC BEVERAGES?	LIMIT "EMPTY" CARBS?
☐☐☐☐ ☐☐☐☐	☐☐ ☐☐	☐☐ ☐☐	☐☐☐ ☐☐☐ ☐☐	☐☐☐ ☐☐☐	Y N	Y N	Y N

WEATHER: SUN WIND RAIN CLOUDY SNOW TEMP:_____

Distance:
Time:
Heart Rate:
i-Rate (1-10)
X-Training:
Sleep Hours:
Weight:
Mood: ☺ 😐 ☹ Other

FRIDAY / Date:

Training notes: _____

Today's goal: _____

FUEL LOG

WATER: 6-8 x 8 OZ.	FRUITS: 2-4	VEGGIES: 3-5	WHOLE GRAIN SERVINGS: 6-11	PROTEIN: 4-6 OZ.	LIMIT FAT?	ALCOHOLIC BEVERAGES?	LIMIT "EMPTY" CARBS?
☐☐☐☐ ☐☐☐☐	☐☐ ☐☐	☐☐ ☐☐	☐☐☐☐☐ ☐☐☐☐☐	☐☐☐ ☐☐☐	Y N	Y N	Y N

WEATHER: SUN WIND RAIN CLOUDY SNOW TEMP: ____

Distance:
Time:
Heart Rate:
i-Rate (1-10)
X-Training:
Sleep Hours:
Weight:
Mood: ☺ ☺ ☹ Other

SATURDAY / Date:

Training notes: _____

Today's goal: _____

FUEL LOG

WATER: 6-8 x 8 OZ.	FRUITS: 2-4	VEGGIES: 3-5	WHOLE GRAIN SERVINGS: 6-11	PROTEIN: 4-6 OZ.	LIMIT FAT?	ALCOHOLIC BEVERAGES?	LIMIT "EMPTY" CARBS?
☐☐☐☐ ☐☐☐☐	☐☐ ☐☐	☐☐ ☐☐	☐☐☐☐☐ ☐☐☐☐☐	☐☐☐ ☐☐☐	Y N	Y N	Y N

WEATHER: SUN WIND RAIN CLOUDY SNOW TEMP: ____

Distance:
Time:
Heart Rate:
i-Rate (1-10)
X-Training:
Sleep Hours:
Weight:
Mood: ☺ ☺ ☹ Other

SUNDAY / Date:

Training notes: _____

Today's goal: _____

FUEL LOG

WATER: 6-8 x 8 OZ.	FRUITS: 2-4	VEGGIES: 3-5	WHOLE GRAIN SERVINGS: 6-11	PROTEIN: 4-6 OZ.	LIMIT FAT?	ALCOHOLIC BEVERAGES?	LIMIT "EMPTY" CARBS?
☐☐☐☐ ☐☐☐☐	☐☐ ☐☐	☐☐ ☐☐	☐☐☐☐☐ ☐☐☐☐☐	☐☐☐ ☐☐☐	Y N	Y N	Y N

WEATHER: SUN WIND RAIN CLOUDY SNOW TEMP: ____

Distance:
Time:
Heart Rate:
i-Rate (1-10)
X-Training:
Sleep Hours:
Weight:
Mood: ☺ ☺ ☹ Other

WEEK OF:

GOALS FOR WEEK:

WEEKLY TOTAL: _____

YEAR-TO-DATE TOTAL:

If the benefits of exercise could be put into a pill, it would be the most prescribed medication of all time.

MONDAY / Date:

Training notes:

Today's goal:

FUEL LOG

WATER: 6-8 x 8 OZ.	FRUITS: 2-4	VEGGIES: 3-5	WHOLE GRAIN SERVINGS: 6-11	PROTEIN: 4-6 OZ.	LIMIT FAT?	ALCOHOLIC BEVERAGES?	LIMIT "EMPTY" CARBS?
☐☐☐☐ ☐☐☐☐	☐☐ ☐☐	☐☐☐ ☐☐	☐☐☐☐☐ ☐	☐☐☐ ☐☐☐	Y N	Y N	Y N

WEATHER: SUN WIND RAIN CLOUDY SNOW
TEMP:____

Distance:
Time:
Heart Rate:
i-Rate (1-10)
X-Training:
Sleep Hours:
Weight:
Mood: ☺ ☺ ☹ Other

TUESDAY / Date:

Training notes:

Today's goal:

FUEL LOG

WATER: 6-8 x 8 OZ.	FRUITS: 2-4	VEGGIES: 3-5	WHOLE GRAIN SERVINGS: 6-11	PROTEIN: 4-6 OZ.	LIMIT FAT?	ALCOHOLIC BEVERAGES?	LIMIT "EMPTY" CARBS?
☐☐☐☐ ☐☐☐☐	☐☐ ☐☐	☐☐☐ ☐☐	☐☐☐☐☐ ☐	☐☐☐ ☐☐☐	Y N	Y N	Y N

WEATHER: SUN WIND RAIN CLOUDY SNOW
TEMP:____

Distance:
Time:
Heart Rate:
i-Rate (1-10)
X-Training:
Sleep Hours:
Weight:
Mood: ☺ ☺ ☹ Other

WEDNESDAY / Date:

Training notes:

Today's goal:

FUEL LOG

WATER: 6-8 x 8 OZ.	FRUITS: 2-4	VEGGIES: 3-5	WHOLE GRAIN SERVINGS: 6-11	PROTEIN: 4-6 OZ.	LIMIT FAT?	ALCOHOLIC BEVERAGES?	LIMIT "EMPTY" CARBS?
☐☐☐☐ ☐☐☐☐	☐☐ ☐☐	☐☐☐ ☐☐	☐☐☐☐☐ ☐	☐☐☐ ☐☐☐	Y N	Y N	Y N

WEATHER: SUN WIND RAIN CLOUDY SNOW
TEMP:____

Distance:
Time:
Heart Rate:
i-Rate (1-10)
X-Training:
Sleep Hours:
Weight:
Mood: ☺ ☺ ☹ Other

THURSDAY / Date:

Training notes:

Today's goal:

FUEL LOG

WATER: 6-8 x 8 OZ.	FRUITS: 2-4	VEGGIES: 3-5	WHOLE GRAIN SERVINGS: 6-11	PROTEIN: 4-6 OZ.	LIMIT FAT?	ALCOHOLIC BEVERAGES?	LIMIT "EMPTY" CARBS?
☐☐☐☐ ☐☐☐☐	☐☐ ☐☐	☐☐☐ ☐☐	☐☐☐☐☐ ☐	☐☐☐ ☐☐☐	Y N	Y N	Y N

WEATHER: SUN WIND RAIN CLOUDY SNOW
TEMP:____

Distance:
Time:
Heart Rate:
i-Rate (1-10)
X-Training:
Sleep Hours:
Weight:
Mood: ☺ ☺ ☹ Other

FRIDAY / Date:

Training notes: _____

Today's goal: _____

| Distance: |
| Time: |
| Heart Rate: |
| i-Rate (1-10) |
| X-Training: |
| Sleep Hours: |
| Weight: |
| Mood: ☺ ☺ ☹ Other |

WEATHER: SUN   WIND   RAIN   CLOUDY   SNOW   TEMP: _____

FUEL LOG

WATER: 6-8 x 8 OZ.	FRUITS: 2-4	VEGGIES: 3-5	WHOLE GRAIN SERVINGS: 6-11	PROTEIN: 4-6 OZ.	LIMIT FAT?	ALCOHOLIC BEVERAGES?	LIMIT "EMPTY" CARBS?
☐☐☐☐ ☐☐☐☐	☐☐ ☐☐	☐☐ ☐☐	☐☐☐☐☐ ☐☐☐☐	☐☐☐ ☐☐☐	Y N	Y N	Y N

SATURDAY / Date:

Training notes: _____

Today's goal: _____

| Distance: |
| Time: |
| Heart Rate: |
| i-Rate (1-10) |
| X-Training: |
| Sleep Hours: |
| Weight: |
| Mood: ☺ ☺ ☹ Other |

WEATHER: SUN   WIND   RAIN   CLOUDY   SNOW   TEMP: _____

FUEL LOG

WATER: 6-8 x 8 OZ.	FRUITS: 2-4	VEGGIES: 3-5	WHOLE GRAIN SERVINGS: 6-11	PROTEIN: 4-6 OZ.	LIMIT FAT?	ALCOHOLIC BEVERAGES?	LIMIT "EMPTY" CARBS?
☐☐☐☐ ☐☐☐☐	☐☐ ☐☐	☐☐ ☐☐	☐☐☐☐☐ ☐☐☐☐	☐☐☐ ☐☐☐	Y N	Y N	Y N

SUNDAY / Date:

Training notes: _____

Today's goal: _____

| Distance: |
| Time: |
| Heart Rate: |
| i-Rate (1-10) |
| X-Training: |
| Sleep Hours: |
| Weight: |
| Mood: ☺ ☺ ☹ Other |

WEATHER: SUN   WIND   RAIN   CLOUDY   SNOW   TEMP: _____

FUEL LOG

WATER: 6-8 x 8 OZ.	FRUITS: 2-4	VEGGIES: 3-5	WHOLE GRAIN SERVINGS: 6-11	PROTEIN: 4-6 OZ.	LIMIT FAT?	ALCOHOLIC BEVERAGES?	LIMIT "EMPTY" CARBS?
☐☐☐☐ ☐☐☐☐	☐☐ ☐☐	☐☐ ☐☐	☐☐☐☐☐ ☐☐☐☐	☐☐☐ ☐☐☐	Y N	Y N	Y N

WEEK OF:

GOALS FOR WEEK:

WEEKLY TOTAL: _____

YEAR-TO-DATE TOTAL: _____

In the beginning, there was you. You'll take the you that you are now and make it the you that you're going to be. But throughout the journey, you are all you'll ever need.

MONDAY / Date:

Today's goal:

Training notes: _____

Distance:
Time:
Heart Rate:
i-Rate (1-10)
X-Training:
Sleep Hours:
Weight:
Mood: 😊 😐 ☹ ⊗ Other

WEATHER:
SUN   WIND
RAIN   CLOUDY
SNOW
TEMP: _____

FUEL LOG

WATER: 6-8 × 8 OZ.	FRUITS: 2-4	VEGGIES: 3-5	WHOLE GRAIN SERVINGS: 6-11	PROTEIN: 4-6 OZ.	LIMIT FAT?	ALCOHOLIC BEVERAGES?	LIMIT "EMPTY" CARBS?
☐☐☐☐ ☐☐☐☐	☐☐ ☐☐	☐☐ ☐☐	☐☐☐☐☐ ☐☐☐☐☐ ☐	☐☐☐ ☐☐☐	Y N	Y N	Y N

TUESDAY / Date:

Today's goal:

Training notes: _____

Distance:
Time:
Heart Rate:
i-Rate (1-10)
X-Training:
Sleep Hours:
Weight:
Mood: 😊 😐 ☹ ⊗ Other

WEATHER:
SUN   WIND
RAIN   CLOUDY
SNOW
TEMP: _____

FUEL LOG

WATER: 6-8 × 8 OZ.	FRUITS: 2-4	VEGGIES: 3-5	WHOLE GRAIN SERVINGS: 6-11	PROTEIN: 4-6 OZ.	LIMIT FAT?	ALCOHOLIC BEVERAGES?	LIMIT "EMPTY" CARBS?
☐☐☐☐ ☐☐☐☐	☐☐ ☐☐	☐☐ ☐☐	☐☐☐☐☐ ☐☐☐☐☐ ☐	☐☐☐ ☐☐☐	Y N	Y N	Y N

WEDNESDAY / Date:

Today's goal:

Training notes: _____

Distance:
Time:
Heart Rate:
i-Rate (1-10)
X-Training:
Sleep Hours:
Weight:
Mood: 😊 😐 ☹ ⊗ Other

WEATHER:
SUN   WIND
RAIN   CLOUDY
SNOW
TEMP: _____

FUEL LOG

WATER: 6-8 × 8 OZ.	FRUITS: 2-4	VEGGIES: 3-5	WHOLE GRAIN SERVINGS: 6-11	PROTEIN: 4-6 OZ.	LIMIT FAT?	ALCOHOLIC BEVERAGES?	LIMIT "EMPTY" CARBS?
☐☐☐☐ ☐☐☐☐	☐☐ ☐☐	☐☐ ☐☐	☐☐☐☐☐ ☐☐☐☐☐ ☐	☐☐☐ ☐☐☐	Y N	Y N	Y N

THURSDAY / Date:

Today's goal:

Training notes: _____

Distance:
Time:
Heart Rate:
i-Rate (1-10)
X-Training:
Sleep Hours:
Weight:
Mood: 😊 😐 ☹ ⊗ Other

WEATHER:
SUN   WIND
RAIN   CLOUDY
SNOW
TEMP: _____

FUEL LOG

WATER: 6-8 × 8 OZ.	FRUITS: 2-4	VEGGIES: 3-5	WHOLE GRAIN SERVINGS: 6-11	PROTEIN: 4-6 OZ.	LIMIT FAT?	ALCOHOLIC BEVERAGES?	LIMIT "EMPTY" CARBS?
☐☐☐☐ ☐☐☐☐	☐☐ ☐☐	☐☐ ☐☐	☐☐☐☐☐ ☐☐☐☐☐ ☐	☐☐☐ ☐☐☐	Y N	Y N	Y N

FRIDAY / Date:

Training notes:

Today's goal:

Distance:
Time:
Heart Rate:
i-Rate (1-10)
X-Training:
Sleep Hours:
Weight:
Mood: ☺ ☺ ☹ Other

WEATHER: SUN WIND RAIN CLOUDY SNOW TEMP: ____

FUEL LOG

WATER: 6-8 × 8 OZ.	FRUITS: 2-4	VEGGIES: 3-5	WHOLE GRAIN SERVINGS: 6-11	PROTEIN: 4-6 OZ.	LIMIT FAT?	ALCOHOLIC BEVERAGES?	LIMIT "EMPTY" CARBS?
☐☐☐☐ ☐☐☐☐	☐☐ ☐☐	☐☐ ☐☐	☐☐☐☐ ☐☐☐☐	☐☐☐ ☐☐☐	Y N	Y N	Y N

SATURDAY / Date:

Training notes:

Today's goal:

Distance:
Time:
Heart Rate:
i-Rate (1-10)
X-Training:
Sleep Hours:
Weight:
Mood: ☺ ☺ ☹ Other

WEATHER: SUN WIND RAIN CLOUDY SNOW TEMP: ____

FUEL LOG

WATER: 6-8 × 8 OZ.	FRUITS: 2-4	VEGGIES: 3-5	WHOLE GRAIN SERVINGS: 6-11	PROTEIN: 4-6 OZ.	LIMIT FAT?	ALCOHOLIC BEVERAGES?	LIMIT "EMPTY" CARBS?
☐☐☐☐ ☐☐☐☐	☐☐ ☐☐	☐☐ ☐☐	☐☐☐☐ ☐☐☐☐	☐☐☐ ☐☐☐	Y N	Y N	Y N

SUNDAY / Date:

Training notes:

Today's goal:

Distance:
Time:
Heart Rate:
i-Rate (1-10)
X-Training:
Sleep Hours:
Weight:
Mood: ☺ ☺ ☹ Other

WEATHER: SUN WIND RAIN CLOUDY SNOW TEMP: ____

FUEL LOG

WATER: 6-8 × 8 OZ.	FRUITS: 2-4	VEGGIES: 3-5	WHOLE GRAIN SERVINGS: 6-11	PROTEIN: 4-6 OZ.	LIMIT FAT?	ALCOHOLIC BEVERAGES?	LIMIT "EMPTY" CARBS?
☐☐☐☐ ☐☐☐☐	☐☐ ☐☐	☐☐ ☐☐	☐☐☐☐ ☐☐☐☐	☐☐☐ ☐☐☐	Y N	Y N	Y N

WEEK OF:

GOALS FOR WEEK:

WEEKLY TOTAL: _____

YEAR-TO-DATE TOTAL:

Don't get so focused on the road ahead that you forget to look around.

MONDAY / Date:

Today's goal:

Training notes: _____

FUEL LOG

WATER: 6-8 x 8 OZ.	FRUITS: 2-4	VEGGIES: 3-5	WHOLE GRAIN SERVINGS: 6-11	PROTEIN: 4-6 OZ.	LIMIT FAT?	ALCOHOLIC BEVERAGES?	LIMIT "EMPTY" CARBS?
☐☐☐☐ ☐☐☐☐	☐☐ ☐☐	☐☐ ☐☐	☐☐☐☐ ☐☐☐	☐☐☐ ☐☐☐	Y N	Y N	Y N

WEATHER: SUN WIND RAIN CLOUDY SNOW   TEMP: _____

Distance:
Time:
Heart Rate:
i-Rate (1-10):
X-Training:
Sleep Hours:
Weight:
Mood: ☺ ☺ ☹ ☹ Other

TUESDAY / Date:

Today's goal:

Training notes: _____

FUEL LOG

WATER: 6-8 x 8 OZ.	FRUITS: 2-4	VEGGIES: 3-5	WHOLE GRAIN SERVINGS: 6-11	PROTEIN: 4-6 OZ.	LIMIT FAT?	ALCOHOLIC BEVERAGES?	LIMIT "EMPTY" CARBS?
☐☐☐☐ ☐☐☐☐	☐☐ ☐☐	☐☐ ☐☐	☐☐☐☐ ☐☐☐	☐☐☐ ☐☐☐	Y N	Y N	Y N

WEATHER: SUN WIND RAIN CLOUDY SNOW   TEMP: _____

Distance:
Time:
Heart Rate:
i-Rate (1-10):
X-Training:
Sleep Hours:
Weight:
Mood: ☺ ☺ ☹ ☹ Other

WEDNESDAY / Date:

Today's goal:

Training notes: _____

FUEL LOG

WATER: 6-8 x 8 OZ.	FRUITS: 2-4	VEGGIES: 3-5	WHOLE GRAIN SERVINGS: 6-11	PROTEIN: 4-6 OZ.	LIMIT FAT?	ALCOHOLIC BEVERAGES?	LIMIT "EMPTY" CARBS?
☐☐☐☐ ☐☐☐☐	☐☐ ☐☐	☐☐ ☐☐	☐☐☐☐ ☐☐☐	☐☐☐ ☐☐☐	Y N	Y N	Y N

WEATHER: SUN WIND RAIN CLOUDY SNOW   TEMP: _____

Distance:
Time:
Heart Rate:
i-Rate (1-10):
X-Training:
Sleep Hours:
Weight:
Mood: ☺ ☺ ☹ ☹ Other

THURSDAY / Date:

Today's goal:

Training notes: _____

FUEL LOG

WATER: 6-8 x 8 OZ.	FRUITS: 2-4	VEGGIES: 3-5	WHOLE GRAIN SERVINGS: 6-11	PROTEIN: 4-6 OZ.	LIMIT FAT?	ALCOHOLIC BEVERAGES?	LIMIT "EMPTY" CARBS?
☐☐☐☐ ☐☐☐☐	☐☐ ☐☐	☐☐ ☐☐	☐☐☐☐ ☐☐☐	☐☐☐ ☐☐☐	Y N	Y N	Y N

WEATHER: SUN WIND RAIN CLOUDY SNOW   TEMP: _____

Distance:
Time:
Heart Rate:
i-Rate (1-10):
X-Training:
Sleep Hours:
Weight:
Mood: ☺ ☺ ☹ ☹ Other

Training notes:

Today's goal:

_____

FUEL LOG

WATER: 6–8 x 8 OZ.	FRUITS: 2–4	VEGGIES: 3–5	WHOLE GRAIN SERVINGS: 6–11	PROTEIN: 4–6 OZ.	LIMIT FAT?	ALCOHOLIC BEVERAGES?	LIMIT "EMPTY" CARBS?
☐☐☐☐ ☐☐	☐☐ ☐☐	☐☐ ☐☐	☐☐☐☐☐ ☐☐	☐☐☐ ☐☐	Y N	Y N	Y N

Distance:
Time:
Heart Rate:
i-Rate (1-10)
X-Training:
Sleep Hours:
Weight:
Mood: ☺ ☹ ☹ Other

WEATHER:
SUN WIND
RAIN CLOUDY
SNOW
TEMP: _____

SATURDAY / Date:

Training notes:

Today's goal:

_____

FUEL LOG

WATER: 6–8 x 8 OZ.	FRUITS: 2–4	VEGGIES: 3–5	WHOLE GRAIN SERVINGS: 6–11	PROTEIN: 4–6 OZ.	LIMIT FAT?	ALCOHOLIC BEVERAGES?	LIMIT "EMPTY" CARBS?
☐☐☐☐ ☐☐	☐☐ ☐☐	☐☐ ☐☐	☐☐☐☐☐ ☐☐	☐☐☐ ☐☐	Y N	Y N	Y N

Distance:
Time:
Heart Rate:
i-Rate (1-10)
X-Training:
Sleep Hours:
Weight:
Mood: ☺ ☹ ☹ Other

WEATHER:
SUN WIND
RAIN CLOUDY
SNOW
TEMP: _____

SUNDAY / Date:

Training notes:

Today's goal:

_____

FUEL LOG

WATER: 6–8 x 8 OZ.	FRUITS: 2–4	VEGGIES: 3–5	WHOLE GRAIN SERVINGS: 6–11	PROTEIN: 4–6 OZ.	LIMIT FAT?	ALCOHOLIC BEVERAGES?	LIMIT "EMPTY" CARBS?
☐☐☐☐ ☐☐	☐☐ ☐☐	☐☐ ☐☐	☐☐☐☐☐ ☐☐	☐☐☐ ☐☐	Y N	Y N	Y N

Distance:
Time:
Heart Rate:
i-Rate (1-10)
X-Training:
Sleep Hours:
Weight:
Mood: ☺ ☹ ☹ Other

WEATHER:
SUN WIND
RAIN CLOUDY
SNOW
TEMP: _____

WEEK OF:

GOALS FOR WEEK:

WEEKLY TOTAL: _____

YEAR-TO-DATE TOTAL:

No one's training program goes exactly as planned. Be ready at any point to rethink your goals.

THE ART OF RUNNING

For thirty years I prided myself on being a craftsman as a musician. I left the art of music to those that I thought had more talent or training. I was content merely to play the right notes, on time, and in tune. I was a player. Nothing more. I gave little attention to my own thoughts and preferences. Loud was as loud as the conductor wanted. Fast was as fast as the music required. What I felt, what I wanted, from the music of the moment was always subject to the whims of those around me.

When I practiced I practiced for that precision. I spent hours perfecting the craft of being able to do what anyone asked. What matter most to me was being able to play what others wanted when they wanted it. They placed the demands. They set the standards. I did my job. The satisfaction came not from pleasing myself, but from pleasing them.

I began to run as a craftsman, focusing mostly on the nuts and bolts of running. I worried about stride length and weekly mileage as though they held the secrets to success and satisfaction. I held to the belief that that arbitrary standards in the sport or running were like the arbitrary standards in the craft of music. If you met the standards you were good. If you didn't, you weren't.

I learned soon that the sport of running has only one true standard. Speed. Speed is the definition that the sport uses to distinguish not just the winners, but the entire hierarchy of best to worst. The pantheon of running gods is listed in order of their personal bests and their record times.

Using those arbitrary standards, my finishing times at every distance were horrible. The truth is, even cutting my finishing times in half wouldn't have made them any good. But, like so many others, in those early years I struggled in frustration against the craft of running. I fought a relentless battle with my own body. I ignored the fun I was having and clung to the despair that I thought I should feel because I was slow.

I struggled against the barriers of speed and distance. I pushed myself to my own personal bests and record times. Despite my efforts, however, the frustration remained. I was getting better. I was going faster and farther, but the joy was nearly gone. Eventually I had to face the bitter truth. Even my very best wasn't going to ever be very good.

It was then that I discovered that running, like music, is best enjoyed with the imprecision of art. Running is more than a craft. Running is more than the mere accumulation of miles. It is more than recording the minutes and seconds of every run. Running, when done with the heart of an artist, becomes a personal expression. It becomes a self-portrait done with water colors, not a black and white snapshot.

As a musical craftsman, there were lots of rights and wrongs. There was always the opportunity to be out of tune, to be early or late, to be too loud or too soft. In thirty years, I never played a perfect concert. As a running craftsman there were also lots of rights and wrongs. There was always the possibility of going out too fast, or training too hard, or having a bad day. I've never run a perfect race.

As an artist, though, there is no right or wrong. Picasso is no more right than Van Gogh. Beethoven is no more right than Bono. A 7 minute mile is no more right than a 7 hour marathon. They each can be a work of art when done with the honesty and integrity of an artist. My running now has become an expression of who I am at the moment that I run. There are days when I am playful and spirited. On those days I run with all the power and stamina that I can summon. There are days when the colors I choose are stark and bold. Days when it is only on the ragged edge of effort that I can truly express myself. But there are also days when my running pallet is filled with muted colors. There are days when the simple act of being out doors running is enough. There are days when I am not the subject of my work of art, only a small character set against the background of that day's run.

And as an artist, I never know for sure what any day will bring. The mystery of the muse is a part of my daily running life. I can't predict what the art of running will demand of me. I can only be prepared to follow my heart in whatever direction my feet decide to go. Waddle on, friends.

MONDAY / Date:

Training notes:

Today's goal:

FUEL LOG

WATER: 6-8 x 8 OZ.	FRUITS: 2-4	VEGGIES: 3-5	WHOLE GRAIN SERVINGS: 6-11	PROTEIN: 4-6 OZ.	LIMIT FAT?	ALCOHOLIC BEVERAGES?	LIMIT "EMPTY" CARBS?
☐☐☐☐	☐☐	☐☐	☐☐☐☐☐	☐☐	Y N	Y N	Y N
☐☐☐☐	☐☐	☐☐	☐☐☐☐☐	☐☐			
			☐☐☐	☐☐			

WEATHER:
SUN WIND
RAIN CLOUDY
SNOW
TEMP:

Distance:
Time:
Heart Rate:
i-Rate (1-10)
X-Training:
Sleep Hours:
Weight:
Mood: ☺ ☺ ☹ ☹ Other

TUESDAY / Date:

Training notes:

Today's goal:

FUEL LOG

WATER: 6-8 x 8 OZ.	FRUITS: 2-4	VEGGIES: 3-5	WHOLE GRAIN SERVINGS: 6-11	PROTEIN: 4-6 OZ.	LIMIT FAT?	ALCOHOLIC BEVERAGES?	LIMIT "EMPTY" CARBS?
☐☐☐☐	☐☐	☐☐	☐☐☐☐☐	☐☐	Y N	Y N	Y N
☐☐☐☐	☐☐	☐☐	☐☐☐☐☐	☐☐			
			☐☐☐	☐☐			

WEATHER:
SUN WIND
RAIN CLOUDY
SNOW
TEMP:

Distance:
Time:
Heart Rate:
i-Rate (1-10)
X-Training:
Sleep Hours:
Weight:
Mood: ☺ ☺ ☹ ☹ Other

WEDNESDAY / Date:

Training notes:

Today's goal:

FUEL LOG

WATER: 6-8 x 8 OZ.	FRUITS: 2-4	VEGGIES: 3-5	WHOLE GRAIN SERVINGS: 6-11	PROTEIN: 4-6 OZ.	LIMIT FAT?	ALCOHOLIC BEVERAGES?	LIMIT "EMPTY" CARBS?
☐☐☐☐	☐☐	☐☐	☐☐☐☐☐	☐☐	Y N	Y N	Y N
☐☐☐☐	☐☐	☐☐	☐☐☐☐☐	☐☐			
			☐☐☐	☐☐			

WEATHER:
SUN WIND
RAIN CLOUDY
SNOW
TEMP:

Distance:
Time:
Heart Rate:
i-Rate (1-10)
X-Training:
Sleep Hours:
Weight:
Mood: ☺ ☺ ☹ ☹ Other

THURSDAY / Date:

Training notes:

Today's goal:

FUEL LOG

WATER: 6-8 x 8 OZ.	FRUITS: 2-4	VEGGIES: 3-5	WHOLE GRAIN SERVINGS: 6-11	PROTEIN: 4-6 OZ.	LIMIT FAT?	ALCOHOLIC BEVERAGES?	LIMIT "EMPTY" CARBS?
☐☐☐☐	☐☐	☐☐	☐☐☐☐☐	☐☐	Y N	Y N	Y N
☐☐☐☐	☐☐	☐☐	☐☐☐☐☐	☐☐			
			☐☐☐	☐☐			

WEATHER:
SUN WIND
RAIN CLOUDY
SNOW
TEMP:

Distance:
Time:
Heart Rate:
i-Rate (1-10)
X-Training:
Sleep Hours:
Weight:
Mood: ☺ ☺ ☹ ☹ Other

FRIDAY / Date:

Training notes:

Today's goal:

Distance:
Time:
Heart Rate:
i-Rate (1-10)
X-Training:
Sleep Hours:
Weight:
Mood: ☺ ☺ ☹ Other

WEATHER: SUN WIND RAIN CLOUDY SNOW   TEMP: _____

FUEL LOG

WATER: 6-8 x 8 OZ.	FRUITS: 2-4	VEGGIES: 3-5	WHOLE GRAIN SERVINGS: 6-11	PROTEIN: 4-6 OZ.	LIMIT FAT?	ALCOHOLIC BEVERAGES?	LIMIT "EMPTY" CARBS?
☐☐☐☐ ☐☐☐☐	☐☐ ☐☐	☐☐ ☐☐	☐☐☐☐ ☐☐☐☐ ☐☐☐	☐☐☐ ☐☐☐	Y N	Y N	Y N

SATURDAY / Date:

Training notes:

Today's goal:

Distance:
Time:
Heart Rate:
i-Rate (1-10)
X-Training:
Sleep Hours:
Weight:
Mood: ☺ ☺ ☹ Other

WEATHER: SUN WIND RAIN CLOUDY SNOW   TEMP: _____

FUEL LOG

WATER: 6-8 x 8 OZ.	FRUITS: 2-4	VEGGIES: 3-5	WHOLE GRAIN SERVINGS: 6-11	PROTEIN: 4-6 OZ.	LIMIT FAT?	ALCOHOLIC BEVERAGES?	LIMIT "EMPTY" CARBS?
☐☐☐☐ ☐☐☐☐	☐☐ ☐☐	☐☐ ☐☐	☐☐☐☐ ☐☐☐☐ ☐☐☐	☐☐☐ ☐☐☐	Y N	Y N	Y N

SUNDAY / Date:

Training notes:

Today's goal:

Distance:
Time:
Heart Rate:
i-Rate (1-10)
X-Training:
Sleep Hours:
Weight:
Mood: ☺ ☺ ☹ Other

WEATHER: SUN WIND RAIN CLOUDY SNOW   TEMP: _____

FUEL LOG

WATER: 6-8 x 8 OZ.	FRUITS: 2-4	VEGGIES: 3-5	WHOLE GRAIN SERVINGS: 6-11	PROTEIN: 4-6 OZ.	LIMIT FAT?	ALCOHOLIC BEVERAGES?	LIMIT "EMPTY" CARBS?
☐☐☐☐ ☐☐☐☐	☐☐ ☐☐	☐☐ ☐☐	☐☐☐☐ ☐☐☐☐ ☐☐☐	☐☐☐ ☐☐☐	Y N	Y N	Y N

WEEK OF:

GOALS FOR WEEK:

WEEKLY TOTAL: _____

YEAR-TO-DATE TOTAL:

Don't look too far ahead in your training. For now it's enough to do what you need to do today and this week. The weeks to come will be here soon enough.

MONDAY / Date:

Today's goal:

Training notes: _____
_____

Distance:
Time:
Heart Rate:
i-Rate (1-10)
X-Training:
Sleep Hours:
Weight:
Mood: ☺ ☺ ☹ Other

WEATHER:
SUN WIND
RAIN CLOUDY
SNOW
TEMP: ____

FUEL LOG

WATER: 6-8 × 8 OZ.	FRUITS: 2-4	VEGGIES: 3-5	WHOLE GRAIN SERVINGS: 6-11	PROTEIN: 4-6 OZ.	LIMIT FAT?	ALCOHOLIC BEVERAGES?	LIMIT "EMPTY" CARBS?
☐☐☐☐ ☐☐☐☐	☐☐ ☐☐	☐☐ ☐☐	☐☐☐☐☐ ☐☐☐☐☐☐	☐☐ ☐☐ ☐☐	Y N	Y N	Y N

TUESDAY / Date:

Today's goal:

Training notes: _____
_____

Distance:
Time:
Heart Rate:
i-Rate (1-10)
X-Training:
Sleep Hours:
Weight:
Mood: ☺ ☺ ☹ Other

WEATHER:
SUN WIND
RAIN CLOUDY
SNOW
TEMP: ____

FUEL LOG

WATER: 6-8 × 8 OZ.	FRUITS: 2-4	VEGGIES: 3-5	WHOLE GRAIN SERVINGS: 6-11	PROTEIN: 4-6 OZ.	LIMIT FAT?	ALCOHOLIC BEVERAGES?	LIMIT "EMPTY" CARBS?
☐☐☐☐ ☐☐☐☐	☐☐ ☐☐	☐☐ ☐☐	☐☐☐☐☐ ☐☐☐☐☐☐	☐☐ ☐☐ ☐☐	Y N	Y N	Y N

WEDNESDAY / Date:

Today's goal:

Training notes: _____
_____

Distance:
Time:
Heart Rate:
i-Rate (1-10)
X-Training:
Sleep Hours:
Weight:
Mood: ☺ ☺ ☹ Other

WEATHER:
SUN WIND
RAIN CLOUDY
SNOW
TEMP: ____

FUEL LOG

WATER: 6-8 × 8 OZ.	FRUITS: 2-4	VEGGIES: 3-5	WHOLE GRAIN SERVINGS: 6-11	PROTEIN: 4-6 OZ.	LIMIT FAT?	ALCOHOLIC BEVERAGES?	LIMIT "EMPTY" CARBS?
☐☐☐☐ ☐☐☐☐	☐☐ ☐☐	☐☐ ☐☐	☐☐☐☐☐ ☐☐☐☐☐☐	☐☐ ☐☐ ☐☐	Y N	Y N	Y N

THURSDAY / Date:

Today's goal:

Training notes: _____
_____

Distance:
Time:
Heart Rate:
i-Rate (1-10)
X-Training:
Sleep Hours:
Weight:
Mood: ☺ ☺ ☹ Other

WEATHER:
SUN WIND
RAIN CLOUDY
SNOW
TEMP: ____

FUEL LOG

WATER: 6-8 × 8 OZ.	FRUITS: 2-4	VEGGIES: 3-5	WHOLE GRAIN SERVINGS: 6-11	PROTEIN: 4-6 OZ.	LIMIT FAT?	ALCOHOLIC BEVERAGES?	LIMIT "EMPTY" CARBS?
☐☐☐☐ ☐☐☐☐	☐☐ ☐☐	☐☐ ☐☐	☐☐☐☐☐ ☐☐☐☐☐☐	☐☐ ☐☐ ☐☐	Y N	Y N	Y N

FRIDAY / Date:

Training notes:

Today's goal:

Distance:
Time:
Heart Rate:
i-Rate (1-10)
X-Training:
Sleep Hours:
Weight:
Mood: ☺ ☺ ☹ Other

WEATHER:
SUN   WIND
RAIN CLOUDY
SNOW
TEMP: _____

FUEL LOG

WATER: 6-8 X 8 OZ.	FRUITS: 2-4	VEGGIES: 3-5	WHOLE GRAIN SERVINGS: 6-11	PROTEIN: 4-6 OZ.	LIMIT FAT?	ALCOHOLIC BEVERAGES?	LIMIT "EMPTY" CARBS?
☐☐☐☐	☐☐	☐☐	☐☐☐☐☐	☐☐☐	Y N	Y N	Y N
☐☐☐☐	☐☐	☐☐	☐☐☐☐☐	☐☐			

SATURDAY / Date:

Training notes:

Today's goal:

Distance:
Time:
Heart Rate:
i-Rate (1-10)
X-Training:
Sleep Hours:
Weight:
Mood: ☺ ☺ ☹ Other

WEATHER:
SUN   WIND
RAIN CLOUDY
SNOW
TEMP: _____

FUEL LOG

WATER: 6-8 X 8 OZ.	FRUITS: 2-4	VEGGIES: 3-5	WHOLE GRAIN SERVINGS: 6-11	PROTEIN: 4-6 OZ.	LIMIT FAT?	ALCOHOLIC BEVERAGES?	LIMIT "EMPTY" CARBS?
☐☐☐☐	☐☐	☐☐	☐☐☐☐☐	☐☐☐	Y N	Y N	Y N
☐☐☐☐	☐☐	☐☐	☐☐☐☐☐	☐☐			

SUNDAY / Date:

Training notes:

Today's goal:

Distance:
Time:
Heart Rate:
i-Rate (1-10)
X-Training:
Sleep Hours:
Weight:
Mood: ☺ ☺ ☹ Other

WEATHER:
SUN   WIND
RAIN CLOUDY
SNOW
TEMP: _____

FUEL LOG

WATER: 6-8 X 8 OZ.	FRUITS: 2-4	VEGGIES: 3-5	WHOLE GRAIN SERVINGS: 6-11	PROTEIN: 4-6 OZ.	LIMIT FAT?	ALCOHOLIC BEVERAGES?	LIMIT "EMPTY" CARBS?
☐☐☐☐	☐☐	☐☐	☐☐☐☐☐	☐☐☐	Y N	Y N	Y N
☐☐☐☐	☐☐	☐☐	☐☐☐☐☐	☐☐			

WEEK OF:

GOALS FOR WEEK:

WEEKLY TOTAL: _____

YEAR-TO-DATE TOTAL:

The Popeye Syndrome: In a training program, there is no easy solution. Eating spinach won't get you through. You need to slowly but surely get fitter one day at a time.

MONDAY / Date: _____

Today's goal: _____

Training notes: _____

FUEL LOG

WATER: 6-8 × 8 OZ.	FRUITS: 2-4	VEGGIES: 3-5	WHOLE GRAIN SERVINGS: 6-11	PROTEIN: 4-6 OZ.	LIMIT FAT?	ALCOHOLIC BEVERAGES?	LIMIT "EMPTY" CARBS?
☐☐☐☐ ☐☐☐☐	☐☐ ☐☐	☐☐ ☐☐	☐☐☐☐☐ ☐☐☐☐☐☐	☐☐☐ ☐☐☐	Y N	Y N	Y N

WEATHER: SUN WIND RAIN CLOUDY SNOW   TEMP: _____

Distance: _____
Time: _____
Heart Rate: _____
i-Rate (1-10): _____
X-Training: _____
Sleep Hours: _____
Weight: _____
Mood: ☺ ☺ ☹ Other

TUESDAY / Date: _____

Today's goal: _____

Training notes: _____

FUEL LOG

WATER: 6-8 × 8 OZ.	FRUITS: 2-4	VEGGIES: 3-5	WHOLE GRAIN SERVINGS: 6-11	PROTEIN: 4-6 OZ.	LIMIT FAT?	ALCOHOLIC BEVERAGES?	LIMIT "EMPTY" CARBS?
☐☐☐☐ ☐☐☐☐	☐☐ ☐☐	☐☐ ☐☐	☐☐☐☐☐ ☐☐☐☐☐☐	☐☐☐ ☐☐☐	Y N	Y N	Y N

WEATHER: SUN WIND RAIN CLOUDY SNOW   TEMP: _____

Distance: _____
Time: _____
Heart Rate: _____
i-Rate (1-10): _____
X-Training: _____
Sleep Hours: _____
Weight: _____
Mood: ☺ ☺ ☹ Other

WEDNESDAY / Date: _____

Today's goal: _____

Training notes: _____

FUEL LOG

WATER: 6-8 × 8 OZ.	FRUITS: 2-4	VEGGIES: 3-5	WHOLE GRAIN SERVINGS: 6-11	PROTEIN: 4-6 OZ.	LIMIT FAT?	ALCOHOLIC BEVERAGES?	LIMIT "EMPTY" CARBS?
☐☐☐☐ ☐☐☐☐	☐☐ ☐☐	☐☐ ☐☐	☐☐☐☐☐ ☐☐☐☐☐☐	☐☐☐ ☐☐☐	Y N	Y N	Y N

WEATHER: SUN WIND RAIN CLOUDY SNOW   TEMP: _____

Distance: _____
Time: _____
Heart Rate: _____
i-Rate (1-10): _____
X-Training: _____
Sleep Hours: _____
Weight: _____
Mood: ☺ ☺ ☹ Other

THURSDAY / Date: _____

Today's goal: _____

Training notes: _____

FUEL LOG

WATER: 6-8 × 8 OZ.	FRUITS: 2-4	VEGGIES: 3-5	WHOLE GRAIN SERVINGS: 6-11	PROTEIN: 4-6 OZ.	LIMIT FAT?	ALCOHOLIC BEVERAGES?	LIMIT "EMPTY" CARBS?
☐☐☐☐ ☐☐☐☐	☐☐ ☐☐	☐☐ ☐☐	☐☐☐☐☐ ☐☐☐☐☐☐	☐☐☐ ☐☐☐	Y N	Y N	Y N

WEATHER: SUN WIND RAIN CLOUDY SNOW   TEMP: _____

Distance: _____
Time: _____
Heart Rate: _____
i-Rate (1-10): _____
X-Training: _____
Sleep Hours: _____
Weight: _____
Mood: ☺ ☺ ☹ Other

FRIDAY / Date:

Training notes: _____

Distance: _____
Time: _____
Heart Rate: _____
i-Rate (1-10): _____
X-Training: _____
Sleep Hours: _____
Weight: _____
Mood: ☺ ☺ ☹ Other

WEATHER:
SUN WIND
RAIN CLOUDY
SNOW
TEMP: _____

Today's goal: _____

FUEL LOG

WATER: 6-8 x 8 OZ.	FRUITS: 2-4	VEGGIES: 3-5	WHOLE GRAIN SERVINGS: 6-11	PROTEIN: 4-6 OZ.	LIMIT FAT?	ALCOHOLIC BEVERAGES?	LIMIT "EMPTY" CARBS?
☐☐☐☐ ☐☐☐☐	☐☐ ☐☐	☐☐ ☐☐	☐☐☐☐☐☐ ☐☐☐☐☐	☐☐☐ ☐☐☐	Y N	Y N	Y N

SATURDAY / Date:

Training notes: _____

Distance: _____
Time: _____
Heart Rate: _____
i-Rate (1-10): _____
X-Training: _____
Sleep Hours: _____
Weight: _____
Mood: ☺ ☺ ☹ Other

WEATHER:
SUN WIND
RAIN CLOUDY
SNOW
TEMP: _____

Today's goal: _____

FUEL LOG

WATER: 6-8 x 8 OZ.	FRUITS: 2-4	VEGGIES: 3-5	WHOLE GRAIN SERVINGS: 6-11	PROTEIN: 4-6 OZ.	LIMIT FAT?	ALCOHOLIC BEVERAGES?	LIMIT "EMPTY" CARBS?
☐☐☐☐ ☐☐☐☐	☐☐ ☐☐	☐☐ ☐☐	☐☐☐☐☐☐ ☐☐☐☐☐	☐☐☐ ☐☐☐	Y N	Y N	Y N

SUNDAY / Date:

Training notes: _____

Distance: _____
Time: _____
Heart Rate: _____
i-Rate (1-10): _____
X-Training: _____
Sleep Hours: _____
Weight: _____
Mood: ☺ ☺ ☹ Other

WEATHER:
SUN WIND
RAIN CLOUDY
SNOW
TEMP: _____

Today's goal: _____

FUEL LOG

WATER: 6-8 x 8 OZ.	FRUITS: 2-4	VEGGIES: 3-5	WHOLE GRAIN SERVINGS: 6-11	PROTEIN: 4-6 OZ.	LIMIT FAT?	ALCOHOLIC BEVERAGES?	LIMIT "EMPTY" CARBS?
☐☐☐☐ ☐☐☐☐	☐☐ ☐☐	☐☐ ☐☐	☐☐☐☐☐☐ ☐☐☐☐☐	☐☐☐ ☐☐☐	Y N	Y N	Y N

WEEK OF:

GOALS FOR WEEK:

WEEKLY TOTAL: _____

YEAR-TO-DATE TOTAL: _____

Every run, every decision to run, becomes a stone in our personal mosaic. Piece by piece we fashion a picture of ourselves that reflects not just who we are, but what we want to become.

MONDAY / Date:

Today's goal:

Training notes: _____

Distance:
Time:
Heart Rate:
i-Rate (1-10)
X-Training:
Sleep Hours:
Weight:
Mood: ☺ 😐 ☹ Other

FUEL LOG

WATER: 6-8 × 8 OZ.	FRUITS: 2-4	VEGGIES: 3-5	WHOLE GRAIN SERVINGS: 6-11	PROTEIN: 4-6 OZ.	LIMIT FAT?	ALCOHOLIC BEVERAGES?	LIMIT "EMPTY" CARBS?	WEATHER: SUN WIND RAIN CLOUDY SNOW
☐☐☐☐ ☐☐☐☐	☐☐ ☐☐	☐☐ ☐☐	☐☐☐ ☐☐☐ ☐	☐☐ ☐☐ ☐☐	Y N	Y N	Y N	TEMP: ____

TUESDAY / Date:

Today's goal:

Training notes: _____

Distance:
Time:
Heart Rate:
i-Rate (1-10)
X-Training:
Sleep Hours:
Weight:
Mood: ☺ 😐 ☹ Other

FUEL LOG

WATER: 6-8 × 8 OZ.	FRUITS: 2-4	VEGGIES: 3-5	WHOLE GRAIN SERVINGS: 6-11	PROTEIN: 4-6 OZ.	LIMIT FAT?	ALCOHOLIC BEVERAGES?	LIMIT "EMPTY" CARBS?	WEATHER: SUN WIND RAIN CLOUDY SNOW
☐☐☐☐ ☐☐☐☐	☐☐ ☐☐	☐☐ ☐☐	☐☐☐ ☐☐☐ ☐	☐☐ ☐☐ ☐☐	Y N	Y N	Y N	TEMP: ____

WEDNESDAY / Date:

Today's goal:

Training notes: _____

Distance:
Time:
Heart Rate:
i-Rate (1-10)
X-Training:
Sleep Hours:
Weight:
Mood: ☺ 😐 ☹ Other

FUEL LOG

WATER: 6-8 × 8 OZ.	FRUITS: 2-4	VEGGIES: 3-5	WHOLE GRAIN SERVINGS: 6-11	PROTEIN: 4-6 OZ.	LIMIT FAT?	ALCOHOLIC BEVERAGES?	LIMIT "EMPTY" CARBS?	WEATHER: SUN WIND RAIN CLOUDY SNOW
☐☐☐☐ ☐☐☐☐	☐☐ ☐☐	☐☐ ☐☐	☐☐☐ ☐☐☐ ☐	☐☐ ☐☐ ☐☐	Y N	Y N	Y N	TEMP: ____

THURSDAY / Date:

Today's goal:

Training notes: _____

Distance:
Time:
Heart Rate:
i-Rate (1-10)
X-Training:
Sleep Hours:
Weight:
Mood: ☺ 😐 ☹ Other

FUEL LOG

WATER: 6-8 × 8 OZ.	FRUITS: 2-4	VEGGIES: 3-5	WHOLE GRAIN SERVINGS: 6-11	PROTEIN: 4-6 OZ.	LIMIT FAT?	ALCOHOLIC BEVERAGES?	LIMIT "EMPTY" CARBS?	WEATHER: SUN WIND RAIN CLOUDY SNOW
☐☐☐☐ ☐☐☐☐	☐☐ ☐☐	☐☐ ☐☐	☐☐☐ ☐☐☐ ☐	☐☐ ☐☐ ☐☐	Y N	Y N	Y N	TEMP: ____

FRIDAY / Date:

Today's goal:

Training notes:

Distance:
Time:
Heart Rate:
i-Rate (1-10)
X-Training:
Sleep Hours:
Weight:
Mood: ☺ ☺ ☹ Other

WEATHER:
SUN   WIND
RAIN CLOUDY
SNOW
TEMP: _____

FUEL LOG

WATER: 6-8 x 8 OZ.	FRUITS: 2-4	VEGGIES: 3-5	WHOLE GRAIN SERVINGS: 6-11	PROTEIN: 4-6 OZ.	LIMIT FAT?	ALCOHOLIC BEVERAGES?	LIMIT "EMPTY" CARBS?
☐☐☐☐ ☐☐☐☐	☐☐ ☐☐	☐☐ ☐☐	☐☐☐ ☐☐☐	☐☐☐ ☐☐☐	Y N	Y N	Y N

SATURDAY / Date:

Today's goal:

Training notes:

Distance:
Time:
Heart Rate:
i-Rate (1-10)
X-Training:
Sleep Hours:
Weight:
Mood: ☺ ☺ ☹ Other

WEATHER:
SUN   WIND
RAIN CLOUDY
SNOW
TEMP: _____

FUEL LOG

WATER: 6-8 x 8 OZ.	FRUITS: 2-4	VEGGIES: 3-5	WHOLE GRAIN SERVINGS: 6-11	PROTEIN: 4-6 OZ.	LIMIT FAT?	ALCOHOLIC BEVERAGES?	LIMIT "EMPTY" CARBS?
☐☐☐☐ ☐☐☐☐	☐☐ ☐☐	☐☐ ☐☐	☐☐☐ ☐☐☐	☐☐☐ ☐☐☐	Y N	Y N	Y N

SUNDAY / Date:

Today's goal:

Training notes:

Distance:
Time:
Heart Rate:
i-Rate (1-10)
X-Training:
Sleep Hours:
Weight:
Mood: ☺ ☺ ☹ Other

WEATHER:
SUN   WIND
RAIN CLOUDY
SNOW
TEMP: _____

FUEL LOG

WATER: 6-8 x 8 OZ.	FRUITS: 2-4	VEGGIES: 3-5	WHOLE GRAIN SERVINGS: 6-11	PROTEIN: 4-6 OZ.	LIMIT FAT?	ALCOHOLIC BEVERAGES?	LIMIT "EMPTY" CARBS?
☐☐☐☐ ☐☐☐☐	☐☐ ☐☐	☐☐ ☐☐	☐☐☐ ☐☐☐	☐☐☐ ☐☐☐	Y N	Y N	Y N

WEEK OF:

GOALS FOR WEEK:

WEEKLY TOTAL: _____

YEAR-TO-DATE TOTAL: _____

Each day of training counts. The short days. The long days. The rest days. Each of them contributes to your success. Yesterday is gone, tomorrow isn't here. Make today's training count.

FAT BOY, SOFT TAIL, ROAD KING

Fat Boy, Soft Tail, Road King: No, those aren't the nicknames of some of my old motorcycling buddies, although they could be. They are actually the model designations of Harley-Davidsons. They represent more than just a piece of equipment. They are characteristics of the image each motorcycle hopes to project.

Ever since Marlon Brando burst into the cultural consciousness in "The Wild One," motorcycles in general and Harley's in particular, have been about image. From the outlaw persona of the Hell's Angels to the inveterate free spirit of Peter Fonda in "Easy Rider," the public has looked past the person and focused on the image that the Harley projects.

In similar fashion, runners, especially those who were a part of the first running boom, understand what the image of a runner is supposed to be. From the tissue paper thin, worn out event t-shirt to the nylon shorts, the old timers knew how a runner was supposed to look, supposed to feel, and supposed to act. And as they did with bikers, the public often looked past the actual person and saw only a runner.

It's not so easy anymore. The new rider who shops online for the lowest interest rate to finance his new Harley and who takes pride in his "American Metal" even though it's really a global mix of parts, still seeks to project the image of the outlaw, free-spirited biker—at least on weekends. There are also runners who feel the need to cling to images that are just as outdated and inaccurate.

Part of the appeal of running is that it is, in its essence, an authentic undertaking. Unlike becoming a biker, there's no way to buy your way into the community of runners. You either run or you don't. You run fast or you don't. You run far or you don't. Whatever kind of runner you are, that's the runner you are. Simple. Authentic. A new leather jacket and a temporary tattoo won't get you in.

And yes, I continue to hear the debate about what it means to be a "real" runner. It's as if we, as a community, have yet to decide on the criteria by which we know and accept each other. It's not just the old school runners who are unwilling to acknowledge the fundamental truth that running is running. Many new runners fall victim to their own false expectations and definitions.

Part of the problem is that even the word runner doesn't mean much inside the running community anymore. 2:30 marathoners are runners. 45-minute 5Kers are runners. Someone who runs 100 miles a week is a runner. Someone who runs 6 miles a week is a runner. Runners are runners, run-walkers are runners and, in some cases, walkers are runners.

What does it take to be an authentic runner? It doesn't take mega-mile weeks. It isn't about speed or method or style. It isn't about the shoes or clothes. It isn't about the image. It's about knowing that it doesn't matter how others define running but that running is a way by which we define ourselves.

The truth of the authentic runner can be found in disparate places--on the streets of small towns and at the starting lines of monster marathons. There you will find the runners. There you will find the people who have discovered that running brings them closer to themselves, closer to others, and closer to the truth. There you will find the people who have discovered that being who you are is much more difficult than pretending to be who you are not.

Fat Boy, Soft Tail, and Road King. Come to think of it, those could be the nicknames of some of my running buddies. Authentic runners every one of them.

Waddle on, friends.

MONDAY / Date:

Today's goal:

Training notes:

FUEL LOG

WATER: 6-8 × 8 OZ.	FRUITS: 2-4	VEGGIES: 3-5	WHOLE GRAIN SERVINGS: 6-11	PROTEIN: 4-6 OZ.	LIMIT FAT?	ALCOHOLIC BEVERAGES?	LIMIT "EMPTY" CARBS?
☐☐☐☐ ☐☐☐☐	☐☐ ☐☐	☐☐ ☐☐	☐☐☐☐☐ ☐☐☐☐☐ ☐	☐☐☐ ☐☐☐	Y N	Y N	Y N

WEATHER: SUN WIND RAIN CLOUDY SNOW
TEMP: _____

Distance:
Time:
Heart Rate:
i-Rate (1-10)
X-Training:
Sleep Hours:
Weight:
Mood: ☺ 😐 ☹ Other

TUESDAY / Date:

Today's goal:

Training notes:

FUEL LOG

WATER: 6-8 × 8 OZ.	FRUITS: 2-4	VEGGIES: 3-5	WHOLE GRAIN SERVINGS: 6-11	PROTEIN: 4-6 OZ.	LIMIT FAT?	ALCOHOLIC BEVERAGES?	LIMIT "EMPTY" CARBS?
☐☐☐☐ ☐☐☐☐	☐☐ ☐☐	☐☐ ☐☐	☐☐☐☐☐ ☐☐☐☐☐ ☐	☐☐☐ ☐☐☐	Y N	Y N	Y N

WEATHER: SUN WIND RAIN CLOUDY SNOW
TEMP: _____

Distance:
Time:
Heart Rate:
i-Rate (1-10)
X-Training:
Sleep Hours:
Weight:
Mood: ☺ 😐 ☹ Other

WEDNESDAY / Date:

Today's goal:

Training notes:

FUEL LOG

WATER: 6-8 × 8 OZ.	FRUITS: 2-4	VEGGIES: 3-5	WHOLE GRAIN SERVINGS: 6-11	PROTEIN: 4-6 OZ.	LIMIT FAT?	ALCOHOLIC BEVERAGES?	LIMIT "EMPTY" CARBS?
☐☐☐☐ ☐☐☐☐	☐☐ ☐☐	☐☐ ☐☐	☐☐☐☐☐ ☐☐☐☐☐ ☐	☐☐☐ ☐☐☐	Y N	Y N	Y N

WEATHER: SUN WIND RAIN CLOUDY SNOW
TEMP: _____

Distance:
Time:
Heart Rate:
i-Rate (1-10)
X-Training:
Sleep Hours:
Weight:
Mood: ☺ 😐 ☹ Other

THURSDAY / Date:

Today's goal:

Training notes:

FUEL LOG

WATER: 6-8 × 8 OZ.	FRUITS: 2-4	VEGGIES: 3-5	WHOLE GRAIN SERVINGS: 6-11	PROTEIN: 4-6 OZ.	LIMIT FAT?	ALCOHOLIC BEVERAGES?	LIMIT "EMPTY" CARBS?
☐☐☐☐ ☐☐☐☐	☐☐ ☐☐	☐☐ ☐☐	☐☐☐☐☐ ☐☐☐☐☐ ☐	☐☐☐ ☐☐☐	Y N	Y N	Y N

WEATHER: SUN WIND RAIN CLOUDY SNOW
TEMP: _____

Distance:
Time:
Heart Rate:
i-Rate (1-10)
X-Training:
Sleep Hours:
Weight:
Mood: ☺ 😐 ☹ Other

FRIDAY / Date:

Today's goal:

Training notes:

Distance:
Time:
Heart Rate:
i-Rate (1-10):
X-Training:
Sleep Hours:
Weight:
Mood: ☺ ☺ ☹ Other

FUEL LOG

WATER: 6-8 x 8 oz.	FRUITS: 2-4	VEGGIES: 3-5	WHOLE GRAIN SERVINGS: 6-11	PROTEIN: 4-6 oz.	LIMIT FAT?	ALCOHOLIC BEVERAGES?	LIMIT "EMPTY" CARBS?
☐☐☐☐ ☐☐☐☐	☐☐ ☐☐	☐☐ ☐☐	☐☐☐☐☐☐ ☐☐☐☐☐	☐☐☐ ☐☐☐	Y N	Y N	Y N

WEATHER: SUN WIND RAIN CLOUDY SNOW TEMP: _____

SATURDAY / Date:

Today's goal:

Training notes:

Distance:
Time:
Heart Rate:
i-Rate (1-10):
X-Training:
Sleep Hours:
Weight:
Mood: ☺ ☺ ☹ Other

FUEL LOG

WATER: 6-8 x 8 oz.	FRUITS: 2-4	VEGGIES: 3-5	WHOLE GRAIN SERVINGS: 6-11	PROTEIN: 4-6 oz.	LIMIT FAT?	ALCOHOLIC BEVERAGES?	LIMIT "EMPTY" CARBS?
☐☐☐☐ ☐☐☐☐	☐☐ ☐☐	☐☐ ☐☐	☐☐☐ ☐☐☐	☐☐☐ ☐☐☐	Y N	Y N	Y N

WEATHER: SUN WIND RAIN CLOUDY SNOW TEMP: _____

SUNDAY / Date:

Today's goal:

Training notes:

Distance:
Time:
Heart Rate:
i-Rate (1-10):
X-Training:
Sleep Hours:
Weight:
Mood: ☺ ☺ ☹ Other

FUEL LOG

WATER: 6-8 x 8 oz.	FRUITS: 2-4	VEGGIES: 3-5	WHOLE GRAIN SERVINGS: 6-11	PROTEIN: 4-6 oz.	LIMIT FAT?	ALCOHOLIC BEVERAGES?	LIMIT "EMPTY" CARBS?
☐☐☐☐ ☐☐☐☐	☐☐ ☐☐	☐☐ ☐☐	☐☐☐ ☐☐☐	☐☐☐ ☐☐☐	Y N	Y N	Y N

WEATHER: SUN WIND RAIN CLOUDY SNOW TEMP: _____

WEEK OF:

GOALS FOR WEEK:

WEEKLY TOTAL: _____

YEAR-TO-DATE TOTAL:

The difference between success and failure has nothing to do with pace or the amount of time you exercise. You must reach into your soul and find the athlete that you want to be.

MONDAY / Date:

Today's goal:

Training notes:
_____
_____
_____

FUEL LOG

WATER: 6-8 × 8 OZ.	FRUITS: 2-4	VEGGIES: 3-5	WHOLE GRAIN SERVINGS: 6-11	PROTEIN: 4-6 OZ.	LIMIT FAT?	ALCOHOLIC BEVERAGES?	LIMIT "EMPTY" CARBS?
☐☐☐☐ ☐☐☐☐	☐☐ ☐☐	☐☐ ☐☐	☐☐☐ ☐☐☐ ☐☐☐ ☐☐	☐☐☐ ☐☐☐	Y N	Y N	Y N

Distance:
Time:
Heart Rate:
i-Rate (1-10)
X-Training:
Sleep Hours:
Weight:
Mood: ☺ ☺ ☹ Other

WEATHER:
SUN WIND
RAIN CLOUDY
SNOW
TEMP: _____

TUESDAY / Date:

Today's goal:

Training notes:
_____
_____
_____

FUEL LOG

WATER: 6-8 × 8 OZ.	FRUITS: 2-4	VEGGIES: 3-5	WHOLE GRAIN SERVINGS: 6-11	PROTEIN: 4-6 OZ.	LIMIT FAT?	ALCOHOLIC BEVERAGES?	LIMIT "EMPTY" CARBS?
☐☐☐☐ ☐☐☐☐	☐☐ ☐☐	☐☐ ☐☐	☐☐☐ ☐☐☐ ☐☐☐ ☐☐	☐☐☐ ☐☐☐	Y N	Y N	Y N

Distance:
Time:
Heart Rate:
i-Rate (1-10)
X-Training:
Sleep Hours:
Weight:
Mood: ☺ ☺ ☹ Other

WEATHER:
SUN WIND
RAIN CLOUDY
SNOW
TEMP: _____

WEDNESDAY / Date:

Today's goal:

Training notes:
_____
_____
_____

FUEL LOG

WATER: 6-8 × 8 OZ.	FRUITS: 2-4	VEGGIES: 3-5	WHOLE GRAIN SERVINGS: 6-11	PROTEIN: 4-6 OZ.	LIMIT FAT?	ALCOHOLIC BEVERAGES?	LIMIT "EMPTY" CARBS?
☐☐☐☐ ☐☐☐☐	☐☐ ☐☐	☐☐ ☐☐	☐☐☐ ☐☐☐ ☐☐☐ ☐☐	☐☐☐ ☐☐☐	Y N	Y N	Y N

Distance:
Time:
Heart Rate:
i-Rate (1-10)
X-Training:
Sleep Hours:
Weight:
Mood: ☺ ☺ ☹ Other

WEATHER:
SUN WIND
RAIN CLOUDY
SNOW
TEMP: _____

THURSDAY / Date:

Today's goal:

Training notes:
_____
_____
_____

FUEL LOG

WATER: 6-8 × 8 OZ.	FRUITS: 2-4	VEGGIES: 3-5	WHOLE GRAIN SERVINGS: 6-11	PROTEIN: 4-6 OZ.	LIMIT FAT?	ALCOHOLIC BEVERAGES?	LIMIT "EMPTY" CARBS?
☐☐☐☐ ☐☐☐☐	☐☐ ☐☐	☐☐ ☐☐	☐☐☐ ☐☐☐ ☐☐☐ ☐☐	☐☐☐ ☐☐☐	Y N	Y N	Y N

Distance:
Time:
Heart Rate:
i-Rate (1-10)
X-Training:
Sleep Hours:
Weight:
Mood: ☺ ☺ ☹ Other

WEATHER:
SUN WIND
RAIN CLOUDY
SNOW
TEMP: _____

FRIDAY / Date:

Today's goal: _____

Training notes: _____

Distance: _____
Time: _____
Heart Rate: _____
i-Rate (1-10): _____
X-Training: _____
Sleep Hours: _____
Weight: _____
Mood: 😊 😐 ☹ Other

WEATHER: SUN WIND RAIN CLOUDY SNOW
TEMP: _____

FUEL LOG

WATER: 6-8 x 8 OZ.	FRUITS: 2-4	VEGGIES: 3-5	WHOLE GRAIN SERVINGS: 6-11	PROTEIN: 4-6 OZ.	LIMIT FAT?	ALCOHOLIC BEVERAGES?	LIMIT "EMPTY" CARBS?
☐☐☐☐ ☐☐☐☐	☐☐ ☐☐	☐☐☐ ☐☐	☐☐☐☐☐ ☐☐☐☐☐	☐☐☐ ☐☐☐	Y N	Y N	Y N

SATURDAY / Date:

Today's goal: _____

Training notes: _____

Distance: _____
Time: _____
Heart Rate: _____
i-Rate (1-10): _____
X-Training: _____
Sleep Hours: _____
Weight: _____
Mood: 😊 😐 ☹ Other

WEATHER: SUN WIND RAIN CLOUDY SNOW
TEMP: _____

FUEL LOG

WATER: 6-8 x 8 OZ.	FRUITS: 2-4	VEGGIES: 3-5	WHOLE GRAIN SERVINGS: 6-11	PROTEIN: 4-6 OZ.	LIMIT FAT?	ALCOHOLIC BEVERAGES?	LIMIT "EMPTY" CARBS?
☐☐☐☐ ☐☐☐☐	☐☐ ☐☐	☐☐☐ ☐☐	☐☐☐☐☐ ☐☐☐☐☐	☐☐☐ ☐☐☐	Y N	Y N	Y N

SUNDAY / Date:

Today's goal: _____

Training notes: _____

Distance: _____
Time: _____
Heart Rate: _____
i-Rate (1-10): _____
X-Training: _____
Sleep Hours: _____
Weight: _____
Mood: 😊 😐 ☹ Other

WEATHER: SUN WIND RAIN CLOUDY SNOW
TEMP: _____

FUEL LOG

WATER: 6-8 x 8 OZ.	FRUITS: 2-4	VEGGIES: 3-5	WHOLE GRAIN SERVINGS: 6-11	PROTEIN: 4-6 OZ.	LIMIT FAT?	ALCOHOLIC BEVERAGES?	LIMIT "EMPTY" CARBS?
☐☐☐☐ ☐☐☐☐	☐☐ ☐☐	☐☐☐ ☐☐	☐☐☐☐☐ ☐☐☐☐☐	☐☐☐ ☐☐☐	Y N	Y N	Y N

WEEK OF:

GOALS FOR WEEK:

Our running shoes are really erasers. Every step erases some memory of a past failure. Every mile brings us closer to a clean slate.

WEEKLY TOTAL: _____

YEAR-TO-DATE TOTAL: _____

MONDAY / Date:

Today's goal:

Training notes:

FUEL LOG

WATER: 6-8 x 8 OZ.	FRUITS: 2-4	VEGGIES: 3-5	WHOLE GRAIN SERVINGS: 6-11	PROTEIN: 4-6 OZ.	LIMIT FAT?	ALCOHOLIC BEVERAGES?	LIMIT "EMPTY" CARBS?
☐☐☐☐ ☐☐☐☐	☐☐ ☐☐	☐☐ ☐	☐☐☐ ☐☐☐	☐☐☐ ☐☐☐	Y N	Y N	Y N

WEATHER: SUN WIND RAIN CLOUDY SNOW TEMP:

Distance:
Time:
Heart Rate:
i-Rate (1-10)
X-Training:
Sleep Hours:
Weight:
Mood: ☺ ☺ ☹ Other

TUESDAY / Date:

Today's goal:

Training notes:

FUEL LOG

WATER: 6-8 x 8 OZ.	FRUITS: 2-4	VEGGIES: 3-5	WHOLE GRAIN SERVINGS: 6-11	PROTEIN: 4-6 OZ.	LIMIT FAT?	ALCOHOLIC BEVERAGES?	LIMIT "EMPTY" CARBS?
☐☐☐☐ ☐☐☐☐	☐☐ ☐☐	☐☐ ☐	☐☐☐ ☐☐☐	☐☐☐ ☐☐☐	Y N	Y N	Y N

WEATHER: SUN WIND RAIN CLOUDY SNOW TEMP:

Distance:
Time:
Heart Rate:
i-Rate (1-10)
X-Training:
Sleep Hours:
Weight:
Mood: ☺ ☺ ☹ Other

WEDNESDAY / Date:

Today's goal:

Training notes:

FUEL LOG

WATER: 6-8 x 8 OZ.	FRUITS: 2-4	VEGGIES: 3-5	WHOLE GRAIN SERVINGS: 6-11	PROTEIN: 4-6 OZ.	LIMIT FAT?	ALCOHOLIC BEVERAGES?	LIMIT "EMPTY" CARBS?
☐☐☐☐ ☐☐☐☐	☐☐ ☐☐	☐☐ ☐	☐☐☐ ☐☐☐	☐☐☐ ☐☐☐	Y N	Y N	Y N

WEATHER: SUN WIND RAIN CLOUDY SNOW TEMP:

Distance:
Time:
Heart Rate:
i-Rate (1-10)
X-Training:
Sleep Hours:
Weight:
Mood: ☺ ☺ ☹ Other

THURSDAY / Date:

Today's goal:

Training notes:

FUEL LOG

WATER: 6-8 x 8 OZ.	FRUITS: 2-4	VEGGIES: 3-5	WHOLE GRAIN SERVINGS: 6-11	PROTEIN: 4-6 OZ.	LIMIT FAT?	ALCOHOLIC BEVERAGES?	LIMIT "EMPTY" CARBS?
☐☐☐☐ ☐☐☐☐	☐☐ ☐☐	☐☐ ☐	☐☐☐ ☐☐☐	☐☐☐ ☐☐☐	Y N	Y N	Y N

WEATHER: SUN WIND RAIN CLOUDY SNOW TEMP:

Distance:
Time:
Heart Rate:
i-Rate (1-10)
X-Training:
Sleep Hours:
Weight:
Mood: ☺ ☺ ☹ Other

FRIDAY / Date:

Training notes:

Today's goal:

Distance:
Time:
Heart Rate:
i-Rate (1-10)
X-Training:
Sleep Hours:
Weight:
Mood: ☺ ☺ ☹ Other

WEATHER:
SUN WIND
RAIN CLOUDY
SNOW
TEMP: _____

FUEL LOG

WATER: 6-8 x 8 OZ.	FRUITS: 2-4	VEGGIES: 3-5	WHOLE GRAIN SERVINGS: 6-11	PROTEIN: 4-6 OZ.	LIMIT FAT?	ALCOHOLIC BEVERAGES?	LIMIT "EMPTY" CARBS?
☐☐☐☐ ☐☐☐☐	☐☐ ☐☐	☐☐ ☐☐	☐☐☐ ☐☐☐ ☐☐☐☐☐	☐☐☐ ☐☐	Y N	Y N	Y N

SATURDAY / Date:

Training notes:

Today's goal:

Distance:
Time:
Heart Rate:
i-Rate (1-10)
X-Training:
Sleep Hours:
Weight:
Mood: ☺ ☺ ☹ Other

WEATHER:
SUN WIND
RAIN CLOUDY
SNOW
TEMP: _____

FUEL LOG

WATER: 6-8 x 8 OZ.	FRUITS: 2-4	VEGGIES: 3-5	WHOLE GRAIN SERVINGS: 6-11	PROTEIN: 4-6 OZ.	LIMIT FAT?	ALCOHOLIC BEVERAGES?	LIMIT "EMPTY" CARBS?
☐☐☐☐ ☐☐☐☐	☐☐ ☐☐	☐☐ ☐☐	☐☐☐ ☐☐☐ ☐☐☐☐☐	☐☐☐ ☐☐	Y N	Y N	Y N

SUNDAY / Date:

Training notes:

Today's goal:

Distance:
Time:
Heart Rate:
i-Rate (1-10)
X-Training:
Sleep Hours:
Weight:
Mood: ☺ ☺ ☹ Other

WEATHER:
SUN WIND
RAIN CLOUDY
SNOW
TEMP: _____

FUEL LOG

WATER: 6-8 x 8 OZ.	FRUITS: 2-4	VEGGIES: 3-5	WHOLE GRAIN SERVINGS: 6-11	PROTEIN: 4-6 OZ.	LIMIT FAT?	ALCOHOLIC BEVERAGES?	LIMIT "EMPTY" CARBS?
☐☐☐☐ ☐☐☐☐	☐☐ ☐☐	☐☐ ☐☐	☐☐☐ ☐☐☐ ☐☐☐☐☐	☐☐☐ ☐☐	Y N	Y N	Y N

WEEK OF:

GOALS FOR WEEK:

WEEKLY TOTAL: _____

YEAR-TO-DATE TOTAL:

We do not march to the beat of a different drummer. We ramble to the syncopation of our own existence.

MONDAY / Date:

Today's goal:

Training notes:

Distance:
Time:
Heart Rate:
i-Rate (1-10)
X-Training:
Sleep Hours:
Weight:
Mood: ☺ ☺ ☺ Other

FUEL LOG

WATER: 6-8 × 8 OZ.	FRUITS: 2-4	VEGGIES: 3-5	WHOLE GRAIN SERVINGS: 6-11	PROTEIN: 4-6 OZ.	LIMIT FAT?	ALCOHOLIC BEVERAGES?	LIMIT "EMPTY" CARBS?
☐☐☐☐ / ☐☐☐☐	☐☐ / ☐☐	☐☐ / ☐☐	☐☐☐ / ☐☐☐ / ☐☐☐	☐☐☐ / ☐☐☐	Y N	Y N	Y N

WEATHER: SUN WIND RAIN CLOUDY SNOW
TEMP: _____

TUESDAY / Date:

Today's goal:

Training notes:

Distance:
Time:
Heart Rate:
i-Rate (1-10)
X-Training:
Sleep Hours:
Weight:
Mood: ☺ ☺ ☺ Other

FUEL LOG

WATER: 6-8 × 8 OZ.	FRUITS: 2-4	VEGGIES: 3-5	WHOLE GRAIN SERVINGS: 6-11	PROTEIN: 4-6 OZ.	LIMIT FAT?	ALCOHOLIC BEVERAGES?	LIMIT "EMPTY" CARBS?
☐☐☐☐ / ☐☐☐☐	☐☐ / ☐☐	☐☐ / ☐☐	☐☐☐ / ☐☐☐ / ☐☐☐	☐☐☐ / ☐☐☐	Y N	Y N	Y N

WEATHER: SUN WIND RAIN CLOUDY SNOW
TEMP: _____

WEDNESDAY / Date:

Today's goal:

Training notes:

Distance:
Time:
Heart Rate:
i-Rate (1-10)
X-Training:
Sleep Hours:
Weight:
Mood: ☺ ☺ ☺ Other

FUEL LOG

WATER: 6-8 × 8 OZ.	FRUITS: 2-4	VEGGIES: 3-5	WHOLE GRAIN SERVINGS: 6-11	PROTEIN: 4-6 OZ.	LIMIT FAT?	ALCOHOLIC BEVERAGES?	LIMIT "EMPTY" CARBS?
☐☐☐☐ / ☐☐☐☐	☐☐ / ☐☐	☐☐ / ☐☐	☐☐☐ / ☐☐☐ / ☐☐☐	☐☐☐ / ☐☐☐	Y N	Y N	Y N

WEATHER: SUN WIND RAIN CLOUDY SNOW
TEMP: _____

THURSDAY / Date:

Today's goal:

Training notes:

Distance:
Time:
Heart Rate:
i-Rate (1-10)
X-Training:
Sleep Hours:
Weight:
Mood: ☺ ☺ ☺ Other

FUEL LOG

WATER: 6-8 × 8 OZ.	FRUITS: 2-4	VEGGIES: 3-5	WHOLE GRAIN SERVINGS: 6-11	PROTEIN: 4-6 OZ.	LIMIT FAT?	ALCOHOLIC BEVERAGES?	LIMIT "EMPTY" CARBS?
☐☐☐☐ / ☐☐☐☐	☐☐ / ☐☐	☐☐ / ☐☐	☐☐☐ / ☐☐☐ / ☐☐☐	☐☐☐ / ☐☐☐	Y N	Y N	Y N

WEATHER: SUN WIND RAIN CLOUDY SNOW
TEMP: _____

FRIDAY / Date: _____

Today's goal: _____

Distance: _____
Time: _____
Heart Rate: _____
i-Rate (1-10): _____
X-Training: _____
Sleep Hours: _____
Weight: _____
Mood: ☺ 😐 ☹ Other

WEATHER:
SUN WIND
RAIN CLOUDY
SNOW
TEMP: _____

Training notes: _____

FUEL LOG

WATER: 6-8 x 8 OZ.	FRUITS: 2-4	VEGGIES: 3-5	WHOLE GRAIN SERVINGS: 6-11	PROTEIN: 4-6 OZ.	LIMIT FAT?	ALCOHOLIC BEVERAGES?	LIMIT "EMPTY" CARBS?
☐☐☐☐ ☐☐☐☐	☐☐ ☐☐	☐☐☐ ☐☐	☐☐☐☐ ☐☐☐☐ ☐☐☐	☐☐☐ ☐☐☐	Y N	Y N	Y N

SATURDAY / Date: _____

Today's goal: _____

Distance: _____
Time: _____
Heart Rate: _____
i-Rate (1-10): _____
X-Training: _____
Sleep Hours: _____
Weight: _____
Mood: ☺ 😐 ☹ Other

WEATHER:
SUN WIND
RAIN CLOUDY
SNOW
TEMP: _____

Training notes: _____

FUEL LOG

WATER: 6-8 x 8 OZ.	FRUITS: 2-4	VEGGIES: 3-5	WHOLE GRAIN SERVINGS: 6-11	PROTEIN: 4-6 OZ.	LIMIT FAT?	ALCOHOLIC BEVERAGES?	LIMIT "EMPTY" CARBS?
☐☐☐☐ ☐☐☐☐	☐☐ ☐☐	☐☐☐ ☐☐	☐☐☐☐ ☐☐☐☐ ☐☐☐	☐☐☐ ☐☐☐	Y N	Y N	Y N

SUNDAY / Date: _____

Today's goal: _____

Distance: _____
Time: _____
Heart Rate: _____
i-Rate (1-10): _____
X-Training: _____
Sleep Hours: _____
Weight: _____
Mood: ☺ 😐 ☹ Other

WEATHER:
SUN WIND
RAIN CLOUDY
SNOW
TEMP: _____

Training notes: _____

FUEL LOG

WATER: 6-8 x 8 OZ.	FRUITS: 2-4	VEGGIES: 3-5	WHOLE GRAIN SERVINGS: 6-11	PROTEIN: 4-6 OZ.	LIMIT FAT?	ALCOHOLIC BEVERAGES?	LIMIT "EMPTY" CARBS?
☐☐☐☐ ☐☐☐☐	☐☐ ☐☐	☐☐☐ ☐☐	☐☐☐☐ ☐☐☐☐ ☐☐☐	☐☐☐ ☐☐☐	Y N	Y N	Y N

WEEK OF: _____

GOALS FOR WEEK: _____

WEEKLY TOTAL: _____

YEAR-TO-DATE TOTAL: _____

The track is where you can learn what works, experience was doesn't, and walk away knowing that you've made true training progress.

MONDAY / Date:

Today's goal:

Training notes:

Distance: ___
Time: ___
Heart Rate: ___
i-Rate (1-10) ___
X-Training: ___
Sleep Hours: ___
Weight: ___
Mood: ☺ ☺ ☹ Other

FUEL LOG

WATER: 6-8 × 8 OZ.	FRUITS: 2-4	VEGGIES: 3-5	WHOLE GRAIN SERVINGS: 6-11	PROTEIN: 4-6 OZ.	LIMIT FAT?	ALCOHOLIC BEVERAGES?	LIMIT "EMPTY" CARBS?
☐☐☐☐ ☐☐☐☐	☐☐ ☐☐	☐☐ ☐☐☐	☐☐☐☐ ☐☐☐☐ ☐☐☐	☐☐☐ ☐☐☐	Y N	Y N	Y N

WEATHER: SUN WIND RAIN CLOUDY SNOW
TEMP: ___

TUESDAY / Date:

Today's goal:

Training notes:

Distance: ___
Time: ___
Heart Rate: ___
i-Rate (1-10) ___
X-Training: ___
Sleep Hours: ___
Weight: ___
Mood: ☺ ☺ ☹ Other

FUEL LOG

WATER: 6-8 × 8 OZ.	FRUITS: 2-4	VEGGIES: 3-5	WHOLE GRAIN SERVINGS: 6-11	PROTEIN: 4-6 OZ.	LIMIT FAT?	ALCOHOLIC BEVERAGES?	LIMIT "EMPTY" CARBS?
☐☐☐☐ ☐☐☐☐	☐☐ ☐☐	☐☐ ☐☐☐	☐☐☐☐ ☐☐☐☐ ☐☐☐	☐☐☐ ☐☐☐	Y N	Y N	Y N

WEATHER: SUN WIND RAIN CLOUDY SNOW
TEMP: ___

WEDNESDAY / Date:

Today's goal:

Training notes:

Distance: ___
Time: ___
Heart Rate: ___
i-Rate (1-10) ___
X-Training: ___
Sleep Hours: ___
Weight: ___
Mood: ☺ ☺ ☹ Other

FUEL LOG

WATER: 6-8 × 8 OZ.	FRUITS: 2-4	VEGGIES: 3-5	WHOLE GRAIN SERVINGS: 6-11	PROTEIN: 4-6 OZ.	LIMIT FAT?	ALCOHOLIC BEVERAGES?	LIMIT "EMPTY" CARBS?
☐☐☐☐ ☐☐☐☐	☐☐ ☐☐	☐☐ ☐☐☐	☐☐☐☐ ☐☐☐☐ ☐☐☐	☐☐☐ ☐☐☐	Y N	Y N	Y N

WEATHER: SUN WIND RAIN CLOUDY SNOW
TEMP: ___

THURSDAY / Date:

Today's goal:

Training notes:

Distance: ___
Time: ___
Heart Rate: ___
i-Rate (1-10) ___
X-Training: ___
Sleep Hours: ___
Weight: ___
Mood: ☺ ☺ ☹ Other

FUEL LOG

WATER: 6-8 × 8 OZ.	FRUITS: 2-4	VEGGIES: 3-5	WHOLE GRAIN SERVINGS: 6-11	PROTEIN: 4-6 OZ.	LIMIT FAT?	ALCOHOLIC BEVERAGES?	LIMIT "EMPTY" CARBS?
☐☐☐☐ ☐☐☐☐	☐☐ ☐☐	☐☐ ☐☐☐	☐☐☐☐ ☐☐☐☐ ☐☐☐	☐☐☐ ☐☐☐	Y N	Y N	Y N

WEATHER: SUN WIND RAIN CLOUDY SNOW
TEMP: ___

FRIDAY / Date:

Training notes: _____

Today's goal: _____

Distance: _____
Time: _____
Heart Rate: _____
i-Rate (1-10): _____
X-Training: _____
Sleep Hours: _____
Weight: _____
Mood: ☺ ☺ ☹ Other

WEATHER: SUN WIND RAIN CLOUDY SNOW
TEMP: _____

FUEL LOG

WATER: 6-8 × 8 OZ.	FRUITS: 2-4	VEGGIES: 3-5	WHOLE GRAIN SERVINGS: 6-11	PROTEIN: 4-6 OZ.	LIMIT FAT?	ALCOHOLIC BEVERAGES?	LIMIT "EMPTY" CARBS?
☐☐☐☐ ☐☐☐☐	☐☐ ☐☐	☐☐☐ ☐☐	☐☐☐☐☐ ☐☐☐☐☐ ☐	☐☐☐ ☐☐	Y N	Y N	Y N

SATURDAY / Date:

Training notes: _____

Today's goal: _____

Distance: _____
Time: _____
Heart Rate: _____
i-Rate (1-10): _____
X-Training: _____
Sleep Hours: _____
Weight: _____
Mood: ☺ ☺ ☹ Other

WEATHER: SUN WIND RAIN CLOUDY SNOW
TEMP: _____

FUEL LOG

WATER: 6-8 × 8 OZ.	FRUITS: 2-4	VEGGIES: 3-5	WHOLE GRAIN SERVINGS: 6-11	PROTEIN: 4-6 OZ.	LIMIT FAT?	ALCOHOLIC BEVERAGES?	LIMIT "EMPTY" CARBS?
☐☐☐☐ ☐☐☐☐	☐☐ ☐☐	☐☐☐ ☐☐	☐☐☐☐☐ ☐☐☐☐☐ ☐	☐☐☐ ☐☐	Y N	Y N	Y N

SUNDAY / Date:

Training notes: _____

Today's goal: _____

Distance: _____
Time: _____
Heart Rate: _____
i-Rate (1-10): _____
X-Training: _____
Sleep Hours: _____
Weight: _____
Mood: ☺ ☺ ☹ Other

WEATHER: SUN WIND RAIN CLOUDY SNOW
TEMP: _____

FUEL LOG

WATER: 6-8 × 8 OZ.	FRUITS: 2-4	VEGGIES: 3-5	WHOLE GRAIN SERVINGS: 6-11	PROTEIN: 4-6 OZ.	LIMIT FAT?	ALCOHOLIC BEVERAGES?	LIMIT "EMPTY" CARBS?
☐☐☐☐ ☐☐☐☐	☐☐ ☐☐	☐☐☐ ☐☐	☐☐☐☐☐ ☐☐☐☐☐ ☐	☐☐☐ ☐☐	Y N	Y N	Y N

As you get deeper and deeper into a training program, the memory of why you started on this journey may start to fade. Think about what exactly motivated you to begin.

WEEK OF:

GOALS FOR WEEK:

WEEKLY TOTAL: _____

YEAR-TO-DATE TOTAL:

HOOP DREAMS

I had my shot. There was one brief moment where my destiny was in my hands. Watching the ball sail off the tip of my fingers I had no idea what that one shot would mean.

Like most twelve-year-old boys, I wanted to be an athlete, so I tried out for the Rhodes Elementary School basketball team. Being a seventh grader, being nearly the youngest in my class, and being short didn't deter me. I'd seen the uniforms, I'd been to the games, and I'd heard the cheerleaders calling out the player's names. I wanted to be on the team.

It may help put this in perspective for you to know that I shot free-throws using the two-handed, between-the-legs technique since I wasn't strong enough to actually shoot the ball overhand. After each practice, I'd stay until I had made twenty baskets from the free-throw line. The coach was impressed with my tenacity, if not my talent.

Then came the moment. We were behind by one point, to our cross-city rivals, there we just a few seconds left when the coach called a time out. "Bingham", he yelled. "Get ready to go in." This was a major shock since I had never actually played *in* a game at that point. The next words out of his mouth stunned everyone.

"Let Bingham take the shot. No one will expect it. No one will be guarding him. Toss him the inbound pass, get out of his way, and get under the basket." Then he turned to me and said: "Just get close enough to shoot a free-throw."

My heart was pounding. My palms were sweating. The coach was right. Not one opposing player came within fifty feet of me.

The inbound pass came to me, I had the ball in my hands, the coach was yelling, the team was yelling, the cheerleaders were yelling. And then it happened. I moved toward the basket. I even managed to dribble once or twice. But instead of taking the under-hand shot that I had practice, I drew the ball up and shot it over-hand. As I pushed to ball off I could feel the room go into a state of suspended animation. The world stopped. So did the ball. Well, it didn't actually stop. It just sort of fell harmlessly to the ground and into the hands of an all too eager opponent who raced past me and scored an easy basket. We lost the game by three points.

Adolescent boys are not the most forgiving people on earth. Neither was the coach. In fact, even the cheerleaders took turns berating me. I'm not sure what was the most humiliating, the taunts by the opponents or by my teammates, but the result was that I never put on the uniform again. I never put on *any* uniform again. And never played on another school sports team.

It was 32 years later that I tried to become an athlete again. 32 years before I worked up the courage to put on a pair of running shoes and pin a race number to my chest. 32 years before I had the nerve to admit that more than anything in my life I had always wanted to be an athlete.

So often we are defined by moments in our lives over which we have little or no control. Too often, that one instant becomes the turning point. Those moments are, after all, just that. Moments. And yet there are so many of us, who, as adult-onset athletes, must first overcome our pasts before we can dream of a future.

I don't know what happened to anyone that was on that team with me. I don't know what happened to the coach. I don't know if any of them have run 24 marathons, or hundreds of 5 and 10K's. But I have. Every starting line is my chance to erase that memory. Every finish line is a chance to redeem myself. And I savor every victory I have over myself.

There are times when I wonder how my life would have changed if I had made the shot. I wonder if there are others, like me, who turned to running because then their failures wouldn't affect the entire team. And I wonder if I might have found out all those years ago what I've only recently discovered, that what really matters most is being in the game. Waddle on, friends.

MONDAY / Date:

Training notes:

Today's goal:

Distance:
Time:
Heart Rate:
i-Rate (1-10)
X-Training:
Sleep Hours:
Weight:
Mood: ☺ ☺ ☹ Other

WEATHER:
SUN WIND
RAIN CLOUDY
SNOW
TEMP: ___

FUEL LOG

WATER: 6-8 x 8 OZ.	FRUITS: 2-4	VEGGIES: 3-5	WHOLE GRAIN SERVINGS: 6-11	PROTEIN: 4-6 OZ.	LIMIT FAT?	ALCOHOLIC BEVERAGES?	LIMIT "EMPTY" CARBS?
☐☐☐☐ ☐☐☐☐	☐☐ ☐☐	☐☐☐ ☐☐	☐☐☐☐ ☐☐☐☐☐ ☐	☐☐☐ ☐☐☐	Y N	Y N	Y N

TUESDAY / Date:

Training notes:

Today's goal:

Distance:
Time:
Heart Rate:
i-Rate (1-10)
X-Training:
Sleep Hours:
Weight:
Mood: ☺ ☺ ☹ Other

WEATHER:
SUN WIND
RAIN CLOUDY
SNOW
TEMP: ___

FUEL LOG

WATER: 6-8 x 8 OZ.	FRUITS: 2-4	VEGGIES: 3-5	WHOLE GRAIN SERVINGS: 6-11	PROTEIN: 4-6 OZ.	LIMIT FAT?	ALCOHOLIC BEVERAGES?	LIMIT "EMPTY" CARBS?
☐☐☐☐ ☐☐☐☐	☐☐ ☐☐	☐☐☐ ☐☐	☐☐☐☐ ☐☐☐☐☐ ☐	☐☐☐ ☐☐☐	Y N	Y N	Y N

WEDNESDAY / Date:

Training notes:

Today's goal:

Distance:
Time:
Heart Rate:
i-Rate (1-10)
X-Training:
Sleep Hours:
Weight:
Mood: ☺ ☺ ☹ Other

WEATHER:
SUN WIND
RAIN CLOUDY
SNOW
TEMP: ___

FUEL LOG

WATER: 6-8 x 8 OZ.	FRUITS: 2-4	VEGGIES: 3-5	WHOLE GRAIN SERVINGS: 6-11	PROTEIN: 4-6 OZ.	LIMIT FAT?	ALCOHOLIC BEVERAGES?	LIMIT "EMPTY" CARBS?
☐☐☐☐ ☐☐☐☐	☐☐ ☐☐	☐☐☐ ☐☐	☐☐☐☐ ☐☐☐☐☐ ☐	☐☐☐ ☐☐☐	Y N	Y N	Y N

THURSDAY / Date:

Training notes:

Today's goal:

Distance:
Time:
Heart Rate:
i-Rate (1-10)
X-Training:
Sleep Hours:
Weight:
Mood: ☺ ☺ ☹ Other

WEATHER:
SUN WIND
RAIN CLOUDY
SNOW
TEMP: ___

FUEL LOG

WATER: 6-8 x 8 OZ.	FRUITS: 2-4	VEGGIES: 3-5	WHOLE GRAIN SERVINGS: 6-11	PROTEIN: 4-6 OZ.	LIMIT FAT?	ALCOHOLIC BEVERAGES?	LIMIT "EMPTY" CARBS?
☐☐☐☐ ☐☐☐☐	☐☐ ☐☐	☐☐☐ ☐☐	☐☐☐☐ ☐☐☐☐☐ ☐	☐☐☐ ☐☐☐	Y N	Y N	Y N

FRIDAY / Date: _____

Today's goal: _____

Training notes: _____

FUEL LOG

WATER: 6-8 x 8 OZ.	FRUITS: 2-4	VEGGIES: 3-5	WHOLE GRAIN SERVINGS: 6-11	PROTEIN: 4-6 OZ.	LIMIT FAT?	ALCOHOLIC BEVERAGES?	LIMIT "EMPTY" CARBS?
☐☐☐☐ ☐☐☐☐	☐☐ ☐☐	☐☐ ☐☐	☐☐☐☐☐ ☐☐☐☐☐☐	☐☐☐ ☐☐☐	Y N	Y N	Y N

WEATHER: SUN WIND RAIN CLOUDY SNOW   TEMP: _____

Distance: _____
Time: _____
Heart Rate: _____
i-Rate (1-10): _____
X-Training: _____
Sleep Hours: _____
Weight: _____
Mood: ☺ ☺ ☹ ☹ Other

SATURDAY / Date: _____

Today's goal: _____

Training notes: _____

FUEL LOG

WATER: 6-8 x 8 OZ.	FRUITS: 2-4	VEGGIES: 3-5	WHOLE GRAIN SERVINGS: 6-11	PROTEIN: 4-6 OZ.	LIMIT FAT?	ALCOHOLIC BEVERAGES?	LIMIT "EMPTY" CARBS?
☐☐☐☐ ☐☐☐☐	☐☐ ☐☐	☐☐ ☐☐	☐☐☐☐☐ ☐☐☐☐☐☐	☐☐☐ ☐☐☐	Y N	Y N	Y N

WEATHER: SUN WIND RAIN CLOUDY SNOW   TEMP: _____

Distance: _____
Time: _____
Heart Rate: _____
i-Rate (1-10): _____
X-Training: _____
Sleep Hours: _____
Weight: _____
Mood: ☺ ☺ ☹ ☹ Other

SUNDAY / Date: _____

Today's goal: _____

Training notes: _____

FUEL LOG

WATER: 6-8 x 8 OZ.	FRUITS: 2-4	VEGGIES: 3-5	WHOLE GRAIN SERVINGS: 6-11	PROTEIN: 4-6 OZ.	LIMIT FAT?	ALCOHOLIC BEVERAGES?	LIMIT "EMPTY" CARBS?
☐☐☐☐ ☐☐☐☐	☐☐ ☐☐	☐☐ ☐☐	☐☐☐☐☐ ☐☐☐☐☐☐	☐☐☐ ☐☐☐	Y N	Y N	Y N

WEATHER: SUN WIND RAIN CLOUDY SNOW   TEMP: _____

Distance: _____
Time: _____
Heart Rate: _____
i-Rate (1-10): _____
X-Training: _____
Sleep Hours: _____
Weight: _____
Mood: ☺ ☺ ☹ ☹ Other

WEEK OF: _____

GOALS FOR WEEK:

It happens to all of us I think. The moment comes when what was impossible is possible, the unthinkable thinkable, the undoable done.

WEEKLY TOTAL: _____

YEAR-TO-DATE TOTAL: _____

MONDAY / Date: _____

Training notes: _____

Distance: _____
Time: _____
Heart Rate: _____
i-Rate (1-10): _____
X-Training: _____
Sleep Hours: _____
Weight: _____
Mood: ☺ ☺ ☹ ☹ Other

Today's goal: _____

FUEL LOG

WATER: 6-8 × 8 OZ.	FRUITS: 2-4	VEGGIES: 3-5	WHOLE GRAIN SERVINGS: 6-11	PROTEIN: 4-6 OZ.	LIMIT FAT?	ALCOHOLIC BEVERAGES?	LIMIT "EMPTY" CARBS?
☐☐☐☐ ☐☐☐☐	☐☐ ☐☐	☐☐☐ ☐☐	☐☐☐☐☐ ☐	☐☐☐ ☐☐	Y N	Y N	Y N

WEATHER: SUN WIND RAIN CLOUDY SNOW
TEMP: _____

TUESDAY / Date: _____

Training notes: _____

Distance: _____
Time: _____
Heart Rate: _____
i-Rate (1-10): _____
X-Training: _____
Sleep Hours: _____
Weight: _____
Mood: ☺ ☺ ☹ ☹ Other

Today's goal: _____

FUEL LOG

WATER: 6-8 × 8 OZ.	FRUITS: 2-4	VEGGIES: 3-5	WHOLE GRAIN SERVINGS: 6-11	PROTEIN: 4-6 OZ.	LIMIT FAT?	ALCOHOLIC BEVERAGES?	LIMIT "EMPTY" CARBS?
☐☐☐☐ ☐☐☐☐	☐☐ ☐☐	☐☐☐ ☐☐	☐☐☐☐☐ ☐	☐☐☐ ☐☐	Y N	Y N	Y N

WEATHER: SUN WIND RAIN CLOUDY SNOW
TEMP: _____

WEDNESDAY / Date: _____

Training notes: _____

Distance: _____
Time: _____
Heart Rate: _____
i-Rate (1-10): _____
X-Training: _____
Sleep Hours: _____
Weight: _____
Mood: ☺ ☺ ☹ ☹ Other

Today's goal: _____

FUEL LOG

WATER: 6-8 × 8 OZ.	FRUITS: 2-4	VEGGIES: 3-5	WHOLE GRAIN SERVINGS: 6-11	PROTEIN: 4-6 OZ.	LIMIT FAT?	ALCOHOLIC BEVERAGES?	LIMIT "EMPTY" CARBS?
☐☐☐☐ ☐☐☐☐	☐☐ ☐☐	☐☐☐ ☐☐	☐☐☐☐☐ ☐	☐☐☐ ☐☐	Y N	Y N	Y N

WEATHER: SUN WIND RAIN CLOUDY SNOW
TEMP: _____

THURSDAY / Date: _____

Training notes: _____

Distance: _____
Time: _____
Heart Rate: _____
i-Rate (1-10): _____
X-Training: _____
Sleep Hours: _____
Weight: _____
Mood: ☺ ☺ ☹ ☹ Other

Today's goal: _____

FUEL LOG

WATER: 6-8 × 8 OZ.	FRUITS: 2-4	VEGGIES: 3-5	WHOLE GRAIN SERVINGS: 6-11	PROTEIN: 4-6 OZ.	LIMIT FAT?	ALCOHOLIC BEVERAGES?	LIMIT "EMPTY" CARBS?
☐☐☐☐ ☐☐☐☐	☐☐ ☐☐	☐☐☐ ☐☐	☐☐☐☐☐ ☐	☐☐☐ ☐☐	Y N	Y N	Y N

WEATHER: SUN WIND RAIN CLOUDY SNOW
TEMP: _____

FRIDAY / Date:

Today's goal:

_____

Distance:
Time:
Heart Rate:
i-Rate (1-10)
X-Training:
Sleep Hours:
Weight:
Mood: ☺ ☺ ☹ ☹ Other

FUEL LOG

WATER: 6-8 × 8 OZ.	FRUITS: 2-4	VEGGIES: 3-5	WHOLE GRAIN SERVINGS: 6-11	PROTEIN: 4-6 OZ.	LIMIT FAT?	ALCOHOLIC BEVERAGES?	LIMIT "EMPTY" CARBS?	WEATHER:
☐☐☐☐ ☐☐☐☐	☐☐ ☐☐	☐☐ ☐☐	☐☐☐☐☐ ☐☐☐☐☐	☐☐☐ ☐☐	Y N	Y N	Y N	SUN WIND RAIN CLOUDY SNOW TEMP:____

SATURDAY / Date:

Today's goal:

Training notes:

_____

Distance:
Time:
Heart Rate:
i-Rate (1-10)
X-Training:
Sleep Hours:
Weight:
Mood: ☺ ☺ ☹ ☹ Other

FUEL LOG

WATER: 6-8 × 8 OZ.	FRUITS: 2-4	VEGGIES: 3-5	WHOLE GRAIN SERVINGS: 6-11	PROTEIN: 4-6 OZ.	LIMIT FAT?	ALCOHOLIC BEVERAGES?	LIMIT "EMPTY" CARBS?	WEATHER:
☐☐☐☐ ☐☐☐☐	☐☐ ☐☐	☐☐ ☐☐	☐☐☐☐☐ ☐☐☐☐☐	☐☐☐ ☐☐	Y N	Y N	Y N	SUN WIND RAIN CLOUDY SNOW TEMP:____

SUNDAY / Date:

Today's goal:

Training notes:

_____

Distance:
Time:
Heart Rate:
i-Rate (1-10)
X-Training:
Sleep Hours:
Weight:
Mood: ☺ ☺ ☹ ☹ Other

FUEL LOG

WATER: 6-8 × 8 OZ.	FRUITS: 2-4	VEGGIES: 3-5	WHOLE GRAIN SERVINGS: 6-11	PROTEIN: 4-6 OZ.	LIMIT FAT?	ALCOHOLIC BEVERAGES?	LIMIT "EMPTY" CARBS?	WEATHER:
☐☐☐☐ ☐☐☐☐	☐☐ ☐☐	☐☐ ☐☐	☐☐☐☐☐ ☐☐☐☐☐	☐☐☐ ☐☐	Y N	Y N	Y N	SUN WIND RAIN CLOUDY SNOW TEMP:____

WEEK OF:

GOALS FOR WEEK:

WEEKLY TOTAL: _____

YEAR-TO-DATE TOTAL:

If you miss a workout or two and have to start a few days back, just remember that the cycle of success is normal.

MONDAY / Date:

Today's goal: _____

Training notes: _____

Distance: _____
Time: _____
Heart Rate: _____
i-Rate (1-10) _____
X-Training: _____
Sleep Hours: _____
Weight: _____
Mood: ☺ ☺ ☹ Other

WEATHER:
SUN   WIND
RAIN   CLOUDY
SNOW
TEMP: _____

FUEL LOG

WATER: 6-8 × 8 OZ.	FRUITS: 2-4	VEGGIES: 3-5	WHOLE GRAIN SERVINGS: 6-11	PROTEIN: 4-6 OZ.	LIMIT FAT?	ALCOHOLIC BEVERAGES?	LIMIT "EMPTY" CARBS?
☐☐☐☐ ☐☐☐☐	☐☐ ☐☐	☐☐ ☐☐	☐☐☐☐ ☐☐☐☐	☐☐☐ ☐☐☐	Y N	Y N	Y N

TUESDAY / Date:

Today's goal: _____

Training notes: _____

Distance: _____
Time: _____
Heart Rate: _____
i-Rate (1-10) _____
X-Training: _____
Sleep Hours: _____
Weight: _____
Mood: ☺ ☺ ☹ Other

WEATHER:
SUN   WIND
RAIN   CLOUDY
SNOW
TEMP: _____

FUEL LOG

WATER: 6-8 × 8 OZ.	FRUITS: 2-4	VEGGIES: 3-5	WHOLE GRAIN SERVINGS: 6-11	PROTEIN: 4-6 OZ.	LIMIT FAT?	ALCOHOLIC BEVERAGES?	LIMIT "EMPTY" CARBS?
☐☐☐☐ ☐☐☐☐	☐☐ ☐☐	☐☐ ☐☐	☐☐☐☐ ☐☐☐☐	☐☐☐ ☐☐☐	Y N	Y N	Y N

WEDNESDAY / Date:

Today's goal: _____

Training notes: _____

Distance: _____
Time: _____
Heart Rate: _____
i-Rate (1-10) _____
X-Training: _____
Sleep Hours: _____
Weight: _____
Mood: ☺ ☺ ☹ Other

WEATHER:
SUN   WIND
RAIN   CLOUDY
SNOW
TEMP: _____

FUEL LOG

WATER: 6-8 × 8 OZ.	FRUITS: 2-4	VEGGIES: 3-5	WHOLE GRAIN SERVINGS: 6-11	PROTEIN: 4-6 OZ.	LIMIT FAT?	ALCOHOLIC BEVERAGES?	LIMIT "EMPTY" CARBS?
☐☐☐☐ ☐☐☐☐	☐☐ ☐☐	☐☐ ☐☐	☐☐☐☐ ☐☐☐☐	☐☐☐ ☐☐☐	Y N	Y N	Y N

THURSDAY / Date:

Today's goal: _____

Training notes: _____

Distance: _____
Time: _____
Heart Rate: _____
i-Rate (1-10) _____
X-Training: _____
Sleep Hours: _____
Weight: _____
Mood: ☺ ☺ ☹ Other

WEATHER:
SUN   WIND
RAIN   CLOUDY
SNOW
TEMP: _____

FUEL LOG

WATER: 6-8 × 8 OZ.	FRUITS: 2-4	VEGGIES: 3-5	WHOLE GRAIN SERVINGS: 6-11	PROTEIN: 4-6 OZ.	LIMIT FAT?	ALCOHOLIC BEVERAGES?	LIMIT "EMPTY" CARBS?
☐☐☐☐ ☐☐☐☐	☐☐ ☐☐	☐☐ ☐☐	☐☐☐☐ ☐☐☐☐	☐☐☐ ☐☐☐	Y N	Y N	Y N

FRIDAY / Date:

Today's goal:

Training notes:

FUEL LOG

WATER: 6-8 x 8 OZ.	FRUITS: 2-4	VEGGIES: 3-5	WHOLE GRAIN SERVINGS: 6-11	PROTEIN: 4-6 OZ.	LIMIT FAT?	ALCOHOLIC BEVERAGES?	LIMIT "EMPTY" CARBS?
☐☐☐☐	☐☐	☐☐	☐☐☐☐	☐☐	Y N	Y N	Y N
☐☐☐☐	☐☐	☐☐	☐☐☐☐	☐☐			

Distance:
Time:
Heart Rate:
i-Rate (1-10):
X-Training:
Sleep Hours:
Weight:
Mood: ☺ ☺ ☹ ☹ Other

WEATHER: SUN WIND RAIN CLOUDY SNOW
TEMP: _____

SATURDAY / Date:

Today's goal:

Training notes:

FUEL LOG

WATER: 6-8 x 8 OZ.	FRUITS: 2-4	VEGGIES: 3-5	WHOLE GRAIN SERVINGS: 6-11	PROTEIN: 4-6 OZ.	LIMIT FAT?	ALCOHOLIC BEVERAGES?	LIMIT "EMPTY" CARBS?
☐☐☐☐	☐☐	☐☐	☐☐☐☐	☐☐	Y N	Y N	Y N
☐☐☐☐	☐☐	☐☐	☐☐☐☐	☐☐			

Distance:
Time:
Heart Rate:
i-Rate (1-10):
X-Training:
Sleep Hours:
Weight:
Mood: ☺ ☺ ☹ ☹ Other

WEATHER: SUN WIND RAIN CLOUDY SNOW
TEMP: _____

SUNDAY / Date:

Today's goal:

Training notes:

FUEL LOG

WATER: 6-8 x 8 OZ.	FRUITS: 2-4	VEGGIES: 3-5	WHOLE GRAIN SERVINGS: 6-11	PROTEIN: 4-6 OZ.	LIMIT FAT?	ALCOHOLIC BEVERAGES?	LIMIT "EMPTY" CARBS?
☐☐☐☐	☐☐	☐☐	☐☐☐☐	☐☐	Y N	Y N	Y N
☐☐☐☐	☐☐	☐☐	☐☐☐☐	☐☐			

Distance:
Time:
Heart Rate:
i-Rate (1-10):
X-Training:
Sleep Hours:
Weight:
Mood: ☺ ☺ ☹ ☹ Other

WEATHER: SUN WIND RAIN CLOUDY SNOW
TEMP: _____

WEEK OF:

GOALS FOR WEEK:

WEEKLY TOTAL: _____

YEAR-TO-DATE TOTAL:

If I'm content too long I get stale. If I push my limits too often I get frustrated. Let the momentum of your training work for you.

MONDAY / Date:

Training notes: _____

Today's goal: _____

Distance: _____
Time: _____
Heart Rate: _____
i-Rate (1-10): _____
X-Training: _____
Sleep Hours: _____
Weight: _____
Mood: ☺ ☺ ☹ ☹ Other

FUEL LOG

WATER: 6-8 × 8 OZ.	FRUITS: 2-4	VEGGIES: 3-5	WHOLE GRAIN SERVINGS: 6-11	PROTEIN: 4-6 OZ.	LIMIT FAT?	ALCOHOLIC BEVERAGES?	LIMIT "EMPTY" CARBS?
☐☐☐☐ ☐☐☐☐	☐☐ ☐☐	☐☐ ☐☐	☐☐☐☐☐ ☐	☐☐☐ ☐☐	Y N	Y N	Y N

WEATHER:
SUN WIND
RAIN CLOUDY
SNOW
TEMP: _____

TUESDAY / Date:

Training notes: _____

Today's goal: _____

Distance: _____
Time: _____
Heart Rate: _____
i-Rate (1-10): _____
X-Training: _____
Sleep Hours: _____
Weight: _____
Mood: ☺ ☺ ☹ ☹ Other

FUEL LOG

WATER: 6-8 × 8 OZ.	FRUITS: 2-4	VEGGIES: 3-5	WHOLE GRAIN SERVINGS: 6-11	PROTEIN: 4-6 OZ.	LIMIT FAT?	ALCOHOLIC BEVERAGES?	LIMIT "EMPTY" CARBS?
☐☐☐☐ ☐☐☐☐	☐☐ ☐☐	☐☐ ☐☐	☐☐☐☐☐ ☐	☐☐☐ ☐☐	Y N	Y N	Y N

WEATHER:
SUN WIND
RAIN CLOUDY
SNOW
TEMP: _____

WEDNESDAY / Date:

Training notes: _____

Today's goal: _____

Distance: _____
Time: _____
Heart Rate: _____
i-Rate (1-10): _____
X-Training: _____
Sleep Hours: _____
Weight: _____
Mood: ☺ ☺ ☹ ☹ Other

FUEL LOG

WATER: 6-8 × 8 OZ.	FRUITS: 2-4	VEGGIES: 3-5	WHOLE GRAIN SERVINGS: 6-11	PROTEIN: 4-6 OZ.	LIMIT FAT?	ALCOHOLIC BEVERAGES?	LIMIT "EMPTY" CARBS?
☐☐☐☐ ☐☐☐☐	☐☐ ☐☐	☐☐ ☐☐	☐☐☐☐☐ ☐	☐☐☐ ☐☐	Y N	Y N	Y N

WEATHER:
SUN WIND
RAIN CLOUDY
SNOW
TEMP: _____

THURSDAY / Date:

Training notes: _____

Today's goal: _____

Distance: _____
Time: _____
Heart Rate: _____
i-Rate (1-10): _____
X-Training: _____
Sleep Hours: _____
Weight: _____
Mood: ☺ ☺ ☹ ☹ Other

FUEL LOG

WATER: 6-8 × 8 OZ.	FRUITS: 2-4	VEGGIES: 3-5	WHOLE GRAIN SERVINGS: 6-11	PROTEIN: 4-6 OZ.	LIMIT FAT?	ALCOHOLIC BEVERAGES?	LIMIT "EMPTY" CARBS?
☐☐☐☐ ☐☐☐☐	☐☐ ☐☐	☐☐ ☐☐	☐☐☐☐☐ ☐	☐☐☐ ☐☐	Y N	Y N	Y N

WEATHER:
SUN WIND
RAIN CLOUDY
SNOW
TEMP: _____

FRIDAY / Date:

Training notes:
_____

Today's goal:

| Distance: |
| Time: |
| Heart Rate: |
| i-Rate (1-10) |
| X-Training: |
| Sleep Hours: |
| Weight: |
| Mood: ☺ ☺ ☹ Other |

FUEL LOG

WATER: 6-8 x 8 OZ.	FRUITS: 2-4	VEGGIES: 3-5	WHOLE GRAIN SERVINGS: 6-11	PROTEIN: 4-6 OZ.	LIMIT FAT?	ALCOHOLIC BEVERAGES?	LIMIT "EMPTY" CARBS?
☐☐☐ ☐☐☐	☐☐ ☐☐	☐☐ ☐☐	☐☐☐ ☐☐☐ ☐☐☐	☐☐☐ ☐☐☐	Y N	Y N	Y N

WEATHER:
SUN WIND
RAIN CLOUDY
SNOW
TEMP: _____

SATURDAY / Date:

Training notes:
_____

Today's goal:

| Distance: |
| Time: |
| Heart Rate: |
| i-Rate (1-10) |
| X-Training: |
| Sleep Hours: |
| Weight: |
| Mood: ☺ ☺ ☹ Other |

FUEL LOG

WATER: 6-8 x 8 OZ.	FRUITS: 2-4	VEGGIES: 3-5	WHOLE GRAIN SERVINGS: 6-11	PROTEIN: 4-6 OZ.	LIMIT FAT?	ALCOHOLIC BEVERAGES?	LIMIT "EMPTY" CARBS?
☐☐☐ ☐☐☐	☐☐ ☐☐	☐☐ ☐☐	☐☐☐ ☐☐☐ ☐☐☐	☐☐☐ ☐☐☐	Y N	Y N	Y N

WEATHER:
SUN WIND
RAIN CLOUDY
SNOW
TEMP: _____

SUNDAY / Date:

Training notes:
_____

Today's goal:

| Distance: |
| Time: |
| Heart Rate: |
| i-Rate (1-10) |
| X-Training: |
| Sleep Hours: |
| Weight: |
| Mood: ☺ ☺ ☹ Other |

FUEL LOG

WATER: 6-8 x 8 OZ.	FRUITS: 2-4	VEGGIES: 3-5	WHOLE GRAIN SERVINGS: 6-11	PROTEIN: 4-6 OZ.	LIMIT FAT?	ALCOHOLIC BEVERAGES?	LIMIT "EMPTY" CARBS?
☐☐☐ ☐☐☐	☐☐ ☐☐	☐☐ ☐☐	☐☐☐ ☐☐☐ ☐☐☐	☐☐☐ ☐☐☐	Y N	Y N	Y N

WEATHER:
SUN WIND
RAIN CLOUDY
SNOW
TEMP: _____

WEEK OF:

GOALS FOR WEEK:

WEEKLY TOTAL: _____

YEAR-TO-DATE TOTAL:

Don't worry about the quality of any particular workout. Focus on the quality of the days and weeks and months that you've already put in.

PRIZED POSSESSIONS

They were all over my parent's house, those monuments to my childhood: the plaster cast of my hand, a Valentine's card I made myself. Now, my home is filled with the same monuments to my son's childhood: the wreath made of rotini pasta that gets hung on the door every Christmas, the rock on which is glued felt feet, head, and tail that, if you have enough imagination, looks very much like a turtle. They are prized possessions.

My home is also filled with the monuments of my return to childhood, of my return to a time of play and joy: my finisher's medals and photos, my race T-shirts, and even a second place trophy from a duathlon where there were only two males competing in the 45-49 age group. These too have become prized possessions. I'm always interested in what other runners do with their medals. I've been to homes where each medal is ceremoniously displayed in a glass-covered case complete with the race number and race shirt, and photo. I don't know how these people do it. I don't understand how they find the time.

My medals are hung around the bedroom doorknob. Why? Because that's where I unpack after a race weekend. I come home, empty the suitcase, and hang the medal on the door. Unceremonious? Sort of. But, as the number of medals has increased, they have become something like a wind chime. Most of the time I don't notice them hanging there. But, when I move the door, their clanging together reminds me of what I have accomplished.

In fact, now, after completing over twenty marathons, I've had to start hanging the medals on both sides of the doorknob. The ribbons are so thick that it's impossible to actually turn the knob. And their combined weight makes me worry about the strength of the hinges. The last thing I want is the door crashing to the ground in the middle of the night.

Recently, I was asked if, after so many marathons, it gets any easier. It might for some, but not for me. Sure, I understand the distance better. I know not to blast off in the early miles, I recognize the brain-fade in the middle miles, and I'm not surprised by the fatigue in the later miles. But, like having more than one cat, no two marathons are ever exactly the same. And the lessons learned in one may be of no use whatever in the next.

The doorknob holds the memories of the good days, and the not so good days, of people who brought great inspiration into my life, and then faded away. There are memories of cities and streets and steps taken towards a finish line that never really seemed to be the end.

Sometimes I think that I should put the medals in a place of greater distinction. I think that I should have them displayed where others can see them. But then I remember why I wanted those medals in the first place. I wanted them not to show to anyone else, but as reminders of my own journey as a runner, and as a person.

And like my son's Rotini wreath, I will prize them not for what they are, but for what they mean to me.

Waddle on, friends.

MONDAY / Date:

Today's goal:

Training notes:

Distance:
Time:
Heart Rate:
i-Rate (1-10)
X-Training:
Sleep Hours:
Weight:
Mood: ☺ ☺ ☹ Other

WEATHER:
SUN WIND
RAIN CLOUDY
SNOW
TEMP:

FUEL LOG

WATER: 6-8 x 8 OZ.	FRUITS: 2-4	VEGGIES: 3-5	WHOLE GRAIN SERVINGS: 6-11	PROTEIN: 4-6 OZ.	LIMIT FAT?	ALCOHOLIC BEVERAGES?	LIMIT "EMPTY" CARBS?
☐☐☐☐ ☐☐☐☐	☐☐ ☐☐	☐☐ ☐☐	☐☐☐ ☐☐☐ ☐☐☐	☐☐ ☐☐ ☐☐	Y N	Y N	Y N

TUESDAY / Date:

Today's goal:

Training notes:

Distance:
Time:
Heart Rate:
i-Rate (1-10)
X-Training:
Sleep Hours:
Weight:
Mood: ☺ ☺ ☹ Other

WEATHER:
SUN WIND
RAIN CLOUDY
SNOW
TEMP:

FUEL LOG

WATER: 6-8 x 8 OZ.	FRUITS: 2-4	VEGGIES: 3-5	WHOLE GRAIN SERVINGS: 6-11	PROTEIN: 4-6 OZ.	LIMIT FAT?	ALCOHOLIC BEVERAGES?	LIMIT "EMPTY" CARBS?
☐☐☐☐ ☐☐☐☐	☐☐ ☐☐	☐☐ ☐☐	☐☐☐ ☐☐☐ ☐☐☐	☐☐ ☐☐ ☐☐	Y N	Y N	Y N

WEDNESDAY / Date:

Today's goal:

Training notes:

Distance:
Time:
Heart Rate:
i-Rate (1-10)
X-Training:
Sleep Hours:
Weight:
Mood: ☺ ☺ ☹ Other

WEATHER:
SUN WIND
RAIN CLOUDY
SNOW
TEMP:

FUEL LOG

WATER: 6-8 x 8 OZ.	FRUITS: 2-4	VEGGIES: 3-5	WHOLE GRAIN SERVINGS: 6-11	PROTEIN: 4-6 OZ.	LIMIT FAT?	ALCOHOLIC BEVERAGES?	LIMIT "EMPTY" CARBS?
☐☐☐☐ ☐☐☐☐	☐☐ ☐☐	☐☐ ☐☐	☐☐☐ ☐☐☐ ☐☐☐	☐☐ ☐☐ ☐☐	Y N	Y N	Y N

THURSDAY / Date:

Today's goal:

Training notes:

Distance:
Time:
Heart Rate:
i-Rate (1-10)
X-Training:
Sleep Hours:
Weight:
Mood: ☺ ☺ ☹ Other

WEATHER:
SUN WIND
RAIN CLOUDY
SNOW
TEMP:

FUEL LOG

WATER: 6-8 x 8 OZ.	FRUITS: 2-4	VEGGIES: 3-5	WHOLE GRAIN SERVINGS: 6-11	PROTEIN: 4-6 OZ.	LIMIT FAT?	ALCOHOLIC BEVERAGES?	LIMIT "EMPTY" CARBS?
☐☐☐☐ ☐☐☐☐	☐☐ ☐☐	☐☐ ☐☐	☐☐☐ ☐☐☐ ☐☐☐	☐☐ ☐☐ ☐☐	Y N	Y N	Y N

FRIDAY / Date: _____

Today's goal: _____

Distance: _____
Time: _____
Heart Rate: _____
i-Rate (1-10): _____
X-Training: _____
Sleep Hours: _____
Weight: _____
Mood: ☺ 😐 ☹ Other ____

Training notes: _____

FUEL LOG

WATER: 6-8 x 8 OZ.	FRUITS: 2-4	VEGGIES: 3-5	WHOLE GRAIN SERVINGS: 6-11	PROTEIN: 4-6 OZ.	LIMIT FAT?	ALCOHOLIC BEVERAGES?	LIMIT "EMPTY" CARBS?
☐☐☐☐ ☐☐☐☐	☐☐ ☐☐	☐☐ ☐	☐☐☐☐☐ ☐☐☐☐☐☐	☐☐☐ ☐☐	Y N	Y N	Y N

WEATHER: SUN WIND RAIN CLOUDY SNOW TEMP: ____

SATURDAY / Date: _____

Today's goal: _____

Distance: _____
Time: _____
Heart Rate: _____
i-Rate (1-10): _____
X-Training: _____
Sleep Hours: _____
Weight: _____
Mood: ☺ 😐 ☹ Other ____

Training notes: _____

FUEL LOG

WATER: 6-8 x 8 OZ.	FRUITS: 2-4	VEGGIES: 3-5	WHOLE GRAIN SERVINGS: 6-11	PROTEIN: 4-6 OZ.	LIMIT FAT?	ALCOHOLIC BEVERAGES?	LIMIT "EMPTY" CARBS?
☐☐☐☐ ☐☐☐☐	☐☐ ☐☐	☐☐ ☐	☐☐☐☐☐ ☐☐☐☐☐☐	☐☐☐ ☐☐	Y N	Y N	Y N

WEATHER: SUN WIND RAIN CLOUDY SNOW TEMP: ____

SUNDAY / Date: _____

Today's goal: _____

Distance: _____
Time: _____
Heart Rate: _____
i-Rate (1-10): _____
X-Training: _____
Sleep Hours: _____
Weight: _____
Mood: ☺ 😐 ☹ Other ____

Training notes: _____

FUEL LOG

WATER: 6-8 x 8 OZ.	FRUITS: 2-4	VEGGIES: 3-5	WHOLE GRAIN SERVINGS: 6-11	PROTEIN: 4-6 OZ.	LIMIT FAT?	ALCOHOLIC BEVERAGES?	LIMIT "EMPTY" CARBS?
☐☐☐☐ ☐☐☐☐	☐☐ ☐☐	☐☐ ☐	☐☐☐☐☐ ☐☐☐☐☐☐	☐☐☐ ☐☐	Y N	Y N	Y N

WEATHER: SUN WIND RAIN CLOUDY SNOW TEMP: ____

WEEK OF: _____

GOALS FOR WEEK: _____

WEEKLY TOTAL: _____

YEAR-TO-DATE TOTAL: _____

> **You've boldly gone where you've never gone before, and you've not only survived but you've gotten stronger. You are becoming what you set out to become: an athlete.**

MONDAY / Date:

Training notes:

Today's goal:

| Distance: |
| Time: |
| Heart Rate: |
| i-Rate (1-10) |
| X-Training: |
| Sleep Hours: |
| Weight: |
| Mood: ☺ ☺ ☹ Other |

WEATHER:
SUN WIND
RAIN CLOUDY
SNOW
TEMP: _____

FUEL LOG

WATER: 6-8 x 8 OZ.	FRUITS: 2-4	VEGGIES: 3-5	WHOLE GRAIN SERVINGS: 6-11	PROTEIN: 4-6 OZ.	LIMIT FAT?	ALCOHOLIC BEVERAGES?	LIMIT "EMPTY" CARBS?
☐☐☐☐ ☐☐☐☐	☐☐ ☐☐	☐☐ ☐☐	☐☐☐☐☐ ☐☐☐☐☐ ☐	☐☐☐ ☐☐☐	Y N	Y N	Y N

TUESDAY / Date:

Training notes:

Today's goal:

| Distance: |
| Time: |
| Heart Rate: |
| i-Rate (1-10) |
| X-Training: |
| Sleep Hours: |
| Weight: |
| Mood: ☺ ☺ ☹ Other |

WEATHER:
SUN WIND
RAIN CLOUDY
SNOW
TEMP: _____

FUEL LOG

WATER: 6-8 x 8 OZ.	FRUITS: 2-4	VEGGIES: 3-5	WHOLE GRAIN SERVINGS: 6-11	PROTEIN: 4-6 OZ.	LIMIT FAT?	ALCOHOLIC BEVERAGES?	LIMIT "EMPTY" CARBS?
☐☐☐☐ ☐☐☐☐	☐☐ ☐☐	☐☐ ☐☐	☐☐☐☐☐ ☐☐☐☐☐ ☐	☐☐☐ ☐☐☐	Y N	Y N	Y N

WEDNESDAY / Date:

Training notes:

Today's goal:

| Distance: |
| Time: |
| Heart Rate: |
| i-Rate (1-10) |
| X-Training: |
| Sleep Hours: |
| Weight: |
| Mood: ☺ ☺ ☹ Other |

WEATHER:
SUN WIND
RAIN CLOUDY
SNOW
TEMP: _____

FUEL LOG

WATER: 6-8 x 8 OZ.	FRUITS: 2-4	VEGGIES: 3-5	WHOLE GRAIN SERVINGS: 6-11	PROTEIN: 4-6 OZ.	LIMIT FAT?	ALCOHOLIC BEVERAGES?	LIMIT "EMPTY" CARBS?
☐☐☐☐ ☐☐☐☐	☐☐ ☐☐	☐☐ ☐☐	☐☐☐☐☐ ☐☐☐☐☐ ☐	☐☐☐ ☐☐☐	Y N	Y N	Y N

THURSDAY / Date:

Training notes:

Today's goal:

| Distance: |
| Time: |
| Heart Rate: |
| i-Rate (1-10) |
| X-Training: |
| Sleep Hours: |
| Weight: |
| Mood: ☺ ☺ ☹ Other |

WEATHER:
SUN WIND
RAIN CLOUDY
SNOW
TEMP: _____

FUEL LOG

WATER: 6-8 x 8 OZ.	FRUITS: 2-4	VEGGIES: 3-5	WHOLE GRAIN SERVINGS: 6-11	PROTEIN: 4-6 OZ.	LIMIT FAT?	ALCOHOLIC BEVERAGES?	LIMIT "EMPTY" CARBS?
☐☐☐☐ ☐☐☐☐	☐☐ ☐☐	☐☐ ☐☐	☐☐☐☐☐ ☐☐☐☐☐ ☐	☐☐☐ ☐☐☐	Y N	Y N	Y N

FRIDAY / Date:

Training notes:

Today's goal:

Distance:
Time:
Heart Rate:
i-Rate (1-10)
X-Training:
Sleep Hours:
Weight:
Mood: ☺ ☺ ☺ Other

WEATHER:
SUN WIND
RAIN CLOUDY
SNOW
TEMP: _____

FUEL LOG

WATER: 6-8 x 8 OZ.	FRUITS: 2-4	VEGGIES: 3-5	WHOLE GRAIN SERVINGS: 6-11	PROTEIN: 4-6 OZ.	LIMIT FAT?	ALCOHOLIC BEVERAGES?	LIMIT "EMPTY" CARBS?
☐☐☐☐ ☐☐☐☐	☐☐ ☐☐	☐☐ ☐☐	☐☐☐☐ ☐☐☐	☐☐ ☐☐ ☐☐	Y N	Y N	Y N

SATURDAY / Date:

Training notes:

Today's goal:

Distance:
Time:
Heart Rate:
i-Rate (1-10)
X-Training:
Sleep Hours:
Weight:
Mood: ☺ ☺ ☺ Other

WEATHER:
SUN WIND
RAIN CLOUDY
SNOW
TEMP: _____

FUEL LOG

WATER: 6-8 x 8 OZ.	FRUITS: 2-4	VEGGIES: 3-5	WHOLE GRAIN SERVINGS: 6-11	PROTEIN: 4-6 OZ.	LIMIT FAT?	ALCOHOLIC BEVERAGES?	LIMIT "EMPTY" CARBS?
☐☐☐☐ ☐☐☐☐	☐☐ ☐☐	☐☐ ☐☐	☐☐☐☐ ☐☐☐	☐☐ ☐☐ ☐☐	Y N	Y N	Y N

SUNDAY / Date:

Training notes:

Today's goal:

Distance:
Time:
Heart Rate:
i-Rate (1-10)
X-Training:
Sleep Hours:
Weight:
Mood: ☺ ☺ ☺ Other

WEATHER:
SUN WIND
RAIN CLOUDY
SNOW
TEMP: _____

FUEL LOG

WATER: 6-8 x 8 OZ.	FRUITS: 2-4	VEGGIES: 3-5	WHOLE GRAIN SERVINGS: 6-11	PROTEIN: 4-6 OZ.	LIMIT FAT?	ALCOHOLIC BEVERAGES?	LIMIT "EMPTY" CARBS?
☐☐☐☐ ☐☐☐☐	☐☐ ☐☐	☐☐ ☐☐	☐☐☐☐ ☐☐☐	☐☐ ☐☐ ☐☐	Y N	Y N	Y N

WEEK OF:

GOALS FOR WEEK:

WEEKLY TOTAL: _____

YEAR-TO-DATE TOTAL:

Energy management is the key to success. And it's not just your physical energy that you've got to monitor and manage, but your emotional and psychic energy as well.

MONDAY / Date:

Training notes: _____

Today's goal: _____

Distance: _____
Time: _____
Heart Rate: _____
i-Rate (1-10) _____
X-Training: _____
Sleep Hours: _____
Weight: _____
Mood: ☺ ☺ ☺ ☹ Other

FUEL LOG

WATER: 6-8 x 8 OZ.	FRUITS: 2-4	VEGGIES: 3-5	WHOLE GRAIN SERVINGS: 6-11	PROTEIN: 4-6 OZ.	LIMIT FAT?	ALCOHOLIC BEVERAGES?	LIMIT "EMPTY" CARBS?
☐☐☐☐ ☐☐☐☐	☐☐ ☐☐	☐☐ ☐☐	☐☐☐☐ ☐☐☐☐ ☐☐☐	☐☐☐ ☐☐☐	Y N	Y N	Y N

WEATHER: SUN WIND RAIN CLOUDY SNOW TEMP: _____

TUESDAY / Date:

Training notes: _____

Today's goal: _____

Distance: _____
Time: _____
Heart Rate: _____
i-Rate (1-10) _____
X-Training: _____
Sleep Hours: _____
Weight: _____
Mood: ☺ ☺ ☺ ☹ Other

FUEL LOG

WATER: 6-8 x 8 OZ.	FRUITS: 2-4	VEGGIES: 3-5	WHOLE GRAIN SERVINGS: 6-11	PROTEIN: 4-6 OZ.	LIMIT FAT?	ALCOHOLIC BEVERAGES?	LIMIT "EMPTY" CARBS?
☐☐☐☐ ☐☐☐☐	☐☐ ☐☐	☐☐ ☐☐	☐☐☐☐ ☐☐☐☐ ☐☐☐	☐☐☐ ☐☐☐	Y N	Y N	Y N

WEATHER: SUN WIND RAIN CLOUDY SNOW TEMP: _____

WEDNESDAY / Date:

Training notes: _____

Today's goal: _____

Distance: _____
Time: _____
Heart Rate: _____
i-Rate (1-10) _____
X-Training: _____
Sleep Hours: _____
Weight: _____
Mood: ☺ ☺ ☺ ☹ Other

FUEL LOG

WATER: 6-8 x 8 OZ.	FRUITS: 2-4	VEGGIES: 3-5	WHOLE GRAIN SERVINGS: 6-11	PROTEIN: 4-6 OZ.	LIMIT FAT?	ALCOHOLIC BEVERAGES?	LIMIT "EMPTY" CARBS?
☐☐☐☐ ☐☐☐☐	☐☐ ☐☐	☐☐ ☐☐	☐☐☐☐ ☐☐☐☐ ☐☐☐	☐☐☐ ☐☐☐	Y N	Y N	Y N

WEATHER: SUN WIND RAIN CLOUDY SNOW TEMP: _____

THURSDAY / Date:

Training notes: _____

Today's goal: _____

Distance: _____
Time: _____
Heart Rate: _____
i-Rate (1-10) _____
X-Training: _____
Sleep Hours: _____
Weight: _____
Mood: ☺ ☺ ☺ ☹ Other

FUEL LOG

WATER: 6-8 x 8 OZ.	FRUITS: 2-4	VEGGIES: 3-5	WHOLE GRAIN SERVINGS: 6-11	PROTEIN: 4-6 OZ.	LIMIT FAT?	ALCOHOLIC BEVERAGES?	LIMIT "EMPTY" CARBS?
☐☐☐☐ ☐☐☐☐	☐☐ ☐☐	☐☐ ☐☐	☐☐☐☐ ☐☐☐☐ ☐☐☐	☐☐☐ ☐☐☐	Y N	Y N	Y N

WEATHER: SUN WIND RAIN CLOUDY SNOW TEMP: _____

FRIDAY / Date:

Training notes:

Today's goal:

Distance:
Time:
Heart Rate:
i-Rate (1-10)
X-Training:
Sleep Hours:
Weight:
Mood: ☺ ☺ ☹ Other

WEATHER: SUN WIND RAIN CLOUDY SNOW TEMP:____

FUEL LOG

WATER: 6-8 × 8 OZ.	FRUITS: 2-4	VEGGIES: 3-5	WHOLE GRAIN SERVINGS: 6-11	PROTEIN: 4-6 OZ.	LIMIT FAT?	ALCOHOLIC BEVERAGES?	LIMIT "EMPTY" CARBS?
☐☐☐☐	☐☐	☐☐	☐☐☐☐	☐☐	Y N	Y N	Y N
☐☐☐☐	☐☐	☐☐	☐☐☐☐	☐☐			

SATURDAY / Date:

Training notes:

Today's goal:

Distance:
Time:
Heart Rate:
i-Rate (1-10)
X-Training:
Sleep Hours:
Weight:
Mood: ☺ ☺ ☹ Other

WEATHER: SUN WIND RAIN CLOUDY SNOW TEMP:____

FUEL LOG

WATER: 6-8 × 8 OZ.	FRUITS: 2-4	VEGGIES: 3-5	WHOLE GRAIN SERVINGS: 6-11	PROTEIN: 4-6 OZ.	LIMIT FAT?	ALCOHOLIC BEVERAGES?	LIMIT "EMPTY" CARBS?
☐☐☐☐	☐☐	☐☐	☐☐☐☐	☐☐	Y N	Y N	Y N
☐☐☐☐	☐☐	☐☐	☐☐☐☐	☐☐			

SUNDAY / Date:

Training notes:

Today's goal:

Distance:
Time:
Heart Rate:
i-Rate (1-10)
X-Training:
Sleep Hours:
Weight:
Mood: ☺ ☺ ☹ Other

WEATHER: SUN WIND RAIN CLOUDY SNOW TEMP:____

FUEL LOG

WATER: 6-8 × 8 OZ.	FRUITS: 2-4	VEGGIES: 3-5	WHOLE GRAIN SERVINGS: 6-11	PROTEIN: 4-6 OZ.	LIMIT FAT?	ALCOHOLIC BEVERAGES?	LIMIT "EMPTY" CARBS?
☐☐☐☐	☐☐	☐☐	☐☐☐☐	☐☐	Y N	Y N	Y N
☐☐☐☐	☐☐	☐☐	☐☐☐☐	☐☐			

WEEK OF:

GOALS FOR WEEK:

WEEKLY TOTAL: _____

YEAR-TO-DATE TOTAL:

Even when I am running alone, I know that somewhere, at the same time, hundreds of other people are doing the same thing. Some, perhaps, for the same reasons.

MONDAY / Date:

Today's goal:

Training notes:

FUEL LOG

WATER: 6-8 x 8 OZ.	FRUITS: 2-4	VEGGIES: 3-5	WHOLE GRAIN SERVINGS: 6-11	PROTEIN: 4-6 OZ.	LIMIT FAT?	ALCOHOLIC BEVERAGES?	LIMIT "EMPTY" CARBS?
☐☐☐☐ ☐☐☐☐	☐☐ ☐☐	☐☐☐ ☐☐	☐☐☐☐☐ ☐	☐☐☐ ☐☐ ☐	Y N	Y N	Y N

WEATHER: SUN WIND RAIN CLOUDY SNOW   TEMP: _____

- Distance:
- Time:
- Heart Rate:
- i-Rate (1-10)
- X-Training:
- Sleep Hours:
- Weight:
- Mood: ☺ ☺ ☹ Other

TUESDAY / Date:

Today's goal:

Training notes:

FUEL LOG

WATER: 6-8 x 8 OZ.	FRUITS: 2-4	VEGGIES: 3-5	WHOLE GRAIN SERVINGS: 6-11	PROTEIN: 4-6 OZ.	LIMIT FAT?	ALCOHOLIC BEVERAGES?	LIMIT "EMPTY" CARBS?
☐☐☐☐ ☐☐☐☐	☐☐ ☐☐	☐☐☐ ☐☐	☐☐☐☐☐ ☐	☐☐☐ ☐☐ ☐	Y N	Y N	Y N

WEATHER: SUN WIND RAIN CLOUDY SNOW   TEMP: _____

- Distance:
- Time:
- Heart Rate:
- i-Rate (1-10)
- X-Training:
- Sleep Hours:
- Weight:
- Mood: ☺ ☺ ☹ Other

WEDNESDAY / Date:

Today's goal:

Training notes:

FUEL LOG

WATER: 6-8 x 8 OZ.	FRUITS: 2-4	VEGGIES: 3-5	WHOLE GRAIN SERVINGS: 6-11	PROTEIN: 4-6 OZ.	LIMIT FAT?	ALCOHOLIC BEVERAGES?	LIMIT "EMPTY" CARBS?
☐☐☐☐ ☐☐☐☐	☐☐ ☐☐	☐☐☐ ☐☐	☐☐☐☐☐ ☐	☐☐☐ ☐☐ ☐	Y N	Y N	Y N

WEATHER: SUN WIND RAIN CLOUDY SNOW   TEMP: _____

- Distance:
- Time:
- Heart Rate:
- i-Rate (1-10)
- X-Training:
- Sleep Hours:
- Weight:
- Mood: ☺ ☺ ☹ Other

THURSDAY / Date:

Today's goal:

Training notes:

FUEL LOG

WATER: 6-8 x 8 OZ.	FRUITS: 2-4	VEGGIES: 3-5	WHOLE GRAIN SERVINGS: 6-11	PROTEIN: 4-6 OZ.	LIMIT FAT?	ALCOHOLIC BEVERAGES?	LIMIT "EMPTY" CARBS?
☐☐☐☐ ☐☐☐☐	☐☐ ☐☐	☐☐☐ ☐☐	☐☐☐☐☐ ☐	☐☐☐ ☐☐ ☐	Y N	Y N	Y N

WEATHER: SUN WIND RAIN CLOUDY SNOW   TEMP: _____

- Distance:
- Time:
- Heart Rate:
- i-Rate (1-10)
- X-Training:
- Sleep Hours:
- Weight:
- Mood: ☺ ☺ ☹ Other

FRIDAY / Date: _____

Training notes: _____

Today's goal: _____
_____
_____

Distance: _____
Time: _____
Heart Rate: _____
i-Rate (1-10): _____
X-Training: _____
Sleep Hours: _____
Weight: _____
Mood: ☺ ☺ ☹ Other

WEATHER:
SUN WIND
RAIN CLOUDY
SNOW
TEMP: _____

FUEL LOG

WATER: 6-8 x 8 oz.	FRUITS: 2-4	VEGGIES: 3-5	WHOLE GRAIN SERVINGS: 6-11	PROTEIN: 4-6 oz.	LIMIT FAT?	ALCOHOLIC BEVERAGES?	LIMIT "EMPTY" CARBS?
☐☐☐☐ ☐☐☐☐	☐☐ ☐☐	☐☐ ☐☐	☐☐☐☐☐☐ ☐☐☐☐☐	☐☐☐ ☐☐☐	Y N	Y N	Y N

SATURDAY / Date: _____

Training notes: _____

Today's goal: _____
_____
_____

Distance: _____
Time: _____
Heart Rate: _____
i-Rate (1-10): _____
X-Training: _____
Sleep Hours: _____
Weight: _____
Mood: ☺ ☺ ☹ Other

WEATHER:
SUN WIND
RAIN CLOUDY
SNOW
TEMP: _____

FUEL LOG

WATER: 6-8 x 8 oz.	FRUITS: 2-4	VEGGIES: 3-5	WHOLE GRAIN SERVINGS: 6-11	PROTEIN: 4-6 oz.	LIMIT FAT?	ALCOHOLIC BEVERAGES?	LIMIT "EMPTY" CARBS?
☐☐☐☐ ☐☐☐☐	☐☐ ☐☐	☐☐ ☐☐	☐☐☐☐☐☐ ☐☐☐☐☐	☐☐☐ ☐☐☐	Y N	Y N	Y N

SUNDAY / Date: _____

Training notes: _____

Today's goal: _____
_____
_____

Distance: _____
Time: _____
Heart Rate: _____
i-Rate (1-10): _____
X-Training: _____
Sleep Hours: _____
Weight: _____
Mood: ☺ ☺ ☹ Other

WEATHER:
SUN WIND
RAIN CLOUDY
SNOW
TEMP: _____

FUEL LOG

WATER: 6-8 x 8 oz.	FRUITS: 2-4	VEGGIES: 3-5	WHOLE GRAIN SERVINGS: 6-11	PROTEIN: 4-6 oz.	LIMIT FAT?	ALCOHOLIC BEVERAGES?	LIMIT "EMPTY" CARBS?
☐☐☐☐ ☐☐☐☐	☐☐ ☐☐	☐☐ ☐☐	☐☐☐☐☐☐ ☐☐☐☐☐	☐☐☐ ☐☐☐	Y N	Y N	Y N

WEEK OF: _____

GOALS FOR WEEK:

WEEKLY TOTAL: _____

YEAR-TO-DATE TOTAL: _____

As an athlete, your equipment is important to you. Take some time to look over your shoes, socks, and running apparel to make sure that they're still working as they should.

RUNNING HOME

There are many advantages to starting to run later in life. Among them is the ability to use running as a means to rediscover memories long forgotten. For me, running is the key that has unlocked the most foreboding doors in the cellar of my psyche.

Having had a life before running means there are many people and places which exist for the pre-running me. As that pre-runner recedes into my past, I've found I need a guide to take me from the person I was to the person I am becoming. Running has become that guide.

The need for that guide became clear on a recent run through my childhood neighborhood. As a child of the 1950s in a small-town Chicago suburb, my house and the elementary school defined the edges of my world. The streets and alleys and playground in the three square blocks around my house were my world.

Running through the old neighborhood, I was struck by how small the houses seemed. Those monuments to the strength of juvenile male bonding and the uncertainties of preadolescent male-female bonding looked positively ordinary. In a few strides I ran past the houses that were the sites of my earliest interpersonal successes and failures. Those adult strides helped me understand both the power and the silliness of my memories.

Running to the elementary school playground brought me face to face with eight years of victories and defeats. From marbles to basketball, baseball, and dodge ball, the images were still painfully clear. It was on this nondescript asphalt that I learned what it felt like to punch and be punched, to be in and out of love, to break a youthful heart, and to have my own heart and spirit broken.

This playground, this absolutely ordinary playground, was my private Roman Coliseum—the place where I often was the lion, but just as often the Christian. This playground was the site of epic battles for turf, for pride, and sometimes for nothing at all. Now, looking at the rusty basketball hoops and chain nets, I wondered what any of it meant.

I ran around the baseball field. I hit the home runs I never hit, stole the bases I never stole, made the sensational catches I had missed, and struck out the best batters. In that moment I reclaimed my right to be a hero, if only in my own mind. Thirty-five years later, I finally was not the last person picked to be on the team.

Running faster, I passed the houses of the childhood friends who taught me about loyalty and the bullies who taught me about pride. I ran again with Lenny and Rich and Lester, but this time I was running in front. This time, I out-kicked Tommy Regala to the corner.

I could have run forever that day. But, just as when I was a child, the time came for me to run home. I had reached the edges of my neighborhood, the edges of my memories, and the edges of my dreams.

That run taught me that there are still playgrounds and ball fields and friends and bullies in my life. The battles I fought as a child are being fought again every day in my adult world. I am still seeking to prove to myself and others that I can play their game, that I should be on their team, and that I shouldn't be picked last.

And I hope I've learned that the daily victories and defeats in my adult world are only as important as I allow them to be.

Waddle on, friends.

MONDAY / Date:

Today's goal:

Training notes:

Distance:
Time:
Heart Rate:
i-Rate (1-10):
X-Training:
Sleep Hours:
Weight:
Mood: ☺ ☺ ☹ Other

FUEL LOG

WATER: 6-8 x 8 oz.	FRUITS: 2-4	VEGGIES: 3-5	WHOLE GRAIN SERVINGS: 6-11	PROTEIN: 4-6 oz.	LIMIT FAT? Y N	ALCOHOLIC BEVERAGES? Y N	LIMIT "EMPTY" CARBS? Y N
☐☐☐☐ ☐☐☐☐	☐☐ ☐☐	☐☐ ☐☐	☐☐☐ ☐☐☐	☐☐ ☐☐			

WEATHER: SUN WIND RAIN CLOUDY SNOW TEMP: _____

TUESDAY / Date:

Today's goal:

Training notes:

Distance:
Time:
Heart Rate:
i-Rate (1-10):
X-Training:
Sleep Hours:
Weight:
Mood: ☺ ☺ ☹ Other

FUEL LOG

WATER: 6-8 x 8 oz.	FRUITS: 2-4	VEGGIES: 3-5	WHOLE GRAIN SERVINGS: 6-11	PROTEIN: 4-6 oz.	LIMIT FAT? Y N	ALCOHOLIC BEVERAGES? Y N	LIMIT "EMPTY" CARBS? Y N
☐☐☐☐ ☐☐☐☐	☐☐ ☐☐	☐☐ ☐☐	☐☐☐ ☐☐☐	☐☐ ☐☐			

WEATHER: SUN WIND RAIN CLOUDY SNOW TEMP: _____

WEDNESDAY / Date:

Today's goal:

Training notes:

Distance:
Time:
Heart Rate:
i-Rate (1-10):
X-Training:
Sleep Hours:
Weight:
Mood: ☺ ☺ ☹ Other

FUEL LOG

WATER: 6-8 x 8 oz.	FRUITS: 2-4	VEGGIES: 3-5	WHOLE GRAIN SERVINGS: 6-11	PROTEIN: 4-6 oz.	LIMIT FAT? Y N	ALCOHOLIC BEVERAGES? Y N	LIMIT "EMPTY" CARBS? Y N
☐☐☐☐ ☐☐☐☐	☐☐ ☐☐	☐☐ ☐☐	☐☐☐ ☐☐☐	☐☐ ☐☐			

WEATHER: SUN WIND RAIN CLOUDY SNOW TEMP: _____

THURSDAY / Date:

Today's goal:

Training notes:

Distance:
Time:
Heart Rate:
i-Rate (1-10):
X-Training:
Sleep Hours:
Weight:
Mood: ☺ ☺ ☹ Other

FUEL LOG

WATER: 6-8 x 8 oz.	FRUITS: 2-4	VEGGIES: 3-5	WHOLE GRAIN SERVINGS: 6-11	PROTEIN: 4-6 oz.	LIMIT FAT? Y N	ALCOHOLIC BEVERAGES? Y N	LIMIT "EMPTY" CARBS? Y N
☐☐☐☐ ☐☐☐☐	☐☐ ☐☐	☐☐ ☐☐	☐☐☐ ☐☐☐	☐☐ ☐☐			

WEATHER: SUN WIND RAIN CLOUDY SNOW TEMP: _____

FRIDAY / Date:

Training notes:

Today's goal:

FUEL LOG

WATER: 6-8 x 8 oz.	FRUITS: 2-4	VEGGIES: 3-5	WHOLE GRAIN SERVINGS: 6-11	PROTEIN: 4-6 oz.	LIMIT FAT?	ALCOHOLIC BEVERAGES?	LIMIT "EMPTY" CARBS?
☐☐☐☐ ☐☐☐☐	☐☐ ☐☐	☐☐ ☐☐	☐☐☐☐ ☐☐☐☐ ☐☐☐	☐☐☐ ☐☐☐	Y N	Y N	Y N

WEATHER: SUN WIND RAIN CLOUDY SNOW   TEMP: _____

Distance:
Time:
Heart Rate:
i-Rate (1-10)
X-Training:
Sleep Hours:
Weight:
Mood: ☺ ☺ ☹ Other

SATURDAY / Date:

Training notes:

Today's goal:

FUEL LOG

WATER: 6-8 x 8 oz.	FRUITS: 2-4	VEGGIES: 3-5	WHOLE GRAIN SERVINGS: 6-11	PROTEIN: 4-6 oz.	LIMIT FAT?	ALCOHOLIC BEVERAGES?	LIMIT "EMPTY" CARBS?
☐☐☐☐ ☐☐☐☐	☐☐ ☐☐	☐☐ ☐☐	☐☐☐☐ ☐☐☐☐ ☐☐☐	☐☐☐ ☐☐☐	Y N	Y N	Y N

WEATHER: SUN WIND RAIN CLOUDY SNOW   TEMP: _____

Distance:
Time:
Heart Rate:
i-Rate (1-10)
X-Training:
Sleep Hours:
Weight:
Mood: ☺ ☺ ☹ Other

SUNDAY / Date:

Training notes:

Today's goal:

FUEL LOG

WATER: 6-8 x 8 oz.	FRUITS: 2-4	VEGGIES: 3-5	WHOLE GRAIN SERVINGS: 6-11	PROTEIN: 4-6 oz.	LIMIT FAT?	ALCOHOLIC BEVERAGES?	LIMIT "EMPTY" CARBS?
☐☐☐☐ ☐☐☐☐	☐☐ ☐☐	☐☐ ☐☐	☐☐☐☐ ☐☐☐☐ ☐☐☐	☐☐☐ ☐☐☐	Y N	Y N	Y N

WEATHER: SUN WIND RAIN CLOUDY SNOW   TEMP: _____

Distance:
Time:
Heart Rate:
i-Rate (1-10)
X-Training:
Sleep Hours:
Weight:
Mood: ☺ ☺ ☹ Other

WEEK OF:

GOALS FOR WEEK:

WEEKLY TOTAL: _____

YEAR-TO-DATE TOTAL:

There are times in your training when the most important element is rest. Take the time to get your head together and let your body heal.

MONDAY / Date:

Today's goal:

Training notes:

FUEL LOG

WATER: 6-8 x 8 OZ.	FRUITS: 2-4	VEGGIES: 3-5	WHOLE GRAIN SERVINGS: 6-11	PROTEIN: 4-6 OZ.	LIMIT FAT?	ALCOHOLIC BEVERAGES?	LIMIT "EMPTY" CARBS?
☐☐☐☐ ☐☐☐☐	☐☐ ☐☐	☐☐ ☐	☐☐☐☐ ☐☐☐☐	☐☐ ☐☐ ☐☐	Y N	Y N	Y N

WEATHER: SUN WIND RAIN CLOUDY SNOW TEMP:_____

Distance:
Time:
Heart Rate:
i-Rate (1-10)
X-Training:
Sleep Hours:
Weight:
Mood: ☺ ☺ ☹ Other

TUESDAY / Date:

Today's goal:

Training notes:

FUEL LOG

WATER: 6-8 x 8 OZ.	FRUITS: 2-4	VEGGIES: 3-5	WHOLE GRAIN SERVINGS: 6-11	PROTEIN: 4-6 OZ.	LIMIT FAT?	ALCOHOLIC BEVERAGES?	LIMIT "EMPTY" CARBS?
☐☐☐☐ ☐☐☐☐	☐☐ ☐☐	☐☐ ☐	☐☐☐☐ ☐☐☐☐	☐☐ ☐☐ ☐☐	Y N	Y N	Y N

WEATHER: SUN WIND RAIN CLOUDY SNOW TEMP:_____

Distance:
Time:
Heart Rate:
i-Rate (1-10)
X-Training:
Sleep Hours:
Weight:
Mood: ☺ ☺ ☹ Other

WEDNESDAY / Date:

Today's goal:

Training notes:

FUEL LOG

WATER: 6-8 x 8 OZ.	FRUITS: 2-4	VEGGIES: 3-5	WHOLE GRAIN SERVINGS: 6-11	PROTEIN: 4-6 OZ.	LIMIT FAT?	ALCOHOLIC BEVERAGES?	LIMIT "EMPTY" CARBS?
☐☐☐☐ ☐☐☐☐	☐☐ ☐☐	☐☐ ☐	☐☐☐☐ ☐☐☐☐	☐☐ ☐☐ ☐☐	Y N	Y N	Y N

WEATHER: SUN WIND RAIN CLOUDY SNOW TEMP:_____

Distance:
Time:
Heart Rate:
i-Rate (1-10)
X-Training:
Sleep Hours:
Weight:
Mood: ☺ ☺ ☹ Other

THURSDAY / Date:

Today's goal:

Training notes:

FUEL LOG

WATER: 6-8 x 8 OZ.	FRUITS: 2-4	VEGGIES: 3-5	WHOLE GRAIN SERVINGS: 6-11	PROTEIN: 4-6 OZ.	LIMIT FAT?	ALCOHOLIC BEVERAGES?	LIMIT "EMPTY" CARBS?
☐☐☐☐ ☐☐☐☐	☐☐ ☐☐	☐☐ ☐	☐☐☐☐ ☐☐☐☐	☐☐ ☐☐ ☐☐	Y N	Y N	Y N

WEATHER: SUN WIND RAIN CLOUDY SNOW TEMP:_____

Distance:
Time:
Heart Rate:
i-Rate (1-10)
X-Training:
Sleep Hours:
Weight:
Mood: ☺ ☺ ☹ Other

FRIDAY / Date:

Training notes:

Today's goal:

FUEL LOG

WATER: 6-8 x 8 OZ.	FRUITS: 2-4	VEGGIES: 3-5	WHOLE GRAIN SERVINGS: 6-11	PROTEIN: 4-6 OZ.	LIMIT FAT?	ALCOHOLIC BEVERAGES?	LIMIT "EMPTY" CARBS?
☐☐☐☐ ☐☐☐☐	☐☐ ☐☐	☐☐☐ ☐☐	☐☐☐☐ ☐☐☐☐ ☐☐☐	☐☐☐ ☐☐☐	Y N	Y N	Y N

WEATHER:
SUN WIND
RAIN CLOUDY
SNOW
TEMP:_____

Distance:
Time:
Heart Rate:
i-Rate (1-10)
X-Training:
Sleep Hours:
Weight:
Mood: ☺ ☺ ☹ Other

SATURDAY / Date:

Training notes:

Today's goal:

FUEL LOG

WATER: 6-8 x 8 OZ.	FRUITS: 2-4	VEGGIES: 3-5	WHOLE GRAIN SERVINGS: 6-11	PROTEIN: 4-6 OZ.	LIMIT FAT?	ALCOHOLIC BEVERAGES?	LIMIT "EMPTY" CARBS?
☐☐☐☐ ☐☐☐☐	☐☐ ☐☐	☐☐☐ ☐☐	☐☐☐☐ ☐☐☐☐ ☐☐☐	☐☐☐ ☐☐☐	Y N	Y N	Y N

WEATHER:
SUN WIND
RAIN CLOUDY
SNOW
TEMP:_____

Distance:
Time:
Heart Rate:
i-Rate (1-10)
X-Training:
Sleep Hours:
Weight:
Mood: ☺ ☺ ☹ Other

SUNDAY / Date:

Training notes:

Today's goal:

FUEL LOG

WATER: 6-8 x 8 OZ.	FRUITS: 2-4	VEGGIES: 3-5	WHOLE GRAIN SERVINGS: 6-11	PROTEIN: 4-6 OZ.	LIMIT FAT?	ALCOHOLIC BEVERAGES?	LIMIT "EMPTY" CARBS?
☐☐☐☐ ☐☐☐☐	☐☐ ☐☐	☐☐☐ ☐☐	☐☐☐☐ ☐☐☐☐ ☐☐☐	☐☐☐ ☐☐☐	Y N	Y N	Y N

WEATHER:
SUN WIND
RAIN CLOUDY
SNOW
TEMP:_____

Distance:
Time:
Heart Rate:
i-Rate (1-10)
X-Training:
Sleep Hours:
Weight:
Mood: ☺ ☺ ☹ Other

WEEK OF:

GOALS FOR WEEK:

WEEKLY TOTAL: _____

YEAR-TO-DATE TOTAL:

Once you get started on a life of fitness you'll need to face the challenges head-on, with courage and conviction.

MONDAY / Date:

Today's goal:

Training notes:

Distance:
Time:
Heart Rate:
i-Rate (1-10)
X-Training:
Sleep Hours:
Weight:
Mood: ☺ ☺ ☹ ☹ Other

FUEL LOG

WATER: 6-8 x 8 OZ.	FRUITS: 2-4	VEGGIES: 3-5	WHOLE GRAIN SERVINGS: 6-11	PROTEIN: 4-6 OZ.	LIMIT FAT?	ALCOHOLIC BEVERAGES?	LIMIT "EMPTY" CARBS?
☐☐☐☐ ☐☐☐☐	☐☐ ☐☐	☐☐☐ ☐☐	☐☐☐☐ ☐☐☐☐ ☐	☐☐☐ ☐☐☐	Y N	Y N	Y N

WEATHER:
SUN WIND
RAIN CLOUDY
SNOW
TEMP:____

TUESDAY / Date:

Today's goal:

Training notes:

Distance:
Time:
Heart Rate:
i-Rate (1-10)
X-Training:
Sleep Hours:
Weight:
Mood: ☺ ☺ ☹ ☹ Other

FUEL LOG

WATER: 6-8 x 8 OZ.	FRUITS: 2-4	VEGGIES: 3-5	WHOLE GRAIN SERVINGS: 6-11	PROTEIN: 4-6 OZ.	LIMIT FAT?	ALCOHOLIC BEVERAGES?	LIMIT "EMPTY" CARBS?
☐☐☐☐ ☐☐☐☐	☐☐ ☐☐	☐☐☐ ☐☐	☐☐☐☐ ☐☐☐☐ ☐	☐☐☐ ☐☐☐	Y N	Y N	Y N

WEATHER:
SUN WIND
RAIN CLOUDY
SNOW
TEMP:____

WEDNESDAY / Date:

Today's goal:

Training notes:

Distance:
Time:
Heart Rate:
i-Rate (1-10)
X-Training:
Sleep Hours:
Weight:
Mood: ☺ ☺ ☹ ☹ Other

FUEL LOG

WATER: 6-8 x 8 OZ.	FRUITS: 2-4	VEGGIES: 3-5	WHOLE GRAIN SERVINGS: 6-11	PROTEIN: 4-6 OZ.	LIMIT FAT?	ALCOHOLIC BEVERAGES?	LIMIT "EMPTY" CARBS?
☐☐☐☐ ☐☐☐☐	☐☐ ☐☐	☐☐☐ ☐☐	☐☐☐☐ ☐☐☐☐ ☐	☐☐☐ ☐☐☐	Y N	Y N	Y N

WEATHER:
SUN WIND
RAIN CLOUDY
SNOW
TEMP:____

THURSDAY / Date:

Today's goal:

Training notes:

Distance:
Time:
Heart Rate:
i-Rate (1-10)
X-Training:
Sleep Hours:
Weight:
Mood: ☺ ☺ ☹ ☹ Other

FUEL LOG

WATER: 6-8 x 8 OZ.	FRUITS: 2-4	VEGGIES: 3-5	WHOLE GRAIN SERVINGS: 6-11	PROTEIN: 4-6 OZ.	LIMIT FAT?	ALCOHOLIC BEVERAGES?	LIMIT "EMPTY" CARBS?
☐☐☐☐ ☐☐☐☐	☐☐ ☐☐	☐☐☐ ☐☐	☐☐☐☐ ☐☐☐☐ ☐	☐☐☐ ☐☐☐	Y N	Y N	Y N

WEATHER:
SUN WIND
RAIN CLOUDY
SNOW
TEMP:____

FRIDAY / Date: _____

Training notes: _____

Today's goal: _____

Distance: _____
Time: _____
Heart Rate: _____
i-Rate (1-10): _____
X-Training: _____
Sleep Hours: _____
Weight: _____
Mood: ☺ ☺ ☹ Other _____

WEATHER:
SUN WIND
RAIN CLOUDY
SNOW
TEMP: _____

FUEL LOG

WATER: 6-8 × 8 OZ.	FRUITS: 2-4	VEGGIES: 3-5	WHOLE GRAIN SERVINGS: 6-11	PROTEIN: 4-6 OZ.	LIMIT FAT?	ALCOHOLIC BEVERAGES?	LIMIT "EMPTY" CARBS?
☐☐☐☐ ☐☐☐☐	☐☐ ☐☐	☐☐ ☐☐	☐☐☐☐☐ ☐☐☐☐☐☐	☐☐☐ ☐☐☐	Y N	Y N	Y N

SATURDAY / Date: _____

Training notes: _____

Today's goal: _____

Distance: _____
Time: _____
Heart Rate: _____
i-Rate (1-10): _____
X-Training: _____
Sleep Hours: _____
Weight: _____
Mood: ☺ ☺ ☹ Other _____

WEATHER:
SUN WIND
RAIN CLOUDY
SNOW
TEMP: _____

FUEL LOG

WATER: 6-8 × 8 OZ.	FRUITS: 2-4	VEGGIES: 3-5	WHOLE GRAIN SERVINGS: 6-11	PROTEIN: 4-6 OZ.	LIMIT FAT?	ALCOHOLIC BEVERAGES?	LIMIT "EMPTY" CARBS?
☐☐☐☐ ☐☐☐☐	☐☐ ☐☐	☐☐ ☐☐	☐☐☐☐☐ ☐☐☐☐☐☐	☐☐☐ ☐☐☐	Y N	Y N	Y N

SUNDAY / Date: _____

Training notes: _____

Today's goal: _____

Distance: _____
Time: _____
Heart Rate: _____
i-Rate (1-10): _____
X-Training: _____
Sleep Hours: _____
Weight: _____
Mood: ☺ ☺ ☹ Other _____

WEATHER:
SUN WIND
RAIN CLOUDY
SNOW
TEMP: _____

FUEL LOG

WATER: 6-8 × 8 OZ.	FRUITS: 2-4	VEGGIES: 3-5	WHOLE GRAIN SERVINGS: 6-11	PROTEIN: 4-6 OZ.	LIMIT FAT?	ALCOHOLIC BEVERAGES?	LIMIT "EMPTY" CARBS?
☐☐☐☐ ☐☐☐☐	☐☐ ☐☐	☐☐ ☐☐	☐☐☐☐☐ ☐☐☐☐☐☐	☐☐☐ ☐☐☐	Y N	Y N	Y N

WEEK OF:

GOALS FOR WEEK:

WEEKLY TOTAL: _____

YEAR-TO-DATE TOTAL: _____

> **My early training was equally divided between sheer lunacy and pure stupidity. I foolishly believed that tearing my body down was the way to build my body up.**

MONDAY / Date:

Today's goal:

Training notes:

FUEL LOG

WATER: 6-8 × 8 OZ.	FRUITS: 2-4	VEGGIES: 3-5	WHOLE GRAIN SERVINGS: 6-11	PROTEIN: 4-6 OZ.	LIMIT FAT?	ALCOHOLIC BEVERAGES?	LIMIT "EMPTY" CARBS?
☐☐☐☐ ☐☐☐☐	☐☐ ☐☐	☐☐ ☐☐	☐☐☐ ☐☐☐	☐☐☐ ☐☐☐	Y N	Y N	Y N

WEATHER: SUN WIND RAIN CLOUDY SNOW TEMP: _____

Distance:
Time:
Heart Rate:
i-Rate (1-10)
X-Training:
Sleep Hours:
Weight:
Mood: ☺ ☺ ☹ Other

TUESDAY / Date:

Today's goal:

Training notes:

FUEL LOG

WATER: 6-8 × 8 OZ.	FRUITS: 2-4	VEGGIES: 3-5	WHOLE GRAIN SERVINGS: 6-11	PROTEIN: 4-6 OZ.	LIMIT FAT?	ALCOHOLIC BEVERAGES?	LIMIT "EMPTY" CARBS?
☐☐☐☐ ☐☐☐☐	☐☐ ☐☐	☐☐ ☐☐	☐☐☐ ☐☐☐	☐☐☐ ☐☐☐	Y N	Y N	Y N

WEATHER: SUN WIND RAIN CLOUDY SNOW TEMP: _____

Distance:
Time:
Heart Rate:
i-Rate (1-10)
X-Training:
Sleep Hours:
Weight:
Mood: ☺ ☺ ☹ Other

WEDNESDAY / Date:

Today's goal:

Training notes:

FUEL LOG

WATER: 6-8 × 8 OZ.	FRUITS: 2-4	VEGGIES: 3-5	WHOLE GRAIN SERVINGS: 6-11	PROTEIN: 4-6 OZ.	LIMIT FAT?	ALCOHOLIC BEVERAGES?	LIMIT "EMPTY" CARBS?
☐☐☐☐ ☐☐☐☐	☐☐ ☐☐	☐☐ ☐☐	☐☐☐ ☐☐☐	☐☐☐ ☐☐☐	Y N	Y N	Y N

WEATHER: SUN WIND RAIN CLOUDY SNOW TEMP: _____

Distance:
Time:
Heart Rate:
i-Rate (1-10)
X-Training:
Sleep Hours:
Weight:
Mood: ☺ ☺ ☹ Other

THURSDAY / Date:

Today's goal:

Training notes:

FUEL LOG

WATER: 6-8 × 8 OZ.	FRUITS: 2-4	VEGGIES: 3-5	WHOLE GRAIN SERVINGS: 6-11	PROTEIN: 4-6 OZ.	LIMIT FAT?	ALCOHOLIC BEVERAGES?	LIMIT "EMPTY" CARBS?
☐☐☐☐ ☐☐☐☐	☐☐ ☐☐	☐☐ ☐☐	☐☐☐ ☐☐☐	☐☐☐ ☐☐☐	Y N	Y N	Y N

WEATHER: SUN WIND RAIN CLOUDY SNOW TEMP: _____

Distance:
Time:
Heart Rate:
i-Rate (1-10)
X-Training:
Sleep Hours:
Weight:
Mood: ☺ ☺ ☹ Other

FRIDAY / Date:

Today's goal: _____

Training notes: _____

Distance: _____
Time: _____
Heart Rate: _____
i-Rate (1-10): _____
X-Training: _____
Sleep Hours: _____
Weight: _____
Mood: ☺ 😐 ☹ Other

WEATHER: SUN WIND RAIN CLOUDY SNOW TEMP: _____

FUEL LOG

WATER: 6-8 × 8 OZ.	FRUITS: 2-4	VEGGIES: 3-5	WHOLE GRAIN SERVINGS: 6-11	PROTEIN: 4-6 OZ.	LIMIT FAT?	ALCOHOLIC BEVERAGES?	LIMIT "EMPTY" CARBS?
☐☐☐☐ ☐☐☐☐	☐☐ ☐☐	☐☐ ☐☐	☐☐☐☐☐ ☐☐☐☐☐ ☐	☐☐☐ ☐☐☐ ☐☐	Y N	Y N	Y N

SATURDAY / Date:

Today's goal: _____

Training notes: _____

Distance: _____
Time: _____
Heart Rate: _____
i-Rate (1-10): _____
X-Training: _____
Sleep Hours: _____
Weight: _____
Mood: ☺ 😐 ☹ Other

WEATHER: SUN WIND RAIN CLOUDY SNOW TEMP: _____

FUEL LOG

WATER: 6-8 × 8 OZ.	FRUITS: 2-4	VEGGIES: 3-5	WHOLE GRAIN SERVINGS: 6-11	PROTEIN: 4-6 OZ.	LIMIT FAT?	ALCOHOLIC BEVERAGES?	LIMIT "EMPTY" CARBS?
☐☐☐☐ ☐☐☐☐	☐☐ ☐☐	☐☐ ☐☐	☐☐☐☐ ☐☐☐☐ ☐	☐☐☐ ☐☐☐ ☐☐	Y N	Y N	Y N

SUNDAY / Date:

Today's goal: _____

Training notes: _____

Distance: _____
Time: _____
Heart Rate: _____
i-Rate (1-10): _____
X-Training: _____
Sleep Hours: _____
Weight: _____
Mood: ☺ 😐 ☹ Other

WEATHER: SUN WIND RAIN CLOUDY SNOW TEMP: _____

FUEL LOG

WATER: 6-8 × 8 OZ.	FRUITS: 2-4	VEGGIES: 3-5	WHOLE GRAIN SERVINGS: 6-11	PROTEIN: 4-6 OZ.	LIMIT FAT?	ALCOHOLIC BEVERAGES?	LIMIT "EMPTY" CARBS?
☐☐☐☐ ☐☐☐☐	☐☐ ☐☐	☐☐ ☐☐	☐☐☐☐ ☐☐☐☐ ☐	☐☐☐ ☐☐☐ ☐☐	Y N	Y N	Y N

WEEK OF:

GOALS FOR WEEK:

WEEKLY TOTAL: _____

YEAR-TO-DATE TOTAL: _____

> **In the old days, races were like final exams. These days the races are the celebration of what you've achieved.**

MONDAY / Date: _____   Training notes: _____

Today's goal: _____

Distance: _____
Time: _____
Heart Rate: _____
i-Rate (1-10): _____
X-Training: _____
Sleep Hours: _____
Weight: _____
Mood: ☺ ☺ ☹ ☹ Other

WEATHER:
SUN WIND
RAIN CLOUDY
SNOW
TEMP: _____

FUEL LOG

WATER: 6-8 × 8 OZ.	FRUITS: 2-4	VEGGIES: 3-5	WHOLE GRAIN SERVINGS: 6-11	PROTEIN: 4-6 OZ.	LIMIT FAT?	ALCOHOLIC BEVERAGES?	LIMIT "EMPTY" CARBS?
☐☐☐☐ ☐☐☐☐	☐☐ ☐☐	☐☐☐ ☐☐	☐☐☐☐ ☐☐☐	☐☐☐ ☐☐☐	Y N	Y N	Y N

TUESDAY / Date: _____   Training notes: _____

Today's goal: _____

Distance: _____
Time: _____
Heart Rate: _____
i-Rate (1-10): _____
X-Training: _____
Sleep Hours: _____
Weight: _____
Mood: ☺ ☺ ☹ ☹ Other

WEATHER:
SUN WIND
RAIN CLOUDY
SNOW
TEMP: _____

FUEL LOG

WATER: 6-8 × 8 OZ.	FRUITS: 2-4	VEGGIES: 3-5	WHOLE GRAIN SERVINGS: 6-11	PROTEIN: 4-6 OZ.	LIMIT FAT?	ALCOHOLIC BEVERAGES?	LIMIT "EMPTY" CARBS?
☐☐☐☐ ☐☐☐☐	☐☐ ☐☐	☐☐☐ ☐☐	☐☐☐☐ ☐☐☐	☐☐☐ ☐☐☐	Y N	Y N	Y N

WEDNESDAY / Date: _____   Training notes: _____

Today's goal: _____

Distance: _____
Time: _____
Heart Rate: _____
i-Rate (1-10): _____
X-Training: _____
Sleep Hours: _____
Weight: _____
Mood: ☺ ☺ ☹ ☹ Other

WEATHER:
SUN WIND
RAIN CLOUDY
SNOW
TEMP: _____

FUEL LOG

WATER: 6-8 × 8 OZ.	FRUITS: 2-4	VEGGIES: 3-5	WHOLE GRAIN SERVINGS: 6-11	PROTEIN: 4-6 OZ.	LIMIT FAT?	ALCOHOLIC BEVERAGES?	LIMIT "EMPTY" CARBS?
☐☐☐☐ ☐☐☐☐	☐☐ ☐☐	☐☐☐ ☐☐	☐☐☐☐ ☐☐☐	☐☐☐ ☐☐☐	Y N	Y N	Y N

THURSDAY / Date: _____   Training notes: _____

Today's goal: _____

Distance: _____
Time: _____
Heart Rate: _____
i-Rate (1-10): _____
X-Training: _____
Sleep Hours: _____
Weight: _____
Mood: ☺ ☺ ☹ ☹ Other

WEATHER:
SUN WIND
RAIN CLOUDY
SNOW
TEMP: _____

FUEL LOG

WATER: 6-8 × 8 OZ.	FRUITS: 2-4	VEGGIES: 3-5	WHOLE GRAIN SERVINGS: 6-11	PROTEIN: 4-6 OZ.	LIMIT FAT?	ALCOHOLIC BEVERAGES?	LIMIT "EMPTY" CARBS?
☐☐☐☐ ☐☐☐☐	☐☐ ☐☐	☐☐☐ ☐☐	☐☐☐☐ ☐☐☐	☐☐☐ ☐☐☐	Y N	Y N	Y N

FRIDAY / Date:

Today's goal:

Training notes:

Distance:
Time:
Heart Rate:
i-Rate (1-10)
X-Training:
Sleep Hours:
Weight:
Mood: ☺ ☺ ☹ ☹

WEATHER:
SUN WIND
RAIN CLOUDY
SNOW
TEMP: _____

FUEL LOG

WATER: 6-8 x 8 OZ.	FRUITS: 2-4	VEGGIES: 3-5	WHOLE GRAIN SERVINGS: 6-11	PROTEIN: 4-6 OZ.	LIMIT FAT?	ALCOHOLIC BEVERAGES?	LIMIT "EMPTY" CARBS?
☐☐☐☐ ☐☐☐☐	☐☐ ☐☐	☐☐☐ ☐☐☐	☐☐☐☐ ☐☐☐☐	☐☐ ☐☐ ☐☐	Y N	Y N	Y N

SATURDAY / Date:

Today's goal:

Training notes:

Distance:
Time:
Heart Rate:
i-Rate (1-10)
X-Training:
Sleep Hours:
Weight:
Mood: ☺ ☺ ☹ ☹

WEATHER:
SUN WIND
RAIN CLOUDY
SNOW
TEMP: _____

FUEL LOG

WATER: 6-8 x 8 OZ.	FRUITS: 2-4	VEGGIES: 3-5	WHOLE GRAIN SERVINGS: 6-11	PROTEIN: 4-6 OZ.	LIMIT FAT?	ALCOHOLIC BEVERAGES?	LIMIT "EMPTY" CARBS?
☐☐☐☐ ☐☐☐☐	☐☐ ☐☐	☐☐☐ ☐☐☐	☐☐☐☐ ☐☐☐☐	☐☐ ☐☐ ☐☐	Y N	Y N	Y N

SUNDAY / Date:

Today's goal:

Training notes:

Distance:
Time:
Heart Rate:
i-Rate (1-10)
X-Training:
Sleep Hours:
Weight:
Mood: ☺ ☺ ☹ ☹

WEATHER:
SUN WIND
RAIN CLOUDY
SNOW
TEMP: _____

FUEL LOG

WATER: 6-8 x 8 OZ.	FRUITS: 2-4	VEGGIES: 3-5	WHOLE GRAIN SERVINGS: 6-11	PROTEIN: 4-6 OZ.	LIMIT FAT?	ALCOHOLIC BEVERAGES?	LIMIT "EMPTY" CARBS?
☐☐☐☐ ☐☐☐☐	☐☐ ☐☐	☐☐☐ ☐☐☐	☐☐☐☐ ☐☐☐☐	☐☐ ☐☐ ☐☐	Y N	Y N	Y N

WEEK OF:

GOALS FOR WEEK:

WEEKLY TOTAL: _____

YEAR-TO-DATE TOTAL:

Some of the best parts of being a runner have nothing to do with running. Knowing the progress I've made has given me the courage to try almost anything.

RUNNING UGLY

Even good runners have bad runs. We all have them. Runs when what we want and what we get are so different that we can't hold it together. Runs when nothing goes right, nothing feels good, and there isn't a thing we can do about it.

I should have known not to expect too much from this one. I hadn't been able to run on the weekend, so this was a mid-day, mid-week, 12-mile, solo make-up run. To make things worse, it was two loops, never the best solution for me.

What made it so ugly? It wasn't the course. I was running my favorite path along the Chicago lakefront, with views of the empty Belmont harbor and geese on the Lincoln Park lagoon. The path isn't crowded in the winter, so there was a quiet peace that disappears with the coming of spring and summer.

It wasn't the day. The weather was fine-cold, with only a little wind. The sky was a beautiful winter blue and the lake was vibrant. The city stood tall and stark against a backdrop of high clouds.

What made it ugly was me. I was angry that I had to run at that time of day, in the middle of the week. I was angry that there wasn't a magic way to log the miles without putting in the time. Nothing about the way I approached the run was good, and nothing about being on the run was going to make it any better.

Looking back I can see I expected too much from that run. I wanted it to build up my mileage base and tear down my emotional walls. I expected my feet to carry me past where my heart was willing to go. I expected the run to set my spirit free while I held my soul hostage to the darkness of my mood. It didn't happen.

The early miles were filled with the kind of hope that often marks my runs. I was a little stiff at first, but I'm often a little stiff. I was grumpy, but my grumpiness often gives way to pleasure as the miles pass. With each foot strike I waited for the magic moment when I would forget everything except the run, the moment when I would be inside of the movement and outside of myself. It never happened.

Starting the second loop was a concession, not a decision. All I really wanted was to stop, feel sorry for myself, and head home. I searched the path for other runners with whom I could share my self-pity. I tried to make eye contact so that I could pass my gloom on to someone else.

I realized I was angry with the runners who were enjoying themselves. I was annoyed that they were taking in the beauty of the day and frustrated by their lack of awareness of how much I was struggling. I was actually shocked at how completely unaware of my plight they seemed to be.

When the run ended, mercifully a mile short of my intended distance, I began the walk home, head down. Once my run was over, I wanted no part of the community of runners still on the path. I wanted no part of their joy, no piece of their satisfaction. I wanted only to wallow in my own pain.

I realized then that, for all the time we spend running with others, it's still easy for us to isolate ourselves from the very people who can help us the most. Running is a solitary activity, but it needn't be an activity of solitude. We may all run alone, but we need never run lonely.

There's no way of knowing what another runner is feeling. There's no telling what they're running to or from. There's no way of knowing what they want or are hoping to find in the day's run. But one thing is certain. They, like we, are runners. And the process of putting one foot in front of the other binds us together.

Every run is a lesson. My ugly run taught me that the battle is still against myself, against the part of me that keeps me separate from people, not just runners. And, it taught me that too often the distance that separates me from others can't be measured in miles. Waddle on, friends.

MONDAY / Date:

Today's goal: _____

Training notes: _____

Distance:
Time:
Heart Rate:
i-Rate (1-10)
X-Training:
Sleep Hours:
Weight:
Mood: ☺ ☺ ☹ Other

WEATHER:
SUN   WIND
RAIN   CLOUDY
SNOW
TEMP: ____

FUEL LOG

WATER: 6-8 x 8 OZ.	FRUITS: 2-4	VEGGIES: 3-5	WHOLE GRAIN SERVINGS: 6-11	PROTEIN: 4-6 OZ.	LIMIT FAT?	ALCOHOLIC BEVERAGES?	LIMIT "EMPTY" CARBS?
☐☐☐☐ ☐☐☐☐	☐☐☐ ☐☐	☐☐☐ ☐☐	☐☐☐☐ ☐☐☐☐ ☐	☐☐☐ ☐☐☐	Y N	Y N	Y N

TUESDAY / Date:

Today's goal: _____

Training notes: _____

Distance:
Time:
Heart Rate:
i-Rate (1-10)
X-Training:
Sleep Hours:
Weight:
Mood: ☺ ☺ ☹ Other

WEATHER:
SUN   WIND
RAIN   CLOUDY
SNOW
TEMP: ____

FUEL LOG

WATER: 6-8 x 8 OZ.	FRUITS: 2-4	VEGGIES: 3-5	WHOLE GRAIN SERVINGS: 6-11	PROTEIN: 4-6 OZ.	LIMIT FAT?	ALCOHOLIC BEVERAGES?	LIMIT "EMPTY" CARBS?
☐☐☐☐ ☐☐☐☐	☐☐☐ ☐☐	☐☐☐ ☐☐	☐☐☐☐ ☐☐☐☐ ☐	☐☐☐ ☐☐☐	Y N	Y N	Y N

WEDNESDAY / Date:

Today's goal: _____

Training notes: _____

Distance:
Time:
Heart Rate:
i-Rate (1-10)
X-Training:
Sleep Hours:
Weight:
Mood: ☺ ☺ ☹ Other

WEATHER:
SUN   WIND
RAIN   CLOUDY
SNOW
TEMP: ____

FUEL LOG

WATER: 6-8 x 8 OZ.	FRUITS: 2-4	VEGGIES: 3-5	WHOLE GRAIN SERVINGS: 6-11	PROTEIN: 4-6 OZ.	LIMIT FAT?	ALCOHOLIC BEVERAGES?	LIMIT "EMPTY" CARBS?
☐☐☐☐ ☐☐☐☐	☐☐☐ ☐☐	☐☐☐ ☐☐	☐☐☐☐ ☐☐☐☐ ☐	☐☐☐ ☐☐☐	Y N	Y N	Y N

THURSDAY / Date:

Today's goal: _____

Training notes: _____

Distance:
Time:
Heart Rate:
i-Rate (1-10)
X-Training:
Sleep Hours:
Weight:
Mood: ☺ ☺ ☹ Other

WEATHER:
SUN   WIND
RAIN   CLOUDY
SNOW
TEMP: ____

FUEL LOG

WATER: 6-8 x 8 OZ.	FRUITS: 2-4	VEGGIES: 3-5	WHOLE GRAIN SERVINGS: 6-11	PROTEIN: 4-6 OZ.	LIMIT FAT?	ALCOHOLIC BEVERAGES?	LIMIT "EMPTY" CARBS?
☐☐☐☐ ☐☐☐☐	☐☐☐ ☐☐	☐☐☐ ☐☐	☐☐☐☐ ☐☐☐☐ ☐	☐☐☐ ☐☐☐	Y N	Y N	Y N

FRIDAY / Date:

Today's goal:

Training notes:

Distance:
Time:
Heart Rate:
i-Rate (1-10)
X-Training:
Sleep Hours:
Weight:
Mood: ☺ ☺ ☹ Other

WEATHER: SUN WIND RAIN CLOUDY SNOW TEMP: ___

FUEL LOG

WATER: 6-8 x 8 OZ.	FRUITS: 2-4	VEGGIES: 3-5	WHOLE GRAIN SERVINGS: 6-11	PROTEIN: 4-6 OZ.	LIMIT FAT?	ALCOHOLIC BEVERAGES?	LIMIT "EMPTY" CARBS?
☐☐☐☐ ☐☐☐☐	☐☐ ☐☐	☐☐ ☐☐ ☐	☐☐☐ ☐☐☐ ☐☐☐ ☐☐	☐☐☐ ☐☐☐	Y N	Y N	Y N

SATURDAY / Date:

Today's goal:

Training notes:

Distance:
Time:
Heart Rate:
i-Rate (1-10)
X-Training:
Sleep Hours:
Weight:
Mood: ☺ ☺ ☹ Other

WEATHER: SUN WIND RAIN CLOUDY SNOW TEMP: ___

FUEL LOG

WATER: 6-8 x 8 OZ.	FRUITS: 2-4	VEGGIES: 3-5	WHOLE GRAIN SERVINGS: 6-11	PROTEIN: 4-6 OZ.	LIMIT FAT?	ALCOHOLIC BEVERAGES?	LIMIT "EMPTY" CARBS?
☐☐☐☐ ☐☐☐☐	☐☐ ☐☐	☐☐ ☐☐ ☐	☐☐☐ ☐☐☐ ☐☐☐ ☐☐	☐☐☐ ☐☐☐	Y N	Y N	Y N

SUNDAY / Date:

Today's goal:

Training notes:

Distance:
Time:
Heart Rate:
i-Rate (1-10)
X-Training:
Sleep Hours:
Weight:
Mood: ☺ ☺ ☹ Other

WEATHER: SUN WIND RAIN CLOUDY SNOW TEMP: ___

FUEL LOG

WATER: 6-8 x 8 OZ.	FRUITS: 2-4	VEGGIES: 3-5	WHOLE GRAIN SERVINGS: 6-11	PROTEIN: 4-6 OZ.	LIMIT FAT?	ALCOHOLIC BEVERAGES?	LIMIT "EMPTY" CARBS?
☐☐☐☐ ☐☐☐☐	☐☐ ☐☐	☐☐ ☐☐ ☐	☐☐☐ ☐☐☐ ☐☐☐ ☐☐	☐☐☐ ☐☐☐	Y N	Y N	Y N

WEEK OF:

GOALS FOR WEEK:

Finishing last in your first race is a sure-fire way to have lots to look forward to in your running career. I know. In my first race I finished just ahead of the ambulance.

WEEKLY TOTAL: _____

YEAR-TO-DATE TOTAL:

MONDAY / Date:

Today's goal: _____

Training notes: _____

Distance: _____
Time: _____
Heart Rate: _____
i-Rate (1-10): _____
X-Training: _____
Sleep Hours: _____
Weight: _____
Mood: ☺ ☺ ☹ Other

FUEL LOG

WATER: 6-8 x 8 oz.	FRUITS: 2-4	VEGGIES: 3-5	WHOLE GRAIN SERVINGS: 6-11	PROTEIN: 4-6 oz.	LIMIT FAT?	ALCOHOLIC BEVERAGES?	LIMIT "EMPTY" CARBS?
☐☐☐☐ ☐☐☐☐	☐☐ ☐☐	☐☐ ☐☐	☐☐☐☐ ☐☐	☐☐ ☐☐ ☐☐	Y N	Y N	Y N

WEATHER: SUN WIND RAIN CLOUDY SNOW   TEMP:____

TUESDAY / Date:

Today's goal: _____

Training notes: _____

Distance: _____
Time: _____
Heart Rate: _____
i-Rate (1-10): _____
X-Training: _____
Sleep Hours: _____
Weight: _____
Mood: ☺ ☺ ☹ Other

FUEL LOG

WATER: 6-8 x 8 oz.	FRUITS: 2-4	VEGGIES: 3-5	WHOLE GRAIN SERVINGS: 6-11	PROTEIN: 4-6 oz.	LIMIT FAT?	ALCOHOLIC BEVERAGES?	LIMIT "EMPTY" CARBS?
☐☐☐☐ ☐☐☐☐	☐☐ ☐☐	☐☐ ☐☐	☐☐☐☐ ☐☐	☐☐ ☐☐ ☐☐	Y N	Y N	Y N

WEATHER: SUN WIND RAIN CLOUDY SNOW   TEMP:____

WEDNESDAY / Date:

Today's goal: _____

Training notes: _____

Distance: _____
Time: _____
Heart Rate: _____
i-Rate (1-10): _____
X-Training: _____
Sleep Hours: _____
Weight: _____
Mood: ☺ ☺ ☹ Other

FUEL LOG

WATER: 6-8 x 8 oz.	FRUITS: 2-4	VEGGIES: 3-5	WHOLE GRAIN SERVINGS: 6-11	PROTEIN: 4-6 oz.	LIMIT FAT?	ALCOHOLIC BEVERAGES?	LIMIT "EMPTY" CARBS?
☐☐☐☐ ☐☐☐☐	☐☐ ☐☐	☐☐ ☐☐	☐☐☐☐ ☐☐	☐☐ ☐☐ ☐☐	Y N	Y N	Y N

WEATHER: SUN WIND RAIN CLOUDY SNOW   TEMP:____

THURSDAY / Date:

Today's goal: _____

Training notes: _____

Distance: _____
Time: _____
Heart Rate: _____
i-Rate (1-10): _____
X-Training: _____
Sleep Hours: _____
Weight: _____
Mood: ☺ ☺ ☹ Other

FUEL LOG

WATER: 6-8 x 8 oz.	FRUITS: 2-4	VEGGIES: 3-5	WHOLE GRAIN SERVINGS: 6-11	PROTEIN: 4-6 oz.	LIMIT FAT?	ALCOHOLIC BEVERAGES?	LIMIT "EMPTY" CARBS?
☐☐☐☐ ☐☐☐☐	☐☐ ☐☐	☐☐ ☐☐	☐☐☐☐ ☐☐	☐☐ ☐☐ ☐☐	Y N	Y N	Y N

WEATHER: SUN WIND RAIN CLOUDY SNOW   TEMP:____

FRIDAY / Date: _____

Today's goal: _____

Training notes: _____

Distance: _____
Time: _____
Heart Rate: _____
i-Rate (1-10): _____
X-Training: _____
Sleep Hours: _____
Weight: _____
Mood: ☺ ☺ ☹ Other

WEATHER:
SUN WIND
RAIN CLOUDY
SNOW
TEMP: _____

FUEL LOG

WATER: 6-8 × 8 OZ.	FRUITS: 2-4	VEGGIES: 3-5	WHOLE GRAIN SERVINGS: 6-11	PROTEIN: 4-6 OZ.	LIMIT FAT?	ALCOHOLIC BEVERAGES?	LIMIT "EMPTY" CARBS?
☐☐☐☐ ☐☐☐☐	☐☐ ☐☐	☐☐ ☐☐	☐☐☐☐☐☐ ☐☐☐☐☐	☐☐☐ ☐☐	Y N	Y N	Y N

SATURDAY / Date: _____

Today's goal: _____

Training notes: _____

Distance: _____
Time: _____
Heart Rate: _____
i-Rate (1-10): _____
X-Training: _____
Sleep Hours: _____
Weight: _____
Mood: ☺ ☺ ☹ Other

WEATHER:
SUN WIND
RAIN CLOUDY
SNOW
TEMP: _____

FUEL LOG

WATER: 6-8 × 8 OZ.	FRUITS: 2-4	VEGGIES: 3-5	WHOLE GRAIN SERVINGS: 6-11	PROTEIN: 4-6 OZ.	LIMIT FAT?	ALCOHOLIC BEVERAGES?	LIMIT "EMPTY" CARBS?
☐☐☐☐ ☐☐☐☐	☐☐ ☐☐	☐☐ ☐☐	☐☐☐☐☐ ☐☐☐☐☐	☐☐☐ ☐☐	Y N	Y N	Y N

SUNDAY / Date: _____

Today's goal: _____

Training notes: _____

Distance: _____
Time: _____
Heart Rate: _____
i-Rate (1-10): _____
X-Training: _____
Sleep Hours: _____
Weight: _____
Mood: ☺ ☺ ☹ Other

WEATHER:
SUN WIND
RAIN CLOUDY
SNOW
TEMP: _____

FUEL LOG

WATER: 6-8 × 8 OZ.	FRUITS: 2-4	VEGGIES: 3-5	WHOLE GRAIN SERVINGS: 6-11	PROTEIN: 4-6 OZ.	LIMIT FAT?	ALCOHOLIC BEVERAGES?	LIMIT "EMPTY" CARBS?
☐☐☐☐ ☐☐☐☐	☐☐ ☐☐	☐☐ ☐☐	☐☐☐☐ ☐☐☐☐	☐☐☐ ☐☐	Y N	Y N	Y N

WEEK OF:

GOALS FOR WEEK:

WEEKLY TOTAL: _____

YEAR-TO-DATE TOTAL:

Learning to train means accepting the physical and emotional ups and downs that come from pushing your limit week after week.

MONDAY / Date:

Today's goal:

Training notes:

Distance:
Time:
Heart Rate:
i-Rate (1-10)
X-Training:
Sleep Hours:
Weight:
Mood: ☺ ☺ ☹ Other

WEATHER:
SUN WIND
RAIN CLOUDY
SNOW
TEMP: _____

FUEL LOG

WATER: 6-8 x 8 OZ.	FRUITS: 2-4	VEGGIES: 3-5	WHOLE GRAIN SERVINGS: 6-11	PROTEIN: 4-6 OZ.	LIMIT FAT?	ALCOHOLIC BEVERAGES?	LIMIT "EMPTY" CARBS?
☐☐☐☐	☐☐	☐☐	☐☐☐☐☐	☐☐☐	Y N	Y N	Y N
☐☐☐☐	☐☐	☐☐	☐☐☐☐☐	☐☐☐			

TUESDAY / Date:

Today's goal:

Training notes:

Distance:
Time:
Heart Rate:
i-Rate (1-10)
X-Training:
Sleep Hours:
Weight:
Mood: ☺ ☺ ☹ Other

WEATHER:
SUN WIND
RAIN CLOUDY
SNOW
TEMP: _____

FUEL LOG

WATER: 6-8 x 8 OZ.	FRUITS: 2-4	VEGGIES: 3-5	WHOLE GRAIN SERVINGS: 6-11	PROTEIN: 4-6 OZ.	LIMIT FAT?	ALCOHOLIC BEVERAGES?	LIMIT "EMPTY" CARBS?
☐☐☐☐	☐☐	☐☐	☐☐☐☐☐	☐☐☐	Y N	Y N	Y N
☐☐☐☐	☐☐	☐☐	☐☐☐☐☐	☐☐☐			

WEDNESDAY / Date:

Today's goal:

Training notes:

Distance:
Time:
Heart Rate:
i-Rate (1-10)
X-Training:
Sleep Hours:
Weight:
Mood: ☺ ☺ ☹ Other

WEATHER:
SUN WIND
RAIN CLOUDY
SNOW
TEMP: _____

FUEL LOG

WATER: 6-8 x 8 OZ.	FRUITS: 2-4	VEGGIES: 3-5	WHOLE GRAIN SERVINGS: 6-11	PROTEIN: 4-6 OZ.	LIMIT FAT?	ALCOHOLIC BEVERAGES?	LIMIT "EMPTY" CARBS?
☐☐☐☐	☐☐	☐☐	☐☐☐☐☐	☐☐☐	Y N	Y N	Y N
☐☐☐☐	☐☐	☐☐	☐☐☐☐☐	☐☐☐			

THURSDAY / Date:

Today's goal:

Training notes:

Distance:
Time:
Heart Rate:
i-Rate (1-10)
X-Training:
Sleep Hours:
Weight:
Mood: ☺ ☺ ☹ Other

WEATHER:
SUN WIND
RAIN CLOUDY
SNOW
TEMP: _____

FUEL LOG

WATER: 6-8 x 8 OZ.	FRUITS: 2-4	VEGGIES: 3-5	WHOLE GRAIN SERVINGS: 6-11	PROTEIN: 4-6 OZ.	LIMIT FAT?	ALCOHOLIC BEVERAGES?	LIMIT "EMPTY" CARBS?
☐☐☐☐	☐☐	☐☐	☐☐☐☐☐	☐☐☐	Y N	Y N	Y N
☐☐☐☐	☐☐	☐☐	☐☐☐☐☐	☐☐☐			

Training notes:

FRIDAY / Date:

Today's goal:

FUEL LOG

WATER: 6-8 × 8 OZ.	FRUITS: 2-4	VEGGIES: 3-5	WHOLE GRAIN SERVINGS: 6-11	PROTEIN: 4-6 OZ.	LIMIT FAT?	ALCOHOLIC BEVERAGES?	LIMIT "EMPTY" CARBS?
☐☐☐☐	☐☐	☐☐	☐☐☐☐	☐☐☐	Y N	Y N	Y N
☐☐☐☐	☐☐	☐☐	☐☐☐☐	☐☐☐			
			☐☐☐				

WEATHER:
SUN   WIND
RAIN   CLOUDY
SNOW
TEMP: _____

Distance:
Time:
Heart Rate:
i-Rate (1-10)
X-Training:
Sleep Hours:
Weight:
Mood: ☺ ☺ ☺ ☹ ☹ Other

Training notes:

SATURDAY / Date:

Today's goal:

FUEL LOG

WATER: 6-8 × 8 OZ.	FRUITS: 2-4	VEGGIES: 3-5	WHOLE GRAIN SERVINGS: 6-11	PROTEIN: 4-6 OZ.	LIMIT FAT?	ALCOHOLIC BEVERAGES?	LIMIT "EMPTY" CARBS?
☐☐☐☐	☐☐	☐☐	☐☐☐☐	☐☐☐	Y N	Y N	Y N
☐☐☐☐	☐☐	☐☐	☐☐☐☐	☐☐☐			
			☐☐☐				

WEATHER:
SUN   WIND
RAIN   CLOUDY
SNOW
TEMP: _____

Distance:
Time:
Heart Rate:
i-Rate (1-10)
X-Training:
Sleep Hours:
Weight:
Mood: ☺ ☺ ☺ ☹ ☹ Other

Training notes:

SUNDAY / Date:

Today's goal:

FUEL LOG

WATER: 6-8 × 8 OZ.	FRUITS: 2-4	VEGGIES: 3-5	WHOLE GRAIN SERVINGS: 6-11	PROTEIN: 4-6 OZ.	LIMIT FAT?	ALCOHOLIC BEVERAGES?	LIMIT "EMPTY" CARBS?
☐☐☐☐	☐☐	☐☐	☐☐☐☐	☐☐☐	Y N	Y N	Y N
☐☐☐☐	☐☐	☐☐	☐☐☐☐	☐☐☐			
			☐☐☐				

WEATHER:
SUN   WIND
RAIN   CLOUDY
SNOW
TEMP: _____

Distance:
Time:
Heart Rate:
i-Rate (1-10)
X-Training:
Sleep Hours:
Weight:
Mood: ☺ ☺ ☺ ☹ ☹ Other

WEEK OF:

GOALS FOR WEEK:

WEEKLY TOTAL: _____

YEAR-TO-DATE TOTAL:

> **I'm not sure exactly when liking to run became longing to run, but there are miles and moments and memories that only converge when the shoe strikes the ground.**

MONDAY / Date:

Today's goal: _____

Training notes: _____

| Distance: |
| Time: |
| Heart Rate: |
| i-Rate (1-10) |
| X-Training: |
| Sleep Hours: |
| Weight: |
| Mood: ☺ ☺ ☹ Other |

WEATHER: SUN WIND RAIN CLOUDY SNOW TEMP: _____

FUEL LOG

WATER: 6-8 x 8 OZ.	FRUITS: 2-4	VEGGIES: 3-5	WHOLE GRAIN SERVINGS: 6-11	PROTEIN: 4-6 OZ.	LIMIT FAT?	ALCOHOLIC BEVERAGES?	LIMIT "EMPTY" CARBS?
☐☐☐☐	☐☐	☐☐	☐☐☐☐☐	☐☐☐	Y N	Y N	Y N
☐☐☐☐	☐☐	☐☐	☐☐☐☐	☐☐☐			

TUESDAY / Date:

Today's goal: _____

Training notes: _____

| Distance: |
| Time: |
| Heart Rate: |
| i-Rate (1-10) |
| X-Training: |
| Sleep Hours: |
| Weight: |
| Mood: ☺ ☺ ☹ Other |

WEATHER: SUN WIND RAIN CLOUDY SNOW TEMP: _____

FUEL LOG

WATER: 6-8 x 8 OZ.	FRUITS: 2-4	VEGGIES: 3-5	WHOLE GRAIN SERVINGS: 6-11	PROTEIN: 4-6 OZ.	LIMIT FAT?	ALCOHOLIC BEVERAGES?	LIMIT "EMPTY" CARBS?
☐☐☐☐	☐☐	☐☐	☐☐☐☐☐	☐☐☐	Y N	Y N	Y N
☐☐☐☐	☐☐	☐☐	☐☐☐☐	☐☐☐			

WEDNESDAY / Date:

Today's goal: _____

Training notes: _____

| Distance: |
| Time: |
| Heart Rate: |
| i-Rate (1-10) |
| X-Training: |
| Sleep Hours: |
| Weight: |
| Mood: ☺ ☺ ☹ Other |

WEATHER: SUN WIND RAIN CLOUDY SNOW TEMP: _____

FUEL LOG

WATER: 6-8 x 8 OZ.	FRUITS: 2-4	VEGGIES: 3-5	WHOLE GRAIN SERVINGS: 6-11	PROTEIN: 4-6 OZ.	LIMIT FAT?	ALCOHOLIC BEVERAGES?	LIMIT "EMPTY" CARBS?
☐☐☐☐	☐☐	☐☐	☐☐☐☐☐	☐☐☐	Y N	Y N	Y N
☐☐☐☐	☐☐	☐☐	☐☐☐☐	☐☐☐			

THURSDAY / Date:

Today's goal: _____

Training notes: _____

| Distance: |
| Time: |
| Heart Rate: |
| i-Rate (1-10) |
| X-Training: |
| Sleep Hours: |
| Weight: |
| Mood: ☺ ☺ ☹ Other |

WEATHER: SUN WIND RAIN CLOUDY SNOW TEMP: _____

FUEL LOG

WATER: 6-8 x 8 OZ.	FRUITS: 2-4	VEGGIES: 3-5	WHOLE GRAIN SERVINGS: 6-11	PROTEIN: 4-6 OZ.	LIMIT FAT?	ALCOHOLIC BEVERAGES?	LIMIT "EMPTY" CARBS?
☐☐☐☐	☐☐	☐☐	☐☐☐☐☐	☐☐☐	Y N	Y N	Y N
☐☐☐☐	☐☐	☐☐	☐☐☐☐	☐☐☐			

FRIDAY / Date:

Today's goal: _____

Training notes: _____

Distance: _____
Time: _____
Heart Rate: _____
i-Rate (1-10): _____
X-Training: _____
Sleep Hours: _____
Weight: _____
Mood: ☺ ☺ ☹ Other

FUEL LOG

WATER: 6-8 x 8 OZ.	FRUITS: 2-4	VEGGIES: 3-5	WHOLE GRAIN SERVINGS: 6-11	PROTEIN: 4-6 OZ.	LIMIT FAT?	ALCOHOLIC BEVERAGES?	LIMIT "EMPTY" CARBS?
☐☐☐☐ ☐☐☐☐	☐☐ ☐☐	☐☐ ☐☐	☐☐☐☐ ☐☐☐	☐☐☐ ☐☐	Y N	Y N	Y N

WEATHER: SUN WIND RAIN CLOUDY SNOW   TEMP: _____

SATURDAY / Date:

Today's goal: _____

Training notes: _____

Distance: _____
Time: _____
Heart Rate: _____
i-Rate (1-10): _____
X-Training: _____
Sleep Hours: _____
Weight: _____
Mood: ☺ ☺ ☹ Other

FUEL LOG

WATER: 6-8 x 8 OZ.	FRUITS: 2-4	VEGGIES: 3-5	WHOLE GRAIN SERVINGS: 6-11	PROTEIN: 4-6 OZ.	LIMIT FAT?	ALCOHOLIC BEVERAGES?	LIMIT "EMPTY" CARBS?
☐☐☐☐ ☐☐☐☐	☐☐ ☐☐	☐☐ ☐☐	☐☐☐☐ ☐☐☐	☐☐☐ ☐☐	Y N	Y N	Y N

WEATHER: SUN WIND RAIN CLOUDY SNOW   TEMP: _____

SUNDAY / Date:

Today's goal: _____

Training notes: _____

Distance: _____
Time: _____
Heart Rate: _____
i-Rate (1-10): _____
X-Training: _____
Sleep Hours: _____
Weight: _____
Mood: ☺ ☺ ☹ Other

FUEL LOG

WATER: 6-8 x 8 OZ.	FRUITS: 2-4	VEGGIES: 3-5	WHOLE GRAIN SERVINGS: 6-11	PROTEIN: 4-6 OZ.	LIMIT FAT?	ALCOHOLIC BEVERAGES?	LIMIT "EMPTY" CARBS?
☐☐☐☐ ☐☐☐☐	☐☐ ☐☐	☐☐ ☐☐	☐☐☐☐ ☐☐☐	☐☐☐ ☐☐	Y N	Y N	Y N

WEATHER: SUN WIND RAIN CLOUDY SNOW   TEMP: _____

WEEK OF:

GOALS FOR WEEK:

WEEKLY TOTAL: _____

YEAR-TO-DATE TOTAL:

> **The magic is in the training. The magic is in the day-to-day dedication to the goal. The magic comes every time you lace up your shoes.**

SETTING THE SAIL

I'm not much of a sailor. I'm sure there are times when the magic of being pushed across the water by the power of the wind is exhilarating, but every time I've tried to sail, the wind has nearly pushed me into the rocks.

It has to do with leeway or, more precisely, the lack of leeway. A boat has two sides: the windward side from which the wind is blowing, and the leeward side that is away from the wind. A sailboat doesn't go in a straight line; it gets pushed to the leeward side. You set the sail and then point the bow slightly to windward with the rudder. The important thing is to leave yourself plenty of leeway. Are you with me so far?

This is fine if the wind never changes and the course you're on is a straight line, but that never happens. The wind moves around; the course twists and turns; and you spend the better part of a sailing day fiddling with an endless array of ropes, cranks, and cleats.

Many of us think that running, like sailing, is a matter of devising a plan, laying out goals and strategies, marking a course to reach our goal, and then sitting back and watching our dreams come true. But our running is fraught with the changing winds of fortune and life. We must create our course anew on a daily basis. And, of course, as runners we never think of giving ourselves the leeway to fail.

This is most obvious to me at the finish line of races. Runners of every age and description cross the finish line, look at the time on the clock, and frown! They're disappointed. The 16-minute 5K runner wants a 15:45. The 40-minute 5K runner yearns to break 35:00. The phenomenon is the same—they don't allow enough leeway.

Their disappointment might be justified if precisely the same set of circumstances could be created over and over again. But that can't happen. Our lives are linear. This sentence won't be the same if you reread it an hour from now. You've changed—you've read the sentence and altered yourself by the simple act of reading the words.

And you're a different runner every time you run. You're in a different race as a different runner each time you toe the starting line. In spite of all your preparation, experience, and drive, you have no idea who the person is who's standing at that starting line in your shoes. You may have brought him or her to the race, but the minute the gun goes off you're just along for the ride.

To be sure, you can set the sail—and the rudder, too. You can train effectively, warm up carefully, stay within yourself, and follow your race plan. But you're still at the mercy of the fates. The day, the course, the runners around you, and a host of other factors outside of your control will effect the outcome. So you'd better give yourself some leeway.

It's important to have goals, but it's more important to be honest about what it takes to achieve them. It's important to assess yourself, to observe and even be critical of yourself, but it can't be done in ignorance or from your position as master of the universe. You're only the runner you are on that day at that moment in time.

Deciding to be a runner is only the first step. Actually being a runner is a daily commitment. It's running when you should and not running when you shouldn't. It's paying attention to yourself as you are today and choosing a course that leads you toward tomorrow. It's a matter of endless fiddling—with schedule, distance, pace, and a dozen other things that effect every daily run.

You may not be able to control the wind, but you *can* set the sail.

Waddle on, friends.

MONDAY / Date:

Today's goal:

Training notes:

Distance:
Time:
Heart Rate:
i-Rate (1-10)
X-Training:
Sleep Hours:
Weight:
Mood: ☺ 😐 ☹ Other

FUEL LOG

WATER: 6-8 × 8 OZ.	FRUITS: 2-4	VEGGIES: 3-5	WHOLE GRAIN SERVINGS: 6-11	PROTEIN: 4-6 OZ.	LIMIT FAT?	ALCOHOLIC BEVERAGES?	LIMIT "EMPTY" CARBS?
☐☐☐☐ ☐☐☐☐	☐☐ ☐☐	☐☐☐ ☐☐	☐☐☐☐ ☐☐☐☐ ☐	☐☐☐ ☐☐☐	Y N	Y N	Y N

WEATHER:
SUN WIND
RAIN CLOUDY
SNOW
TEMP: _____

TUESDAY / Date:

Today's goal:

Training notes:

Distance:
Time:
Heart Rate:
i-Rate (1-10)
X-Training:
Sleep Hours:
Weight:
Mood: ☺ 😐 ☹ Other

FUEL LOG

WATER: 6-8 × 8 OZ.	FRUITS: 2-4	VEGGIES: 3-5	WHOLE GRAIN SERVINGS: 6-11	PROTEIN: 4-6 OZ.	LIMIT FAT?	ALCOHOLIC BEVERAGES?	LIMIT "EMPTY" CARBS?
☐☐☐☐ ☐☐☐☐	☐☐ ☐☐	☐☐☐ ☐☐	☐☐☐☐ ☐☐☐☐ ☐	☐☐☐ ☐☐☐	Y N	Y N	Y N

WEATHER:
SUN WIND
RAIN CLOUDY
SNOW
TEMP: _____

WEDNESDAY / Date:

Today's goal:

Training notes:

Distance:
Time:
Heart Rate:
i-Rate (1-10)
X-Training:
Sleep Hours:
Weight:
Mood: ☺ 😐 ☹ Other

FUEL LOG

WATER: 6-8 × 8 OZ.	FRUITS: 2-4	VEGGIES: 3-5	WHOLE GRAIN SERVINGS: 6-11	PROTEIN: 4-6 OZ.	LIMIT FAT?	ALCOHOLIC BEVERAGES?	LIMIT "EMPTY" CARBS?
☐☐☐☐ ☐☐☐☐	☐☐ ☐☐	☐☐☐ ☐☐	☐☐☐☐ ☐☐☐☐ ☐	☐☐☐ ☐☐☐	Y N	Y N	Y N

WEATHER:
SUN WIND
RAIN CLOUDY
SNOW
TEMP: _____

THURSDAY / Date:

Today's goal:

Training notes:

Distance:
Time:
Heart Rate:
i-Rate (1-10)
X-Training:
Sleep Hours:
Weight:
Mood: ☺ 😐 ☹ Other

FUEL LOG

WATER: 6-8 × 8 OZ.	FRUITS: 2-4	VEGGIES: 3-5	WHOLE GRAIN SERVINGS: 6-11	PROTEIN: 4-6 OZ.	LIMIT FAT?	ALCOHOLIC BEVERAGES?	LIMIT "EMPTY" CARBS?
☐☐☐☐ ☐☐☐☐	☐☐ ☐☐	☐☐☐ ☐☐	☐☐☐☐ ☐☐☐☐ ☐	☐☐☐ ☐☐☐	Y N	Y N	Y N

WEATHER:
SUN WIND
RAIN CLOUDY
SNOW
TEMP: _____

FRIDAY / Date:

Training notes:

Today's goal:

Distance:
Time:
Heart Rate:
i-Rate (1-10)
X-Training:
Sleep Hours:
Weight:
Mood: ☺ ☺ ☹ Other

WEATHER:
SUN WIND
RAIN CLOUDY
SNOW
TEMP: _____

FUEL LOG

WATER: 6-8 x 8 OZ.	FRUITS: 2-4	VEGGIES: 3-5	WHOLE GRAIN SERVINGS: 6-11	PROTEIN: 4-6 OZ.	LIMIT FAT?	ALCOHOLIC BEVERAGES?	LIMIT "EMPTY" CARBS?
☐☐☐☐ ☐☐☐☐	☐☐ ☐☐	☐☐ ☐☐	☐☐☐☐☐ ☐☐☐☐☐ ☐	☐☐☐ ☐☐☐	Y N	Y N	Y N

SATURDAY / Date:

Training notes:

Today's goal:

Distance:
Time:
Heart Rate:
i-Rate (1-10)
X-Training:
Sleep Hours:
Weight:
Mood: ☺ ☺ ☹ Other

WEATHER:
SUN WIND
RAIN CLOUDY
SNOW
TEMP: _____

FUEL LOG

WATER: 6-8 x 8 OZ.	FRUITS: 2-4	VEGGIES: 3-5	WHOLE GRAIN SERVINGS: 6-11	PROTEIN: 4-6 OZ.	LIMIT FAT?	ALCOHOLIC BEVERAGES?	LIMIT "EMPTY" CARBS?
☐☐☐☐ ☐☐☐☐	☐☐ ☐☐	☐☐ ☐☐	☐☐☐☐☐ ☐☐☐☐☐ ☐	☐☐☐ ☐☐☐	Y N	Y N	Y N

SUNDAY / Date:

Training notes:

Today's goal:

Distance:
Time:
Heart Rate:
i-Rate (1-10)
X-Training:
Sleep Hours:
Weight:
Mood: ☺ ☺ ☹ Other

WEATHER:
SUN WIND
RAIN CLOUDY
SNOW
TEMP: _____

FUEL LOG

WATER: 6-8 x 8 OZ.	FRUITS: 2-4	VEGGIES: 3-5	WHOLE GRAIN SERVINGS: 6-11	PROTEIN: 4-6 OZ.	LIMIT FAT?	ALCOHOLIC BEVERAGES?	LIMIT "EMPTY" CARBS?
☐☐☐☐ ☐☐☐☐	☐☐ ☐☐	☐☐ ☐☐	☐☐☐☐☐ ☐☐☐☐☐ ☐	☐☐☐ ☐☐☐	Y N	Y N	Y N

WEEK OF:

GOALS FOR WEEK:

WEEKLY TOTAL: _____

YEAR-TO-DATE TOTAL:

My running shoes are like soldiers in my war against the ravages of aging and a less-than-healthy previous lifestyle. And I am the general.

MONDAY / Date: _____

Today's goal: _____

Training notes: _____

| Distance: |
| Time: |
| Heart Rate: |
| i-Rate (1-10) |
| X-Training: |
| Sleep Hours: |
| Weight: |
| Mood: ☺ ☺ ☹ Other |

WEATHER:
SUN   WIND
RAIN   CLOUDY
SNOW
TEMP: _____

FUEL LOG

WATER: 6-8 x 8 OZ.	FRUITS: 2-4	VEGGIES: 3-5	WHOLE GRAIN SERVINGS: 6-11	PROTEIN: 4-6 OZ.	LIMIT FAT?	ALCOHOLIC BEVERAGES?	LIMIT "EMPTY" CARBS?
☐☐☐☐	☐☐	☐☐	☐☐☐☐☐☐	☐☐☐	Y N	Y N	Y N
☐☐☐☐	☐☐	☐☐	☐☐☐☐☐	☐☐☐			

TUESDAY / Date: _____

Today's goal: _____

Training notes: _____

| Distance: |
| Time: |
| Heart Rate: |
| i-Rate (1-10) |
| X-Training: |
| Sleep Hours: |
| Weight: |
| Mood: ☺ ☺ ☹ Other |

WEATHER:
SUN   WIND
RAIN   CLOUDY
SNOW
TEMP: _____

FUEL LOG

WATER: 6-8 x 8 OZ.	FRUITS: 2-4	VEGGIES: 3-5	WHOLE GRAIN SERVINGS: 6-11	PROTEIN: 4-6 OZ.	LIMIT FAT?	ALCOHOLIC BEVERAGES?	LIMIT "EMPTY" CARBS?
☐☐☐☐	☐☐	☐☐	☐☐☐☐☐☐	☐☐☐	Y N	Y N	Y N
☐☐☐☐	☐☐	☐☐	☐☐☐☐☐	☐☐☐			

WEDNESDAY / Date: _____

Today's goal: _____

Training notes: _____

| Distance: |
| Time: |
| Heart Rate: |
| i-Rate (1-10) |
| X-Training: |
| Sleep Hours: |
| Weight: |
| Mood: ☺ ☺ ☹ Other |

WEATHER:
SUN   WIND
RAIN   CLOUDY
SNOW
TEMP: _____

FUEL LOG

WATER: 6-8 x 8 OZ.	FRUITS: 2-4	VEGGIES: 3-5	WHOLE GRAIN SERVINGS: 6-11	PROTEIN: 4-6 OZ.	LIMIT FAT?	ALCOHOLIC BEVERAGES?	LIMIT "EMPTY" CARBS?
☐☐☐☐	☐☐	☐☐	☐☐☐☐☐☐	☐☐☐	Y N	Y N	Y N
☐☐☐☐	☐☐	☐☐	☐☐☐☐☐	☐☐☐			

THURSDAY / Date: _____

Today's goal: _____

Training notes: _____

| Distance: |
| Time: |
| Heart Rate: |
| i-Rate (1-10) |
| X-Training: |
| Sleep Hours: |
| Weight: |
| Mood: ☺ ☺ ☹ Other |

WEATHER:
SUN   WIND
RAIN   CLOUDY
SNOW
TEMP: _____

FUEL LOG

WATER: 6-8 x 8 OZ.	FRUITS: 2-4	VEGGIES: 3-5	WHOLE GRAIN SERVINGS: 6-11	PROTEIN: 4-6 OZ.	LIMIT FAT?	ALCOHOLIC BEVERAGES?	LIMIT "EMPTY" CARBS?
☐☐☐☐	☐☐	☐☐	☐☐☐☐☐☐	☐☐☐	Y N	Y N	Y N
☐☐☐☐	☐☐	☐☐	☐☐☐☐☐	☐☐☐			

FRIDAY / Date: Training notes:

Today's goal:

Distance:
Time:
Heart Rate:
i-Rate (1-10)
X-Training:
Sleep Hours:
Weight:
Mood: ☺ ☺ ☹ Other

WEATHER:
SUN WIND
RAIN CLOUDY
SNOW
TEMP:_____

FUEL LOG

WATER: 6-8 x 8 OZ.	FRUITS: 2-4	VEGGIES: 3-5	WHOLE GRAIN SERVINGS: 6-11	PROTEIN: 4-6 OZ.	LIMIT FAT?	ALCOHOLIC BEVERAGES?	LIMIT "EMPTY" CARBS?
☐☐☐☐ ☐☐☐☐	☐☐ ☐☐	☐☐☐ ☐☐	☐☐☐☐ ☐☐☐☐ ☐☐☐	☐☐☐ ☐☐	Y N	Y N	Y N

SATURDAY / Date: Training notes:

Today's goal:

Distance:
Time:
Heart Rate:
i-Rate (1-10)
X-Training:
Sleep Hours:
Weight:
Mood: ☺ ☺ ☹ Other

WEATHER:
SUN WIND
RAIN CLOUDY
SNOW
TEMP:_____

FUEL LOG

WATER: 6-8 x 8 OZ.	FRUITS: 2-4	VEGGIES: 3-5	WHOLE GRAIN SERVINGS: 6-11	PROTEIN: 4-6 OZ.	LIMIT FAT?	ALCOHOLIC BEVERAGES?	LIMIT "EMPTY" CARBS?
☐☐☐☐ ☐☐☐☐	☐☐ ☐☐	☐☐☐ ☐☐	☐☐☐☐ ☐☐☐☐ ☐☐☐	☐☐☐ ☐☐	Y N	Y N	Y N

SUNDAY / Date: Training notes:

Today's goal:

Distance:
Time:
Heart Rate:
i-Rate (1-10)
X-Training:
Sleep Hours:
Weight:
Mood: ☺ ☺ ☹ Other

WEATHER:
SUN WIND
RAIN CLOUDY
SNOW
TEMP:_____

FUEL LOG

WATER: 6-8 x 8 OZ.	FRUITS: 2-4	VEGGIES: 3-5	WHOLE GRAIN SERVINGS: 6-11	PROTEIN: 4-6 OZ.	LIMIT FAT?	ALCOHOLIC BEVERAGES?	LIMIT "EMPTY" CARBS?
☐☐☐☐ ☐☐☐☐	☐☐ ☐☐	☐☐☐ ☐☐	☐☐☐☐ ☐☐☐☐ ☐☐☐	☐☐☐ ☐☐	Y N	Y N	Y N

WEEK OF:

GOALS FOR WEEK:

WEEKLY TOTAL: _____

YEAR-TO-DATE TOTAL:

To paraphrase an old poster: Today is the first day of the rest of your training.

MONDAY / Date: _____

Training notes: _____

Today's goal: _____

FUEL LOG

WATER: 6-8 × 8 OZ.	FRUITS: 2-4	VEGGIES: 3-5	WHOLE GRAIN SERVINGS: 6-11	PROTEIN: 4-6 OZ.	LIMIT FAT?	ALCOHOLIC BEVERAGES?	LIMIT "EMPTY" CARBS?
☐☐☐☐ ☐☐☐☐	☐☐ ☐☐	☐☐☐ ☐☐	☐☐☐☐ ☐☐☐☐ ☐	☐☐☐ ☐☐☐	Y N	Y N	Y N

WEATHER: SUN WIND RAIN CLOUDY SNOW TEMP: _____

Distance: _____
Time: _____
Heart Rate: _____
i-Rate (1-10): _____
X-Training: _____
Sleep Hours: _____
Weight: _____
Mood: ☺ ☺ ☹ ☹ Other

TUESDAY / Date: _____

Training notes: _____

Today's goal: _____

FUEL LOG

WATER: 6-8 × 8 OZ.	FRUITS: 2-4	VEGGIES: 3-5	WHOLE GRAIN SERVINGS: 6-11	PROTEIN: 4-6 OZ.	LIMIT FAT?	ALCOHOLIC BEVERAGES?	LIMIT "EMPTY" CARBS?
☐☐☐☐ ☐☐☐☐	☐☐ ☐☐	☐☐☐ ☐☐	☐☐☐☐ ☐☐☐☐ ☐	☐☐☐ ☐☐☐	Y N	Y N	Y N

WEATHER: SUN WIND RAIN CLOUDY SNOW TEMP: _____

Distance: _____
Time: _____
Heart Rate: _____
i-Rate (1-10): _____
X-Training: _____
Sleep Hours: _____
Weight: _____
Mood: ☺ ☺ ☹ Other

WEDNESDAY / Date: _____

Training notes: _____

Today's goal: _____

FUEL LOG

WATER: 6-8 × 8 OZ.	FRUITS: 2-4	VEGGIES: 3-5	WHOLE GRAIN SERVINGS: 6-11	PROTEIN: 4-6 OZ.	LIMIT FAT?	ALCOHOLIC BEVERAGES?	LIMIT "EMPTY" CARBS?
☐☐☐☐ ☐☐☐☐	☐☐ ☐☐	☐☐☐ ☐☐	☐☐☐☐ ☐☐☐☐ ☐	☐☐☐ ☐☐☐	Y N	Y N	Y N

WEATHER: SUN WIND RAIN CLOUDY SNOW TEMP: _____

Distance: _____
Time: _____
Heart Rate: _____
i-Rate (1-10): _____
X-Training: _____
Sleep Hours: _____
Weight: _____
Mood: ☺ ☺ ☹ Other

THURSDAY / Date: _____

Training notes: _____

Today's goal: _____

FUEL LOG

WATER: 6-8 × 8 OZ.	FRUITS: 2-4	VEGGIES: 3-5	WHOLE GRAIN SERVINGS: 6-11	PROTEIN: 4-6 OZ.	LIMIT FAT?	ALCOHOLIC BEVERAGES?	LIMIT "EMPTY" CARBS?
☐☐☐☐ ☐☐☐☐	☐☐ ☐☐	☐☐☐ ☐☐	☐☐☐☐ ☐☐☐☐ ☐	☐☐☐ ☐☐☐	Y N	Y N	Y N

WEATHER: SUN WIND RAIN CLOUDY SNOW TEMP: _____

Distance: _____
Time: _____
Heart Rate: _____
i-Rate (1-10): _____
X-Training: _____
Sleep Hours: _____
Weight: _____
Mood: ☺ ☺ ☹ Other

FRIDAY / Date:

Training notes:

Today's goal:

Distance:
Time:
Heart Rate:
i-Rate (1-10)
X-Training:
Sleep Hours:
Weight:
Mood: ☺ ☺ ☹ Other

FUEL LOG

WEATHER:
SUN   WIND
RAIN CLOUDY
SNOW
TEMP: _____

WATER: 6-8 x 8 OZ.	FRUITS: 2-4	VEGGIES: 3-5	WHOLE GRAIN SERVINGS: 6-11	PROTEIN: 4-6 OZ.	LIMIT FAT?	ALCOHOLIC BEVERAGES?	LIMIT "EMPTY" CARBS?
☐☐☐☐ ☐☐☐☐	☐☐ ☐☐	☐☐ ☐	☐☐☐ ☐☐☐	☐☐☐ ☐☐	Y N	Y N	Y N

SATURDAY / Date:

Training notes:

Today's goal:

Distance:
Time:
Heart Rate:
i-Rate (1-10)
X-Training:
Sleep Hours:
Weight:
Mood: ☺ ☺ ☹ Other

FUEL LOG

WEATHER:
SUN   WIND
RAIN CLOUDY
SNOW
TEMP: _____

WATER: 6-8 x 8 OZ.	FRUITS: 2-4	VEGGIES: 3-5	WHOLE GRAIN SERVINGS: 6-11	PROTEIN: 4-6 OZ.	LIMIT FAT?	ALCOHOLIC BEVERAGES?	LIMIT "EMPTY" CARBS?
☐☐☐☐ ☐☐☐☐	☐☐ ☐☐	☐☐ ☐	☐☐☐ ☐☐☐	☐☐☐ ☐☐	Y N	Y N	Y N

SUNDAY / Date:

Training notes:

Today's goal:

Distance:
Time:
Heart Rate:
i-Rate (1-10)
X-Training:
Sleep Hours:
Weight:
Mood: ☺ ☺ ☹ Other

FUEL LOG

WEATHER:
SUN   WIND
RAIN CLOUDY
SNOW
TEMP: _____

WATER: 6-8 x 8 OZ.	FRUITS: 2-4	VEGGIES: 3-5	WHOLE GRAIN SERVINGS: 6-11	PROTEIN: 4-6 OZ.	LIMIT FAT?	ALCOHOLIC BEVERAGES?	LIMIT "EMPTY" CARBS?
☐☐☐☐ ☐☐☐☐	☐☐ ☐☐	☐☐ ☐	☐☐☐ ☐☐☐	☐☐☐ ☐☐	Y N	Y N	Y N

WEEK OF:

GOALS FOR WEEK:

WEEKLY TOTAL: _____

YEAR-TO-DATE TOTAL:

Part of the appeal of running is that it is an authentic undertaking. You either run or you don't.

MONDAY / Date:

Today's goal:

Training notes:

Distance:
Time:
Heart Rate:
i-Rate (1-10)
X-Training:
Sleep Hours:
Weight:
Mood: ☺ ☺ ☹ Other

WEATHER:
SUN WIND
RAIN CLOUDY
SNOW
TEMP: _____

FUEL LOG

WATER: 6-8 x 8 OZ.	FRUITS: 2-4	VEGGIES: 3-5	WHOLE GRAIN SERVINGS: 6-11	PROTEIN: 4-6 OZ.	LIMIT FAT?	ALCOHOLIC BEVERAGES?	LIMIT "EMPTY" CARBS?
☐☐☐☐ ☐☐☐☐	☐☐ ☐☐	☐☐ ☐	☐☐☐☐☐ ☐☐☐☐☐ ☐	☐☐☐ ☐☐☐	Y N	Y N	Y N

TUESDAY / Date:

Today's goal:

Training notes:

Distance:
Time:
Heart Rate:
i-Rate (1-10)
X-Training:
Sleep Hours:
Weight:
Mood: ☺ ☺ ☹ Other

WEATHER:
SUN WIND
RAIN CLOUDY
SNOW
TEMP: _____

FUEL LOG

WATER: 6-8 x 8 OZ.	FRUITS: 2-4	VEGGIES: 3-5	WHOLE GRAIN SERVINGS: 6-11	PROTEIN: 4-6 OZ.	LIMIT FAT?	ALCOHOLIC BEVERAGES?	LIMIT "EMPTY" CARBS?
☐☐☐☐ ☐☐☐☐	☐☐ ☐☐	☐☐ ☐	☐☐☐☐☐ ☐☐☐☐☐ ☐	☐☐☐ ☐☐☐	Y N	Y N	Y N

WEDNESDAY / Date:

Today's goal:

Training notes:

Distance:
Time:
Heart Rate:
i-Rate (1-10)
X-Training:
Sleep Hours:
Weight:
Mood: ☺ ☺ ☹ Other

WEATHER:
SUN WIND
RAIN CLOUDY
SNOW
TEMP: _____

FUEL LOG

WATER: 6-8 x 8 OZ.	FRUITS: 2-4	VEGGIES: 3-5	WHOLE GRAIN SERVINGS: 6-11	PROTEIN: 4-6 OZ.	LIMIT FAT?	ALCOHOLIC BEVERAGES?	LIMIT "EMPTY" CARBS?
☐☐☐☐ ☐☐☐☐	☐☐ ☐☐	☐☐ ☐	☐☐☐☐☐ ☐☐☐☐☐ ☐	☐☐☐ ☐☐☐	Y N	Y N	Y N

THURSDAY / Date:

Today's goal:

Training notes:

Distance:
Time:
Heart Rate:
i-Rate (1-10)
X-Training:
Sleep Hours:
Weight:
Mood: ☺ ☺ ☹ Other

WEATHER:
SUN WIND
RAIN CLOUDY
SNOW
TEMP: _____

FUEL LOG

WATER: 6-8 x 8 OZ.	FRUITS: 2-4	VEGGIES: 3-5	WHOLE GRAIN SERVINGS: 6-11	PROTEIN: 4-6 OZ.	LIMIT FAT?	ALCOHOLIC BEVERAGES?	LIMIT "EMPTY" CARBS?
☐☐☐☐ ☐☐☐☐	☐☐ ☐☐	☐☐ ☐	☐☐☐☐☐ ☐☐☐☐☐ ☐	☐☐☐ ☐☐☐	Y N	Y N	Y N

FRIDAY / Date:

Training notes:

Today's goal:

FUEL LOG

WATER: 6-8 × 8 OZ.	FRUITS: 2-4	VEGGIES: 3-5	WHOLE GRAIN SERVINGS: 6-11	PROTEIN: 4-6 OZ.	LIMIT FAT?	ALCOHOLIC BEVERAGES?	LIMIT "EMPTY" CARBS?
☐☐☐☐ ☐☐☐☐	☐☐ ☐☐	☐☐ ☐☐	☐☐☐☐☐ ☐☐☐☐☐ ☐	☐☐☐ ☐☐☐	Y N	Y N	Y N

Distance:
Time:
Heart Rate:
i-Rate (1-10)
X-Training:
Sleep Hours:
Weight:
Mood: ☺ ☺ ☹

WEATHER:
SUN WIND
RAIN CLOUDY
SNOW
TEMP: _____

SATURDAY / Date:

Training notes:

Today's goal:

FUEL LOG

WATER: 6-8 × 8 OZ.	FRUITS: 2-4	VEGGIES: 3-5	WHOLE GRAIN SERVINGS: 6-11	PROTEIN: 4-6 OZ.	LIMIT FAT?	ALCOHOLIC BEVERAGES?	LIMIT "EMPTY" CARBS?
☐☐☐☐ ☐☐☐☐	☐☐ ☐☐	☐☐ ☐☐	☐☐☐☐☐ ☐☐☐☐☐ ☐	☐☐☐ ☐☐☐	Y N	Y N	Y N

Distance:
Time:
Heart Rate:
i-Rate (1-10)
X-Training:
Sleep Hours:
Weight:
Mood: ☺ ☺ ☹

WEATHER:
SUN WIND
RAIN CLOUDY
SNOW
TEMP: _____

SUNDAY / Date:

Training notes:

Today's goal:

FUEL LOG

WATER: 6-8 × 8 OZ.	FRUITS: 2-4	VEGGIES: 3-5	WHOLE GRAIN SERVINGS: 6-11	PROTEIN: 4-6 OZ.	LIMIT FAT?	ALCOHOLIC BEVERAGES?	LIMIT "EMPTY" CARBS?
☐☐☐☐ ☐☐☐☐	☐☐ ☐☐	☐☐ ☐☐	☐☐☐☐☐ ☐☐☐☐☐ ☐	☐☐☐ ☐☐☐	Y N	Y N	Y N

Distance:
Time:
Heart Rate:
i-Rate (1-10)
X-Training:
Sleep Hours:
Weight:
Mood: ☺ ☺ ☹

WEATHER:
SUN WIND
RAIN CLOUDY
SNOW
TEMP: _____

WEEK OF:

GOALS FOR WEEK:

WEEKLY TOTAL: _____

YEAR-TO-DATE TOTAL:

I remember how much I looked forward to the recess bell when I was young. It didn't matter what I was doing; nothing was more important than recess. Now training is my recess.

THE INNER PENGUIN

I'm a 90s guy. Or at least I was. That all seems so . . . "20th Century" now. I'm not ready to call myself a "zero" guy, but I'll bet there are others that might. I'm in touch with my feminine side, I know all about male bounding, and I am way too in touch with my inner child. But, I am just beginning to learn how to be in touch with my inner Penguin.

I didn't even know that there WAS an inner penguin at first. I thought that being a penguin was about being satisfied with what I had, about finding the joy in the movement of running and the moment of running. I thought that being a penguin was looking past other's expectations and getting to the truth about ourselves. I thought that being a penguin was about being slow.

Not long ago a 30 minute-ish 10K runner introduced himself to me as a Penguin. I was astonished. How could this be? He had talent, he had skill, and he had the body of an elite runner. How could HE be a penguin? I thought he was just being kind so I told him that he must be wrong.

"No" he said smiling. "I don't run like a penguin, but I'm in touch with my inner Penguin." He went on to say that he struggled against his limitations just like I did. He was honest enough to tell me of his frustrations as he tried to break through the 35-minute barrier, and then 34 and 33. He was talking about his training, but he was telling me about himself.

He explained that there were days when he would just cruise through a run at about a 6:30 pace and enjoy the sights and sounds and smells of the day. That, he said, was his inner penguin at work. I explained that I too often cruised through runs, but at something like a 12 minute pace. That, I told him, was my inner penguin at work, and my outer penguin at play.

As we laughed I began to understand that we were talking about the same phenomenon. We were both talking about releasing ourselves from the pressures of training, from the demands of travel and schedules, and were allowing ourselves to simply enjoy the most fundamental component of being a runner. Running.

I learned again that I have more in common with a 6-minute miler than with someone who has never tasted their own sweat. I learned that I have more in common with a sub 3-hour marathoner than with someone who has never felt the flush of achievement or the ache of failure. I learned that it is mostly about what goes on inside of our souls that unites as runners... and as penguins.

Since then I've come to view those in front of me somewhat differently. I no longer believe that their speed relative to mine is any reason to deny them the joy of being a penguin. I see now that it is possible to improve one's speed, to increase one's distance, and not lose sight of the essential pleasure of running.

That insight has caused me to rethink some of my own goals and aspirations. I have always feared reaching for my own running potential because I thought it would mean losing the pleasure. I have been frightened to let go of my comfort to find the real limits of my body and mind. I thought it would mean that I was no longer a penguin.

But, I now see that being a penguin is more about what's inside that out, more about what I feel than what I accomplish, and more about what a can do than what I can't. Being a penguin isn't about what someone does, but about why someone does it.

Waddle on, friends.

MONDAY / Date:

Today's goal:

Training notes:

Distance:
Time:
Heart Rate:
i-Rate (1-10)
X-Training:
Sleep Hours:
Weight:
Mood: ☺ ☺ ☺ ☹ Other

FUEL LOG

WATER: 6-8 × 8 OZ.	FRUITS: 2-4	VEGGIES: 3-5	WHOLE GRAIN SERVINGS: 6-11	PROTEIN: 4-6 OZ.	LIMIT FAT?	ALCOHOLIC BEVERAGES?	LIMIT "EMPTY" CARBS?
☐☐☐☐ ☐☐☐☐	☐☐ ☐☐	☐☐ ☐☐	☐☐☐ ☐☐☐	☐☐☐ ☐☐☐	Y N	Y N	Y N

WEATHER:
SUN   WIND
RAIN CLOUDY
SNOW
TEMP:_____

TUESDAY / Date:

Today's goal:

Training notes:

Distance:
Time:
Heart Rate:
i-Rate (1-10)
X-Training:
Sleep Hours:
Weight:
Mood: ☺ ☺ ☺ ☹ Other

FUEL LOG

WATER: 6-8 × 8 OZ.	FRUITS: 2-4	VEGGIES: 3-5	WHOLE GRAIN SERVINGS: 6-11	PROTEIN: 4-6 OZ.	LIMIT FAT?	ALCOHOLIC BEVERAGES?	LIMIT "EMPTY" CARBS?
☐☐☐☐ ☐☐☐☐	☐☐ ☐☐	☐☐ ☐☐	☐☐☐ ☐☐☐	☐☐☐ ☐☐☐	Y N	Y N	Y N

WEATHER:
SUN   WIND
RAIN CLOUDY
SNOW
TEMP:_____

WEDNESDAY / Date:

Today's goal:

Training notes:

Distance:
Time:
Heart Rate:
i-Rate (1-10)
X-Training:
Sleep Hours:
Weight:
Mood: ☺ ☺ ☺ ☹ Other

FUEL LOG

WATER: 6-8 × 8 OZ.	FRUITS: 2-4	VEGGIES: 3-5	WHOLE GRAIN SERVINGS: 6-11	PROTEIN: 4-6 OZ.	LIMIT FAT?	ALCOHOLIC BEVERAGES?	LIMIT "EMPTY" CARBS?
☐☐☐☐ ☐☐☐☐	☐☐ ☐☐	☐☐ ☐☐	☐☐☐ ☐☐☐	☐☐☐ ☐☐☐	Y N	Y N	Y N

WEATHER:
SUN   WIND
RAIN CLOUDY
SNOW
TEMP:_____

THURSDAY / Date:

Today's goal:

Training notes:

Distance:
Time:
Heart Rate:
i-Rate (1-10)
X-Training:
Sleep Hours:
Weight:
Mood: ☺ ☺ ☺ ☹ Other

FUEL LOG

WATER: 6-8 × 8 OZ.	FRUITS: 2-4	VEGGIES: 3-5	WHOLE GRAIN SERVINGS: 6-11	PROTEIN: 4-6 OZ.	LIMIT FAT?	ALCOHOLIC BEVERAGES?	LIMIT "EMPTY" CARBS?
☐☐☐☐ ☐☐☐☐	☐☐ ☐☐	☐☐ ☐☐	☐☐☐ ☐☐☐	☐☐☐ ☐☐☐	Y N	Y N	Y N

WEATHER:
SUN   WIND
RAIN CLOUDY
SNOW
TEMP:_____

FRIDAY / Date:

Today's goal:

Training notes: _____

Distance:
Time:
Heart Rate:
i-Rate (1-10)
X-Training:
Sleep Hours:
Weight:
Mood: ☺ ☺ ☹ Other

WEATHER:
SUN   WIND
RAIN CLOUDY
SNOW
TEMP: ____

FUEL LOG

WATER: 6-8 × 8 OZ.	FRUITS: 2-4	VEGGIES: 3-5	WHOLE GRAIN SERVINGS: 6-11	PROTEIN: 4-6 OZ.	LIMIT FAT?	ALCOHOLIC BEVERAGES?	LIMIT "EMPTY" CARBS?
☐☐☐☐ ☐☐☐☐	☐☐	☐☐	☐☐☐☐☐☐	☐☐☐ ☐☐☐	Y N	Y N	Y N

SATURDAY / Date:

Today's goal:

Training notes: _____

Distance:
Time:
Heart Rate:
i-Rate (1-10)
X-Training:
Sleep Hours:
Weight:
Mood: ☺ ☺ ☹ Other

WEATHER:
SUN   WIND
RAIN CLOUDY
SNOW
TEMP: ____

FUEL LOG

WATER: 6-8 × 8 OZ.	FRUITS: 2-4	VEGGIES: 3-5	WHOLE GRAIN SERVINGS: 6-11	PROTEIN: 4-6 OZ.	LIMIT FAT?	ALCOHOLIC BEVERAGES?	LIMIT "EMPTY" CARBS?
☐☐☐☐ ☐☐☐☐	☐☐	☐☐	☐☐☐☐☐☐	☐☐☐ ☐☐☐	Y N	Y N	Y N

SUNDAY / Date:

Today's goal:

Training notes: _____

Distance:
Time:
Heart Rate:
i-Rate (1-10)
X-Training:
Sleep Hours:
Weight:
Mood: ☺ ☺ ☹ Other

WEATHER:
SUN   WIND
RAIN CLOUDY
SNOW
TEMP: ____

FUEL LOG

WATER: 6-8 × 8 OZ.	FRUITS: 2-4	VEGGIES: 3-5	WHOLE GRAIN SERVINGS: 6-11	PROTEIN: 4-6 OZ.	LIMIT FAT?	ALCOHOLIC BEVERAGES?	LIMIT "EMPTY" CARBS?
☐☐☐☐ ☐☐☐☐	☐☐	☐☐	☐☐☐☐☐☐	☐☐☐ ☐☐☐	Y N	Y N	Y N

WEEK OF:

GOALS FOR WEEK:

WEEKLY TOTAL: _____

YEAR-TO-DATE TOTAL:

> **When I began running, the act of moving was more important than stride length and foot strikes. The movement of my body reflected the movement of my spirit.**

MONDAY / Date: _____

Today's goal: _____

Training notes: _____

FUEL LOG

WATER: 6-8 x 8 OZ.	FRUITS: 2-4	VEGGIES: 3-5	WHOLE GRAIN SERVINGS: 6-11	PROTEIN: 4-6 OZ.	LIMIT FAT?	ALCOHOLIC BEVERAGES?	LIMIT "EMPTY" CARBS?
☐☐☐☐ ☐☐☐☐	☐☐ ☐☐	☐☐ ☐☐	☐☐☐☐ ☐☐☐☐	☐☐☐ ☐☐☐	Y N	Y N	Y N

WEATHER: SUN WIND RAIN CLOUDY SNOW TEMP: _____

Distance: _____
Time: _____
Heart Rate: _____
i-Rate (1-10): _____
X-Training: _____
Sleep Hours: _____
Weight: _____
Mood: ☺ ☺ ☹ Other

TUESDAY / Date: _____

Today's goal: _____

Training notes: _____

FUEL LOG

WATER: 6-8 x 8 OZ.	FRUITS: 2-4	VEGGIES: 3-5	WHOLE GRAIN SERVINGS: 6-11	PROTEIN: 4-6 OZ.	LIMIT FAT?	ALCOHOLIC BEVERAGES?	LIMIT "EMPTY" CARBS?
☐☐☐☐ ☐☐☐☐	☐☐ ☐☐	☐☐ ☐☐	☐☐☐ ☐☐☐	☐☐☐ ☐☐☐	Y N	Y N	Y N

WEATHER: SUN WIND RAIN CLOUDY SNOW TEMP: _____

Distance: _____
Time: _____
Heart Rate: _____
i-Rate (1-10): _____
X-Training: _____
Sleep Hours: _____
Weight: _____
Mood: ☺ ☺ ☹ Other

WEDNESDAY / Date: _____

Today's goal: _____

Training notes: _____

FUEL LOG

WATER: 6-8 x 8 OZ.	FRUITS: 2-4	VEGGIES: 3-5	WHOLE GRAIN SERVINGS: 6-11	PROTEIN: 4-6 OZ.	LIMIT FAT?	ALCOHOLIC BEVERAGES?	LIMIT "EMPTY" CARBS?
☐☐☐☐ ☐☐☐☐	☐☐ ☐☐	☐☐ ☐☐	☐☐☐ ☐☐☐	☐☐☐ ☐☐☐	Y N	Y N	Y N

WEATHER: SUN WIND RAIN CLOUDY SNOW TEMP: _____

Distance: _____
Time: _____
Heart Rate: _____
i-Rate (1-10): _____
X-Training: _____
Sleep Hours: _____
Weight: _____
Mood: ☺ ☺ ☹ Other

THURSDAY / Date: _____

Today's goal: _____

Training notes: _____

FUEL LOG

WATER: 6-8 x 8 OZ.	FRUITS: 2-4	VEGGIES: 3-5	WHOLE GRAIN SERVINGS: 6-11	PROTEIN: 4-6 OZ.	LIMIT FAT?	ALCOHOLIC BEVERAGES?	LIMIT "EMPTY" CARBS?
☐☐☐☐ ☐☐☐☐	☐☐ ☐☐	☐☐ ☐☐	☐☐☐ ☐☐☐	☐☐☐ ☐☐☐	Y N	Y N	Y N

WEATHER: SUN WIND RAIN CLOUDY SNOW TEMP: _____

Distance: _____
Time: _____
Heart Rate: _____
i-Rate (1-10): _____
X-Training: _____
Sleep Hours: _____
Weight: _____
Mood: ☺ ☺ ☹ Other

FRIDAY / Date:

Training notes:

Today's goal:

_____

FUEL LOG

WATER: 6-8 x 8 OZ.	FRUITS: 2-4	VEGGIES: 3-5	WHOLE GRAIN SERVINGS: 6-11	PROTEIN: 4-6 OZ.	LIMIT FAT?	ALCOHOLIC BEVERAGES?	LIMIT "EMPTY" CARBS?
☐☐☐☐ ☐☐☐☐	☐☐ ☐☐	☐☐☐ ☐☐	☐☐☐☐☐ ☐☐☐☐☐☐	☐☐☐ ☐☐	Y N	Y N	Y N

WEATHER:
SUN WIND
RAIN CLOUDY
SNOW
TEMP: _____

Distance:
Time:
Heart Rate:
i-Rate (1-10)
X-Training:
Sleep Hours:
Weight:
Mood: ☺ ☺ ☹ ☹ Other

SATURDAY / Date:

Training notes:

Today's goal:

_____

FUEL LOG

WATER: 6-8 x 8 OZ.	FRUITS: 2-4	VEGGIES: 3-5	WHOLE GRAIN SERVINGS: 6-11	PROTEIN: 4-6 OZ.	LIMIT FAT?	ALCOHOLIC BEVERAGES?	LIMIT "EMPTY" CARBS?
☐☐☐☐ ☐☐☐☐	☐☐ ☐☐	☐☐☐ ☐☐	☐☐☐☐☐ ☐☐☐☐☐☐	☐☐☐ ☐☐	Y N	Y N	Y N

WEATHER:
SUN WIND
RAIN CLOUDY
SNOW
TEMP: _____

Distance:
Time:
Heart Rate:
i-Rate (1-10)
X-Training:
Sleep Hours:
Weight:
Mood: ☺ ☺ ☹ ☹ Other

SUNDAY / Date:

Training notes:

Today's goal:

_____

FUEL LOG

WATER: 6-8 x 8 OZ.	FRUITS: 2-4	VEGGIES: 3-5	WHOLE GRAIN SERVINGS: 6-11	PROTEIN: 4-6 OZ.	LIMIT FAT?	ALCOHOLIC BEVERAGES?	LIMIT "EMPTY" CARBS?
☐☐☐☐ ☐☐☐☐	☐☐ ☐☐	☐☐☐ ☐☐	☐☐☐☐☐ ☐☐☐☐☐☐	☐☐☐ ☐☐	Y N	Y N	Y N

WEATHER:
SUN WIND
RAIN CLOUDY
SNOW
TEMP: _____

Distance:
Time:
Heart Rate:
i-Rate (1-10)
X-Training:
Sleep Hours:
Weight:
Mood: ☺ ☺ ☹ ☹ Other

WEEK OF:

GOALS FOR WEEK:

There's nothing like a track workout to make you feel like an athlete.

WEEKLY TOTAL: _____

YEAR-TO-DATE TOTAL:

MONDAY / Date: _____

Today's goal:

Training notes:

| Distance: |
| Time: |
| Heart Rate: |
| i-Rate (1-10) |
| X-Training: |
| Sleep Hours: |
| Weight: |
| Mood: ☺ ☺ ☹ Other |

FUEL LOG

WATER: 6-8 × 8 OZ.	FRUITS: 2-4	VEGGIES: 3-5	WHOLE GRAIN SERVINGS: 6-11	PROTEIN: 4-6 OZ.	LIMIT FAT?	ALCOHOLIC BEVERAGES?	LIMIT "EMPTY" CARBS?
☐☐☐☐ ☐☐☐☐	☐☐ ☐☐	☐☐☐ ☐☐	☐☐☐☐☐ ☐☐☐☐☐ ☐	☐☐☐ ☐☐☐	Y N	Y N	Y N

WEATHER: SUN WIND RAIN CLOUDY SNOW TEMP: _____

TUESDAY / Date: _____

Today's goal:

Training notes:

| Distance: |
| Time: |
| Heart Rate: |
| i-Rate (1-10) |
| X-Training: |
| Sleep Hours: |
| Weight: |
| Mood: ☺ ☺ ☹ Other |

FUEL LOG

WATER: 6-8 × 8 OZ.	FRUITS: 2-4	VEGGIES: 3-5	WHOLE GRAIN SERVINGS: 6-11	PROTEIN: 4-6 OZ.	LIMIT FAT?	ALCOHOLIC BEVERAGES?	LIMIT "EMPTY" CARBS?
☐☐☐☐ ☐☐☐☐	☐☐ ☐☐	☐☐☐ ☐☐	☐☐☐☐☐ ☐☐☐☐☐ ☐	☐☐☐ ☐☐☐	Y N	Y N	Y N

WEATHER: SUN WIND RAIN CLOUDY SNOW TEMP: _____

WEDNESDAY / Date: _____

Today's goal:

Training notes:

| Distance: |
| Time: |
| Heart Rate: |
| i-Rate (1-10) |
| X-Training: |
| Sleep Hours: |
| Weight: |
| Mood: ☺ ☺ ☹ Other |

FUEL LOG

WATER: 6-8 × 8 OZ.	FRUITS: 2-4	VEGGIES: 3-5	WHOLE GRAIN SERVINGS: 6-11	PROTEIN: 4-6 OZ.	LIMIT FAT?	ALCOHOLIC BEVERAGES?	LIMIT "EMPTY" CARBS?
☐☐☐☐ ☐☐☐☐	☐☐ ☐☐	☐☐☐ ☐☐	☐☐☐☐☐ ☐☐☐☐☐ ☐	☐☐☐ ☐☐☐	Y N	Y N	Y N

WEATHER: SUN WIND RAIN CLOUDY SNOW TEMP: _____

THURSDAY / Date: _____

Today's goal:

Training notes:

| Distance: |
| Time: |
| Heart Rate: |
| i-Rate (1-10) |
| X-Training: |
| Sleep Hours: |
| Weight: |
| Mood: ☺ ☺ ☹ Other |

FUEL LOG

WATER: 6-8 × 8 OZ.	FRUITS: 2-4	VEGGIES: 3-5	WHOLE GRAIN SERVINGS: 6-11	PROTEIN: 4-6 OZ.	LIMIT FAT?	ALCOHOLIC BEVERAGES?	LIMIT "EMPTY" CARBS?
☐☐☐☐ ☐☐☐☐	☐☐ ☐☐	☐☐☐ ☐☐	☐☐☐☐☐ ☐☐☐☐☐ ☐	☐☐☐ ☐☐☐	Y N	Y N	Y N

WEATHER: SUN WIND RAIN CLOUDY SNOW TEMP: _____

FRIDAY / Date:

Training notes:

Today's goal:

Distance:
Time:
Heart Rate:
i-Rate (1-10)
X-Training:
Sleep Hours:
Weight:
Mood: ☺ ☺ ☹ Other

WEATHER:
SUN   WIND
RAIN CLOUDY
SNOW
TEMP: _____

FUEL LOG

WATER: 6-8 x 8 OZ.	FRUITS: 2-4	VEGGIES: 3-5	WHOLE GRAIN SERVINGS: 6-11	PROTEIN: 4-6 OZ.	LIMIT FAT?	ALCOHOLIC BEVERAGES?	LIMIT "EMPTY" CARBS?
☐☐☐☐ ☐☐☐☐	☐☐ ☐☐	☐☐ ☐☐	☐☐☐☐ ☐☐☐☐ ☐☐☐	☐☐☐ ☐☐☐	Y N	Y N	Y N

SATURDAY / Date:

Training notes:

Today's goal:

Distance:
Time:
Heart Rate:
i-Rate (1-10)
X-Training:
Sleep Hours:
Weight:
Mood: ☺ ☺ ☹ Other

WEATHER:
SUN   WIND
RAIN CLOUDY
SNOW
TEMP: _____

FUEL LOG

WATER: 6-8 x 8 OZ.	FRUITS: 2-4	VEGGIES: 3-5	WHOLE GRAIN SERVINGS: 6-11	PROTEIN: 4-6 OZ.	LIMIT FAT?	ALCOHOLIC BEVERAGES?	LIMIT "EMPTY" CARBS?
☐☐☐☐ ☐☐☐☐	☐☐ ☐☐	☐☐ ☐☐	☐☐☐☐ ☐☐☐☐ ☐☐☐	☐☐☐ ☐☐☐	Y N	Y N	Y N

SUNDAY / Date:

Training notes:

Today's goal:

Distance:
Time:
Heart Rate:
i-Rate (1-10)
X-Training:
Sleep Hours:
Weight:
Mood: ☺ ☺ ☹ Other

WEATHER:
SUN   WIND
RAIN CLOUDY
SNOW
TEMP: _____

FUEL LOG

WATER: 6-8 x 8 OZ.	FRUITS: 2-4	VEGGIES: 3-5	WHOLE GRAIN SERVINGS: 6-11	PROTEIN: 4-6 OZ.	LIMIT FAT?	ALCOHOLIC BEVERAGES?	LIMIT "EMPTY" CARBS?
☐☐☐☐ ☐☐☐☐	☐☐ ☐☐	☐☐ ☐☐	☐☐☐☐ ☐☐☐☐ ☐☐☐	☐☐☐ ☐☐☐	Y N	Y N	Y N

WEEK OF:

GOALS FOR WEEK:

Every now and then, look backward to where you started, the road that you've traveled, and how far you've come.

WEEKLY TOTAL: _____

YEAR-TO-DATE TOTAL:

MONDAY / Date:

Training notes: _____

Today's goal:

FUEL LOG

WATER: 6-8 x 8 OZ.	FRUITS: 2-4	VEGGIES: 3-5	WHOLE GRAIN SERVINGS: 6-11	PROTEIN: 4-6 OZ.	LIMIT FAT?	ALCOHOLIC BEVERAGES?	LIMIT "EMPTY" CARBS?
☐☐☐☐ ☐☐☐☐	☐☐ ☐☐	☐☐☐ ☐☐	☐☐☐☐☐ ☐☐☐☐☐ ☐	☐☐☐ ☐☐☐	Y N	Y N	Y N

Distance:
Time:
Heart Rate:
i-Rate (1-10):
X-Training:
Sleep Hours:
Weight:
Mood: ☺ ☺ ☹

WEATHER: SUN WIND RAIN CLOUDY SNOW
TEMP: _____
Other

TUESDAY / Date:

Training notes: _____

Today's goal:

FUEL LOG

WATER: 6-8 x 8 OZ.	FRUITS: 2-4	VEGGIES: 3-5	WHOLE GRAIN SERVINGS: 6-11	PROTEIN: 4-6 OZ.	LIMIT FAT?	ALCOHOLIC BEVERAGES?	LIMIT "EMPTY" CARBS?
☐☐☐☐ ☐☐☐☐	☐☐ ☐☐	☐☐☐ ☐☐	☐☐☐☐☐ ☐☐☐☐☐ ☐	☐☐☐ ☐☐☐	Y N	Y N	Y N

Distance:
Time:
Heart Rate:
i-Rate (1-10):
X-Training:
Sleep Hours:
Weight:
Mood: ☺ ☺ ☹

WEATHER: SUN WIND RAIN CLOUDY SNOW
TEMP: _____
Other

WEDNESDAY / Date:

Training notes: _____

Today's goal:

FUEL LOG

WATER: 6-8 x 8 OZ.	FRUITS: 2-4	VEGGIES: 3-5	WHOLE GRAIN SERVINGS: 6-11	PROTEIN: 4-6 OZ.	LIMIT FAT?	ALCOHOLIC BEVERAGES?	LIMIT "EMPTY" CARBS?
☐☐☐☐ ☐☐☐☐	☐☐ ☐☐	☐☐☐ ☐☐	☐☐☐☐☐ ☐☐☐☐☐ ☐	☐☐☐ ☐☐☐	Y N	Y N	Y N

Distance:
Time:
Heart Rate:
i-Rate (1-10):
X-Training:
Sleep Hours:
Weight:
Mood: ☺ ☺ ☹

WEATHER: SUN WIND RAIN CLOUDY SNOW
TEMP: _____
Other

THURSDAY / Date:

Training notes: _____

Today's goal:

FUEL LOG

WATER: 6-8 x 8 OZ.	FRUITS: 2-4	VEGGIES: 3-5	WHOLE GRAIN SERVINGS: 6-11	PROTEIN: 4-6 OZ.	LIMIT FAT?	ALCOHOLIC BEVERAGES?	LIMIT "EMPTY" CARBS?
☐☐☐☐ ☐☐☐☐	☐☐ ☐☐	☐☐☐ ☐☐	☐☐☐☐☐ ☐☐☐☐☐ ☐	☐☐☐ ☐☐☐	Y N	Y N	Y N

Distance:
Time:
Heart Rate:
i-Rate (1-10):
X-Training:
Sleep Hours:
Weight:
Mood: ☺ ☺ ☹

WEATHER: SUN WIND RAIN CLOUDY SNOW
TEMP: _____
Other

FRIDAY / Date:

Distance:
Time:
Heart Rate:
i-Rate (1-10):
X-Training:
Sleep Hours:
Weight:
Mood: ☺ 😐 ☹ Other

Today's goal:

Training notes:

WEATHER:
SUN WIND
RAIN CLOUDY
SNOW
TEMP:

FUEL LOG

WATER: 6-8 x 8 OZ.	FRUITS: 2-4	VEGGIES: 3-5	WHOLE GRAIN SERVINGS: 6-11	PROTEIN: 4-6 OZ.	LIMIT FAT?	ALCOHOLIC BEVERAGES?	LIMIT "EMPTY" CARBS?
☐☐☐☐ ☐☐☐☐	☐☐ ☐☐	☐☐☐ ☐☐	☐☐☐☐ ☐☐☐☐ ☐☐☐	☐☐☐ ☐☐☐	Y N	Y N	Y N

SATURDAY / Date:

Distance:
Time:
Heart Rate:
i-Rate (1-10):
X-Training:
Sleep Hours:
Weight:
Mood: ☺ 😐 ☹ Other

Today's goal:

Training notes:

WEATHER:
SUN WIND
RAIN CLOUDY
SNOW
TEMP:

FUEL LOG

WATER: 6-8 x 8 OZ.	FRUITS: 2-4	VEGGIES: 3-5	WHOLE GRAIN SERVINGS: 6-11	PROTEIN: 4-6 OZ.	LIMIT FAT?	ALCOHOLIC BEVERAGES?	LIMIT "EMPTY" CARBS?
☐☐☐☐ ☐☐☐☐	☐☐ ☐☐	☐☐☐ ☐☐	☐☐☐☐ ☐☐☐☐ ☐☐☐	☐☐☐ ☐☐☐	Y N	Y N	Y N

SUNDAY / Date:

Distance:
Time:
Heart Rate:
i-Rate (1-10):
X-Training:
Sleep Hours:
Weight:
Mood: ☺ 😐 ☹ Other

Today's goal:

Training notes:

WEATHER:
SUN WIND
RAIN CLOUDY
SNOW
TEMP:

FUEL LOG

WATER: 6-8 x 8 OZ.	FRUITS: 2-4	VEGGIES: 3-5	WHOLE GRAIN SERVINGS: 6-11	PROTEIN: 4-6 OZ.	LIMIT FAT?	ALCOHOLIC BEVERAGES?	LIMIT "EMPTY" CARBS?
☐☐☐☐ ☐☐☐☐	☐☐ ☐☐	☐☐☐ ☐☐	☐☐☐☐ ☐☐☐☐ ☐☐☐	☐☐☐ ☐☐☐	Y N	Y N	Y N

WEEK OF:

GOALS FOR WEEK:

WEEKLY TOTAL: _____

YEAR-TO-DATE TOTAL:

The reward of training is a lifetime sense of having accomplished something that most people can't even dream of attempting.

MONDAY / Date:

Today's goal: _____

Training notes: _____

FUEL LOG

WATER: 6-8 x 8 OZ.	FRUITS: 2-4	VEGGIES: 3-5	WHOLE GRAIN SERVINGS: 6-11	PROTEIN: 4-6 OZ.	LIMIT FAT?	ALCOHOLIC BEVERAGES?	LIMIT "EMPTY" CARBS?
☐☐☐☐ ☐☐☐☐	☐☐ ☐☐	☐☐☐ ☐☐	☐☐☐☐ ☐☐☐	☐☐☐ ☐☐☐	Y N	Y N	Y N

WEATHER: SUN WIND RAIN CLOUDY SNOW TEMP: _____

Distance: \
Time: \
Heart Rate: \
i-Rate (1-10): \
X-Training: \
Sleep Hours: \
Weight: \
Mood: ☺ ☺ ☹ ☹ Other

TUESDAY / Date:

Today's goal: _____

Training notes: _____

FUEL LOG

WATER: 6-8 x 8 OZ.	FRUITS: 2-4	VEGGIES: 3-5	WHOLE GRAIN SERVINGS: 6-11	PROTEIN: 4-6 OZ.	LIMIT FAT?	ALCOHOLIC BEVERAGES?	LIMIT "EMPTY" CARBS?
☐☐☐☐ ☐☐☐☐	☐☐ ☐☐	☐☐☐ ☐☐	☐☐☐☐ ☐☐☐	☐☐☐ ☐☐☐	Y N	Y N	Y N

WEATHER: SUN WIND RAIN CLOUDY SNOW TEMP: _____

Distance: \
Time: \
Heart Rate: \
i-Rate (1-10): \
X-Training: \
Sleep Hours: \
Weight: \
Mood: ☺ ☺ ☹ ☹ Other

WEDNESDAY / Date:

Today's goal: _____

Training notes: _____

FUEL LOG

WATER: 6-8 x 8 OZ.	FRUITS: 2-4	VEGGIES: 3-5	WHOLE GRAIN SERVINGS: 6-11	PROTEIN: 4-6 OZ.	LIMIT FAT?	ALCOHOLIC BEVERAGES?	LIMIT "EMPTY" CARBS?
☐☐☐☐ ☐☐☐☐	☐☐ ☐☐	☐☐☐ ☐☐	☐☐☐☐ ☐☐☐	☐☐☐ ☐☐☐	Y N	Y N	Y N

WEATHER: SUN WIND RAIN CLOUDY SNOW TEMP: _____

Distance: \
Time: \
Heart Rate: \
i-Rate (1-10): \
X-Training: \
Sleep Hours: \
Weight: \
Mood: ☺ ☺ ☹ ☹ Other

THURSDAY / Date:

Today's goal: _____

Training notes: _____

FUEL LOG

WATER: 6-8 x 8 OZ.	FRUITS: 2-4	VEGGIES: 3-5	WHOLE GRAIN SERVINGS: 6-11	PROTEIN: 4-6 OZ.	LIMIT FAT?	ALCOHOLIC BEVERAGES?	LIMIT "EMPTY" CARBS?
☐☐☐☐ ☐☐☐☐	☐☐ ☐☐	☐☐☐ ☐☐	☐☐☐☐ ☐☐☐	☐☐☐ ☐☐☐	Y N	Y N	Y N

WEATHER: SUN WIND RAIN CLOUDY SNOW TEMP: _____

Distance: \
Time: \
Heart Rate: \
i-Rate (1-10): \
X-Training: \
Sleep Hours: \
Weight: \
Mood: ☺ ☺ ☹ ☹ Other

FRIDAY / Date:

Training notes: _____

Today's goal: _____

Distance: _____
Time: _____
Heart Rate: _____
i-Rate (1-10): _____
X-Training: _____
Sleep Hours: _____
Weight: _____
Mood: ☺ ☺ ☹ Other

WEATHER:
SUN WIND
RAIN CLOUDY
SNOW
TEMP: _____

FUEL LOG

WATER: 6-8 × 8 OZ.	FRUITS: 2-4	VEGGIES: 3-5	WHOLE GRAIN SERVINGS: 6-11	PROTEIN: 4-6 OZ.	LIMIT FAT?	ALCOHOLIC BEVERAGES?	LIMIT "EMPTY" CARBS?
☐☐☐☐ ☐☐☐☐	☐☐ ☐☐	☐☐ ☐	☐☐☐ ☐☐☐	☐☐ ☐☐	Y N	Y N	Y N

SATURDAY / Date:

Training notes: _____

Today's goal: _____

Distance: _____
Time: _____
Heart Rate: _____
i-Rate (1-10): _____
X-Training: _____
Sleep Hours: _____
Weight: _____
Mood: ☺ ☺ ☹ Other

WEATHER:
SUN WIND
RAIN CLOUDY
SNOW
TEMP: _____

FUEL LOG

WATER: 6-8 × 8 OZ.	FRUITS: 2-4	VEGGIES: 3-5	WHOLE GRAIN SERVINGS: 6-11	PROTEIN: 4-6 OZ.	LIMIT FAT?	ALCOHOLIC BEVERAGES?	LIMIT "EMPTY" CARBS?
☐☐☐☐ ☐☐☐☐	☐☐ ☐☐	☐☐ ☐	☐☐☐ ☐☐☐	☐☐ ☐☐	Y N	Y N	Y N

SUNDAY / Date:

Training notes: _____

Today's goal: _____

Distance: _____
Time: _____
Heart Rate: _____
i-Rate (1-10): _____
X-Training: _____
Sleep Hours: _____
Weight: _____
Mood: ☺ ☺ ☹ Other

WEATHER:
SUN WIND
RAIN CLOUDY
SNOW
TEMP: _____

FUEL LOG

WATER: 6-8 × 8 OZ.	FRUITS: 2-4	VEGGIES: 3-5	WHOLE GRAIN SERVINGS: 6-11	PROTEIN: 4-6 OZ.	LIMIT FAT?	ALCOHOLIC BEVERAGES?	LIMIT "EMPTY" CARBS?
☐☐☐☐ ☐☐☐☐	☐☐ ☐☐	☐☐ ☐	☐☐☐ ☐☐☐	☐☐ ☐☐	Y N	Y N	Y N

WEEK OF:

GOALS FOR WEEK:

WEEKLY TOTAL: _____

YEAR-TO-DATE TOTAL:

Treat yourself to something that helps make your running fun.

TIED IN NOTS

I recently received an email from a person who wanted to become more active. They wanted to start walking and running and maybe even compete in a few local 5K and 10K races. They thought that being more active might be a good way to lose some weight and feel better. So far, not a bad plan.

But, they went on, they were not willing to change their eating habits, they were not willing to drink less, and they were not willing to quit smoking. Their question to me was how much activity did I think they would need to overcome the rest of their lifestyle. I didn't know how to answer.

You'd think that this approach would be unusual, but it isn't. I can remember coming in from my early runs and sitting on the sofa and lighting up. It made my son crazy. How could I do that? He would ask. Easy. Like my email friend, in those days I was tied in nots.

I was angry that I was 43 years old and 100 pounds overweight but I was *not* going to change any more than I had to. I was angry that it was getting more and more difficult to walk up steps, or mow the lawn, or wash the car but I was *not* going to stop doing the things I enjoyed. I was angry that I couldn't live an irresponsible lifestyle and still be thin, fit, and healthy.

So, when it finally occurred to me that I would have to be more active, it wasn't as though I relished the idea and jumped in with enthusiasm. Sure, I liked the idea that I was wogging [my combination of waddling and jogging] several days a week. I liked the idea that I was actually running in running shoes. And, I liked the idea that I had a few race t-shirts in my closet.

But, I was not ready to give in to the idea that my life was going to have to change. I was not ready to start thinking like an athlete. I was not ready to be a runner when I wasn't running. I was *not* going to become one of *those* people.

No... not me. I was going to be the one who found the way to be both decadent *and* fit. I was going to be the one who could overeat *and* overtrain. I was going to be the one who was *not* giving in to the benefits of being more active. And for the better part of a year, I managed to be both what I had been, and what I was trying to be.

Eventually, though, I began to realize that my priorities were changing. The more miles I had behind me, the more I began to think about the miles ahead of me. The more I ran, the more I was a runner. It became more and more difficult to *not* be an athlete. Not by design, but by default.

And I wasn't all that happy about it at first. Standing at a starting line in sub-freezing temperatures one Saturday morning I found myself questioning my own sanity. Surely there was another way. What happened to the person who drank hot coffee and smoked cigarettes on cold weekend mornings? Where had he gone? Surely he had enough sense to stay inside.

I was not that person anymore. I was a runner. I was one of those people who ran in the cold and rain and the heat and humidity. I was one of those people who wore shorts and tights in public. I was one of those people who stood in line at the grocery store and stretched.

Even now that I have been running for eight years I'm still amused at all the things I am. But more, I'm amazed at all the things I'm not. I'm not angry any more. I'm not fighting with my own destiny. I am not afraid to find out where my limits are. And I am not afraid to accept those limits.

But more than anything, I am not afraid to change, to learn, to grow, and to look past all the things I can't be to those few that I can.

Waddle on, friends.

MONDAY / Date: _____

Today's goal: _____

Training notes: _____

FUEL LOG

WATER: 6-8 × 8 OZ.	FRUITS: 2-4	VEGGIES: 3-5	WHOLE GRAIN SERVINGS: 6-11	PROTEIN: 4-6 OZ.	LIMIT FAT? Y N	ALCOHOLIC BEVERAGES? Y N	LIMIT "EMPTY" CARBS? Y N
☐☐☐☐ ☐☐☐☐	☐☐ ☐☐	☐☐ ☐☐	☐☐☐☐ ☐☐☐☐ ☐	☐☐ ☐☐ ☐☐			

Distance: _____
Time: _____
Heart Rate: _____
i-Rate (1-10): _____
X-Training: _____
Sleep Hours: _____
Weight: _____
Mood: ☺ ☺ ☹ Other

WEATHER: SUN WIND RAIN CLOUDY SNOW — TEMP: _____

TUESDAY / Date: _____

Today's goal: _____

Training notes: _____

FUEL LOG

WATER: 6-8 × 8 OZ.	FRUITS: 2-4	VEGGIES: 3-5	WHOLE GRAIN SERVINGS: 6-11	PROTEIN: 4-6 OZ.	LIMIT FAT? Y N	ALCOHOLIC BEVERAGES? Y N	LIMIT "EMPTY" CARBS? Y N
☐☐☐☐ ☐☐☐☐	☐☐ ☐☐	☐☐ ☐☐	☐☐☐☐ ☐☐☐☐ ☐	☐☐ ☐☐ ☐☐			

Distance: _____
Time: _____
Heart Rate: _____
i-Rate (1-10): _____
X-Training: _____
Sleep Hours: _____
Weight: _____
Mood: ☺ ☺ ☹ Other

WEATHER: SUN WIND RAIN CLOUDY SNOW — TEMP: _____

WEDNESDAY / Date: _____

Today's goal: _____

Training notes: _____

FUEL LOG

WATER: 6-8 × 8 OZ.	FRUITS: 2-4	VEGGIES: 3-5	WHOLE GRAIN SERVINGS: 6-11	PROTEIN: 4-6 OZ.	LIMIT FAT? Y N	ALCOHOLIC BEVERAGES? Y N	LIMIT "EMPTY" CARBS? Y N
☐☐☐☐ ☐☐☐☐	☐☐ ☐☐	☐☐ ☐☐	☐☐☐☐ ☐☐☐☐ ☐	☐☐ ☐☐ ☐☐			

Distance: _____
Time: _____
Heart Rate: _____
i-Rate (1-10): _____
X-Training: _____
Sleep Hours: _____
Weight: _____
Mood: ☺ ☺ ☹ Other

WEATHER: SUN WIND RAIN CLOUDY SNOW — TEMP: _____

THURSDAY / Date: _____

Today's goal: _____

Training notes: _____

FUEL LOG

WATER: 6-8 × 8 OZ.	FRUITS: 2-4	VEGGIES: 3-5	WHOLE GRAIN SERVINGS: 6-11	PROTEIN: 4-6 OZ.	LIMIT FAT? Y N	ALCOHOLIC BEVERAGES? Y N	LIMIT "EMPTY" CARBS? Y N
☐☐☐☐ ☐☐☐☐	☐☐ ☐☐	☐☐ ☐☐	☐☐☐☐ ☐☐☐☐ ☐	☐☐ ☐☐ ☐☐			

Distance: _____
Time: _____
Heart Rate: _____
i-Rate (1-10): _____
X-Training: _____
Sleep Hours: _____
Weight: _____
Mood: ☺ ☺ ☹ Other

WEATHER: SUN WIND RAIN CLOUDY SNOW — TEMP: _____

FRIDAY / Date: _____

Training notes: _____

Today's goal: _____

FUEL LOG

WATER: 6-8 x 8 OZ.	FRUITS: 2-4	VEGGIES: 3-5	WHOLE GRAIN SERVINGS: 6-11	PROTEIN: 4-6 OZ.	LIMIT FAT?	ALCOHOLIC BEVERAGES?	LIMIT "EMPTY" CARBS?
☐☐☐☐ ☐☐☐☐	☐☐ ☐☐	☐☐ ☐☐	☐☐☐☐☐ ☐☐☐☐☐ ☐	☐☐☐ ☐☐☐	Y N	Y N	Y N

WEATHER:
SUN   WIND
RAIN CLOUDY
SNOW
TEMP: _____

Distance: _____
Time: _____
Heart Rate: _____
i-Rate (1-10) _____
X-Training: _____
Sleep Hours: _____
Weight: _____
Mood: ☺ ☺ ☹ ☹ Other

SATURDAY / Date: _____

Training notes: _____

Today's goal: _____

FUEL LOG

WATER: 6-8 x 8 OZ.	FRUITS: 2-4	VEGGIES: 3-5	WHOLE GRAIN SERVINGS: 6-11	PROTEIN: 4-6 OZ.	LIMIT FAT?	ALCOHOLIC BEVERAGES?	LIMIT "EMPTY" CARBS?
☐☐☐☐ ☐☐☐☐	☐☐ ☐☐	☐☐ ☐☐	☐☐☐☐☐ ☐☐☐☐☐ ☐	☐☐☐ ☐☐☐	Y N	Y N	Y N

WEATHER:
SUN   WIND
RAIN CLOUDY
SNOW
TEMP: _____

Distance: _____
Time: _____
Heart Rate: _____
i-Rate (1-10) _____
X-Training: _____
Sleep Hours: _____
Weight: _____
Mood: ☺ ☺ ☹ ☹ Other

SUNDAY / Date: _____

Training notes: _____

Today's goal: _____

FUEL LOG

WATER: 6-8 x 8 OZ.	FRUITS: 2-4	VEGGIES: 3-5	WHOLE GRAIN SERVINGS: 6-11	PROTEIN: 4-6 OZ.	LIMIT FAT?	ALCOHOLIC BEVERAGES?	LIMIT "EMPTY" CARBS?
☐☐☐☐ ☐☐☐☐	☐☐ ☐☐	☐☐ ☐☐	☐☐☐☐☐ ☐☐☐☐☐ ☐	☐☐☐ ☐☐☐	Y N	Y N	Y N

WEATHER:
SUN   WIND
RAIN CLOUDY
SNOW
TEMP: _____

Distance: _____
Time: _____
Heart Rate: _____
i-Rate (1-10) _____
X-Training: _____
Sleep Hours: _____
Weight: _____
Mood: ☺ ☺ ☹ ☹ Other

WEEK OF:

GOALS FOR WEEK:

WEEKLY TOTAL: _____

YEAR-TO-DATE TOTAL: _____

Your log book is more than just a record of the miles you've trained. It's a history lesson, a memoir, and a best friend.

MONDAY / Date:

Today's goal:

Training notes: _____
_____

FUEL LOG

WATER: 6-8 x 8 OZ.	FRUITS: 2-4	VEGGIES: 3-5	WHOLE GRAIN SERVINGS: 6-11	PROTEIN: 4-6 OZ.	LIMIT FAT?	ALCOHOLIC BEVERAGES?	LIMIT "EMPTY" CARBS?
☐☐☐☐ ☐☐☐☐	☐☐ ☐☐	☐☐ ☐☐	☐☐☐☐☐☐ ☐☐☐☐☐	☐☐ ☐☐ ☐☐	Y N	Y N	Y N

WEATHER: SUN WIND RAIN CLOUDY SNOW TEMP: _____

Distance: _____
Time: _____
Heart Rate: _____
i-Rate (1-10): _____
X-Training: _____
Sleep Hours: _____
Weight: _____
Mood: ☺ ☺ ☹ Other

TUESDAY / Date:

Today's goal:

Training notes: _____
_____

FUEL LOG

WATER: 6-8 x 8 OZ.	FRUITS: 2-4	VEGGIES: 3-5	WHOLE GRAIN SERVINGS: 6-11	PROTEIN: 4-6 OZ.	LIMIT FAT?	ALCOHOLIC BEVERAGES?	LIMIT "EMPTY" CARBS?
☐☐☐☐ ☐☐☐☐	☐☐ ☐☐	☐☐ ☐☐	☐☐☐☐☐☐ ☐☐☐☐☐	☐☐ ☐☐ ☐☐	Y N	Y N	Y N

WEATHER: SUN WIND RAIN CLOUDY SNOW TEMP: _____

Distance: _____
Time: _____
Heart Rate: _____
i-Rate (1-10): _____
X-Training: _____
Sleep Hours: _____
Weight: _____
Mood: ☺ ☺ ☹ Other

WEDNESDAY / Date:

Today's goal:

Training notes: _____
_____

FUEL LOG

WATER: 6-8 x 8 OZ.	FRUITS: 2-4	VEGGIES: 3-5	WHOLE GRAIN SERVINGS: 6-11	PROTEIN: 4-6 OZ.	LIMIT FAT?	ALCOHOLIC BEVERAGES?	LIMIT "EMPTY" CARBS?
☐☐☐☐ ☐☐☐☐	☐☐ ☐☐	☐☐ ☐☐	☐☐☐☐☐☐ ☐☐☐☐☐	☐☐ ☐☐ ☐☐	Y N	Y N	Y N

WEATHER: SUN WIND RAIN CLOUDY SNOW TEMP: _____

Distance: _____
Time: _____
Heart Rate: _____
i-Rate (1-10): _____
X-Training: _____
Sleep Hours: _____
Weight: _____
Mood: ☺ ☺ ☹ Other

THURSDAY / Date:

Today's goal:

Training notes: _____
_____

FUEL LOG

WATER: 6-8 x 8 OZ.	FRUITS: 2-4	VEGGIES: 3-5	WHOLE GRAIN SERVINGS: 6-11	PROTEIN: 4-6 OZ.	LIMIT FAT?	ALCOHOLIC BEVERAGES?	LIMIT "EMPTY" CARBS?
☐☐☐☐ ☐☐☐☐	☐☐ ☐☐	☐☐ ☐☐	☐☐☐☐☐☐ ☐☐☐☐☐	☐☐ ☐☐ ☐☐	Y N	Y N	Y N

WEATHER: SUN WIND RAIN CLOUDY SNOW TEMP: _____

Distance: _____
Time: _____
Heart Rate: _____
i-Rate (1-10): _____
X-Training: _____
Sleep Hours: _____
Weight: _____
Mood: ☺ ☺ ☹ Other

Today's goal:

_____

FUEL LOG

WATER: 6-8 × 8 OZ.	FRUITS: 2-4	VEGGIES: 3-5	WHOLE GRAIN SERVINGS: 6-11	PROTEIN: 4-6 OZ.	LIMIT FAT?	ALCOHOLIC BEVERAGES?	LIMIT "EMPTY" CARBS?
☐☐☐☐ ☐☐☐☐	☐☐ ☐☐	☐☐ ☐☐	☐☐☐☐ ☐☐☐☐	☐☐☐ ☐☐	Y N	Y N	Y N

Distance:
Time:
Heart Rate:
i-Rate (1-10)
X-Training:
Sleep Hours:
Weight:
Mood: ☺ ☺ ☹ Other

WEATHER:
SUN WIND
RAIN CLOUDY
SNOW
TEMP: ____

SATURDAY / Date:

Today's goal:

Training notes:

FUEL LOG

WATER: 6-8 × 8 OZ.	FRUITS: 2-4	VEGGIES: 3-5	WHOLE GRAIN SERVINGS: 6-11	PROTEIN: 4-6 OZ.	LIMIT FAT?	ALCOHOLIC BEVERAGES?	LIMIT "EMPTY" CARBS?
☐☐☐☐ ☐☐☐☐	☐☐ ☐☐	☐☐ ☐☐	☐☐☐☐ ☐☐☐☐	☐☐☐ ☐☐	Y N	Y N	Y N

Distance:
Time:
Heart Rate:
i-Rate (1-10)
X-Training:
Sleep Hours:
Weight:
Mood: ☺ ☺ ☹ Other

WEATHER:
SUN WIND
RAIN CLOUDY
SNOW
TEMP: ____

SUNDAY / Date:

Today's goal:

Training notes:

FUEL LOG

WATER: 6-8 × 8 OZ.	FRUITS: 2-4	VEGGIES: 3-5	WHOLE GRAIN SERVINGS: 6-11	PROTEIN: 4-6 OZ.	LIMIT FAT?	ALCOHOLIC BEVERAGES?	LIMIT "EMPTY" CARBS?
☐☐☐☐ ☐☐☐☐	☐☐ ☐☐	☐☐ ☐☐	☐☐ ☐☐☐☐	☐☐☐ ☐☐	Y N	Y N	Y N

Distance:
Time:
Heart Rate:
i-Rate (1-10)
X-Training:
Sleep Hours:
Weight:
Mood: ☺ ☺ ☹ Other

WEATHER:
SUN WIND
RAIN CLOUDY
SNOW
TEMP: ____

WEEK OF:

GOALS FOR WEEK:

WEEKLY TOTAL: _____

YEAR-TO-DATE TOTAL:

It's important to have goals, but it's more important to be honest about what it takes to achieve them. It's important to assess yourself, to observe and even be critical of yourself.

MONDAY / Date:

Today's goal:

Training notes:

Distance:
Time:
Heart Rate:
i-Rate (1-10)
X-Training:
Sleep Hours:
Weight:
Mood: ☺ ☺ ☹ Other

FUEL LOG

WATER: 6-8 × 8 OZ.	FRUITS: 2-4	VEGGIES: 3-5	WHOLE GRAIN SERVINGS: 6-11	PROTEIN: 4-6 OZ.	LIMIT FAT?	ALCOHOLIC BEVERAGES?	LIMIT "EMPTY" CARBS?
☐☐☐☐ ☐☐☐☐	☐☐ ☐☐	☐☐ ☐☐	☐☐☐☐☐ ☐☐☐☐☐ ☐	☐☐☐ ☐☐☐	Y N	Y N	Y N

WEATHER:
SUN WIND
RAIN CLOUDY
SNOW
TEMP: _____

TUESDAY / Date:

Today's goal:

Training notes:

Distance:
Time:
Heart Rate:
i-Rate (1-10)
X-Training:
Sleep Hours:
Weight:
Mood: ☺ ☺ ☹ Other

FUEL LOG

WATER: 6-8 × 8 OZ.	FRUITS: 2-4	VEGGIES: 3-5	WHOLE GRAIN SERVINGS: 6-11	PROTEIN: 4-6 OZ.	LIMIT FAT?	ALCOHOLIC BEVERAGES?	LIMIT "EMPTY" CARBS?
☐☐☐☐ ☐☐☐☐	☐☐ ☐☐	☐☐ ☐☐	☐☐☐☐☐ ☐☐☐☐☐ ☐	☐☐☐ ☐☐☐	Y N	Y N	Y N

WEATHER:
SUN WIND
RAIN CLOUDY
SNOW
TEMP: _____

WEDNESDAY / Date:

Today's goal:

Training notes:

Distance:
Time:
Heart Rate:
i-Rate (1-10)
X-Training:
Sleep Hours:
Weight:
Mood: ☺ ☺ ☹ Other

FUEL LOG

WATER: 6-8 × 8 OZ.	FRUITS: 2-4	VEGGIES: 3-5	WHOLE GRAIN SERVINGS: 6-11	PROTEIN: 4-6 OZ.	LIMIT FAT?	ALCOHOLIC BEVERAGES?	LIMIT "EMPTY" CARBS?
☐☐☐☐ ☐☐☐☐	☐☐ ☐☐	☐☐ ☐☐	☐☐☐☐☐ ☐☐☐☐☐ ☐	☐☐☐ ☐☐☐	Y N	Y N	Y N

WEATHER:
SUN WIND
RAIN CLOUDY
SNOW
TEMP: _____

THURSDAY / Date:

Today's goal:

Training notes:

Distance:
Time:
Heart Rate:
i-Rate (1-10)
X-Training:
Sleep Hours:
Weight:
Mood: ☺ ☺ ☹ Other

FUEL LOG

WATER: 6-8 × 8 OZ.	FRUITS: 2-4	VEGGIES: 3-5	WHOLE GRAIN SERVINGS: 6-11	PROTEIN: 4-6 OZ.	LIMIT FAT?	ALCOHOLIC BEVERAGES?	LIMIT "EMPTY" CARBS?
☐☐☐☐ ☐☐☐☐	☐☐ ☐☐	☐☐ ☐☐	☐☐☐☐☐ ☐☐☐☐☐ ☐	☐☐☐ ☐☐☐	Y N	Y N	Y N

WEATHER:
SUN WIND
RAIN CLOUDY
SNOW
TEMP: _____

FRIDAY / Date:

Today's goal:

FUEL LOG

WATER: 6-8 x 8 OZ.	FRUITS: 2-4	VEGGIES: 3-5	WHOLE GRAIN SERVINGS: 6-11	PROTEIN: 4-6 OZ.	LIMIT FAT?	ALCOHOLIC BEVERAGES?	LIMIT "EMPTY" CARBS?
☐☐☐☐ ☐☐☐☐	☐☐ ☐☐	☐☐☐ ☐☐	☐☐☐☐☐ ☐☐☐☐☐ ☐	☐☐☐ ☐☐☐	Y N	Y N	Y N

Training notes:

Distance:
Time:
Heart Rate:
i-Rate (1-10)
X-Training:
Sleep Hours:
Weight:
Mood: ☺ ☺ ☹ Other

WEATHER:
SUN WIND
RAIN CLOUDY
SNOW
TEMP: ____

SATURDAY / Date:

Today's goal:

FUEL LOG

WATER: 6-8 x 8 OZ.	FRUITS: 2-4	VEGGIES: 3-5	WHOLE GRAIN SERVINGS: 6-11	PROTEIN: 4-6 OZ.	LIMIT FAT?	ALCOHOLIC BEVERAGES?	LIMIT "EMPTY" CARBS?
☐☐☐☐ ☐☐☐☐	☐☐ ☐☐	☐☐☐ ☐☐	☐☐☐☐☐ ☐☐☐☐☐ ☐	☐☐☐ ☐☐☐	Y N	Y N	Y N

Training notes:

Distance:
Time:
Heart Rate:
i-Rate (1-10)
X-Training:
Sleep Hours:
Weight:
Mood: ☺ ☺ ☹ Other

WEATHER:
SUN WIND
RAIN CLOUDY
SNOW
TEMP: ____

SUNDAY / Date:

Today's goal:

FUEL LOG

WATER: 6-8 x 8 OZ.	FRUITS: 2-4	VEGGIES: 3-5	WHOLE GRAIN SERVINGS: 6-11	PROTEIN: 4-6 OZ.	LIMIT FAT?	ALCOHOLIC BEVERAGES?	LIMIT "EMPTY" CARBS?
☐☐☐☐ ☐☐☐☐	☐☐ ☐☐	☐☐☐ ☐☐	☐☐☐☐☐ ☐☐☐☐☐ ☐	☐☐☐ ☐☐☐	Y N	Y N	Y N

Training notes:

Distance:
Time:
Heart Rate:
i-Rate (1-10)
X-Training:
Sleep Hours:
Weight:
Mood: ☺ ☺ ☹ Other

WEATHER:
SUN WIND
RAIN CLOUDY
SNOW
TEMP: ____

WEEK OF:

GOALS FOR WEEK:

WEEKLY TOTAL: _____

YEAR-TO-DATE TOTAL:

Deciding to be a runner is only the first step. Actually being a runner is a daily commitment.

MONDAY / Date:

Today's goal:

Training notes: _____

Distance: _____
Time: _____
Heart Rate: _____
i-Rate (1-10): _____
X-Training: _____
Sleep Hours: _____
Weight: _____
Mood: ☺ ☺ ☹ Other

WEATHER:
SUN   WIND
RAIN CLOUDY
SNOW
TEMP: _____

FUEL LOG

WATER: 6-8 x 8 oz.	FRUITS: 2-4	VEGGIES: 3-5	WHOLE GRAIN SERVINGS: 6-11	PROTEIN: 4-6 oz.	LIMIT FAT?	ALCOHOLIC BEVERAGES?	LIMIT "EMPTY" CARBS?
☐☐☐☐ ☐☐☐☐	☐☐☐ ☐☐	☐☐☐ ☐☐	☐☐☐☐☐☐ ☐☐☐☐☐	☐☐☐ ☐☐☐	Y N	Y N	Y N

TUESDAY / Date:

Today's goal:

Training notes: _____

Distance: _____
Time: _____
Heart Rate: _____
i-Rate (1-10): _____
X-Training: _____
Sleep Hours: _____
Weight: _____
Mood: ☺ ☺ ☹ Other

WEATHER:
SUN   WIND
RAIN CLOUDY
SNOW
TEMP: _____

FUEL LOG

WATER: 6-8 x 8 oz.	FRUITS: 2-4	VEGGIES: 3-5	WHOLE GRAIN SERVINGS: 6-11	PROTEIN: 4-6 oz.	LIMIT FAT?	ALCOHOLIC BEVERAGES?	LIMIT "EMPTY" CARBS?
☐☐☐☐ ☐☐☐☐	☐☐☐ ☐☐	☐☐☐ ☐☐	☐☐☐☐☐☐ ☐☐☐☐☐	☐☐☐ ☐☐☐	Y N	Y N	Y N

WEDNESDAY / Date:

Today's goal:

Training notes: _____

Distance: _____
Time: _____
Heart Rate: _____
i-Rate (1-10): _____
X-Training: _____
Sleep Hours: _____
Weight: _____
Mood: ☺ ☺ ☹ Other

WEATHER:
SUN   WIND
RAIN CLOUDY
SNOW
TEMP: _____

FUEL LOG

WATER: 6-8 x 8 oz.	FRUITS: 2-4	VEGGIES: 3-5	WHOLE GRAIN SERVINGS: 6-11	PROTEIN: 4-6 oz.	LIMIT FAT?	ALCOHOLIC BEVERAGES?	LIMIT "EMPTY" CARBS?
☐☐☐☐ ☐☐☐☐	☐☐☐ ☐☐	☐☐☐ ☐☐	☐☐☐☐☐☐ ☐☐☐☐☐	☐☐☐ ☐☐☐	Y N	Y N	Y N

THURSDAY / Date:

Today's goal:

Training notes: _____

Distance: _____
Time: _____
Heart Rate: _____
i-Rate (1-10): _____
X-Training: _____
Sleep Hours: _____
Weight: _____
Mood: ☺ ☺ ☹ Other

WEATHER:
SUN   WIND
RAIN CLOUDY
SNOW
TEMP: _____

FUEL LOG

WATER: 6-8 x 8 oz.	FRUITS: 2-4	VEGGIES: 3-5	WHOLE GRAIN SERVINGS: 6-11	PROTEIN: 4-6 oz.	LIMIT FAT?	ALCOHOLIC BEVERAGES?	LIMIT "EMPTY" CARBS?
☐☐☐☐ ☐☐☐☐	☐☐☐ ☐☐	☐☐☐ ☐☐	☐☐☐☐☐☐ ☐☐☐☐☐	☐☐☐ ☐☐☐	Y N	Y N	Y N

FRIDAY / Date:

Today's goal: _____

Distance: _____
Time: _____
Heart Rate: _____
i-Rate (1-10) _____
X-Training: _____
Sleep Hours: _____
Weight: _____
Mood: ☺ ☺ ☹ Other

FUEL LOG

WATER: 6-8 × 8 OZ.	FRUITS: 2-4	VEGGIES: 3-5	WHOLE GRAIN SERVINGS: 6-11	PROTEIN: 4-6 OZ.	LIMIT FAT?	ALCOHOLIC BEVERAGES?	LIMIT "EMPTY" CARBS?
□□□□ □□□□	□□ □□	□□ □□	□□□□ □□□□	□□ □□	Y N	Y N	Y N

WEATHER:
SUN WIND
RAIN CLOUDY
SNOW
TEMP: _____

SATURDAY / Date:

Today's goal: _____

Training notes: _____

Distance: _____
Time: _____
Heart Rate: _____
i-Rate (1-10) _____
X-Training: _____
Sleep Hours: _____
Weight: _____
Mood: ☺ ☺ ☹ Other

FUEL LOG

WATER: 6-8 × 8 OZ.	FRUITS: 2-4	VEGGIES: 3-5	WHOLE GRAIN SERVINGS: 6-11	PROTEIN: 4-6 OZ.	LIMIT FAT?	ALCOHOLIC BEVERAGES?	LIMIT "EMPTY" CARBS?
□□□□ □□□□	□□ □□	□□ □□	□□□□ □□□□	□□ □□	Y N	Y N	Y N

WEATHER:
SUN WIND
RAIN CLOUDY
SNOW
TEMP: _____

SUNDAY / Date:

Today's goal: _____

Training notes: _____

Distance: _____
Time: _____
Heart Rate: _____
i-Rate (1-10) _____
X-Training: _____
Sleep Hours: _____
Weight: _____
Mood: ☺ ☺ ☹ Other

FUEL LOG

WATER: 6-8 × 8 OZ.	FRUITS: 2-4	VEGGIES: 3-5	WHOLE GRAIN SERVINGS: 6-11	PROTEIN: 4-6 OZ.	LIMIT FAT?	ALCOHOLIC BEVERAGES?	LIMIT "EMPTY" CARBS?
□□□□ □□□□	□□ □□	□□ □□	□□□□ □□□□	□□ □□	Y N	Y N	Y N

WEATHER:
SUN WIND
RAIN CLOUDY
SNOW
TEMP: _____

WEEK OF:

GOALS FOR WEEK:

WEEKLY TOTAL: _____

YEAR-TO-DATE TOTAL: _____

You're building a savings account of muscle, will, and determination. It's the most valuable savings account you will ever have. It's an investment in yourself that no one can ever take away.

WHITE LINE FEVER

Until I discovered running, there had only been two real passions in my life: music and motorcycles. Being a freelance musician is best described as serial unemployment. The upside was that this provided the time to ride. It was for many years the perfect solution. Work long enough to build a financial base, then ride long enough to need a job. This delicate balance of time versus money can be tricky at times, but with care and a willingness to consume nothing more than peanut butter and beer for long stretches, it can be done.

Most of my friends didn't understand my consuming passion for motorcycles. It wasn't the bikes themselves that astounded them; it was my need to ride. Riding wasn't about transportation, it was about transformation. Sitting in the saddle, straddling the motor, feeling the power just below me was intoxicating. But more than that, it was watching the world pass beneath my feet that stirred my spirit. I had, so my friends would tell me, a terminal case of white line fever.

Little did I know then that I would discover the same feeling, that same sense of moving over and through the world, the moment I put on a pair of running shoes and felt the asphalt pounding against the soles of my feet. I had no idea that moving slowly across the ground could feel just as satisfying as moving fast. It turned out, for me at least, it was the act of motion not the rate of speed that made it feel so good.

I think that this is why I can't ever remember having a bad run. I can't remember having a bad ride either. As a runner and a biker

I've been hotter than I wanted to be, colder, wetter, and more tired. I've been ready to stop hours before I could, and have ridden roads and run courses that I swear I'll never do again. But none of it was bad.

I'm not sure how it could be bad. I suppose if being comfortable is a criterion for happiness than being soaked to the skin and knowing that you still had 200 miles to ride, or 10 miles to run would be bad. But I don't think so. I suppose if being so cold that you could barely grip the handlebars, or being so hot that you could nearly feel your brain turning to soufflé made you unhappy then you might have a bad ride or a bad run. But I don't understand why.

There are countless stories of the nearly limitless physical reserves of the human body. Men and women have endured hardships that would make even the most difficult run seem like a walk in the park. We have the capacity to simultaneously detach ourselves from the discomfort we feel and experience completely what our bodies are feeling. At the most extreme levels, it is almost a schizophrenia as we tell ourselves that we really should stop what were doing while continuing to enjoy every minute.

Somewhere in between there is that point of balance. Somewhere between the runs that are too easy and the runs that are too hard are the hundreds of runs that are just right. Those are the runs when we've read our body and our spirits accurately, and have found that place where we can simply go along for the ride. And it's in that place that we catch the fever.

I'm not sure exactly when liking to run became longing to run. I'm not sure when wanting to run became needing to run. And I'm not sure exactly when the pursuit of a running passion became the passion for running. I only know that just as there were roads that had to be ridden, there are roads and trails and courses that must be run. There are miles and moments and memories that only converge when the shoe strikes the ground. In that white-hot instant, the world makes sense.

And I also know that once you've caught the fever, once you've felt for yourself the heat of that passion, there is no cure.

Waddle on, friends.

MONDAY / Date: _____   Training notes: _____

Today's goal: _____

FUEL LOG

WATER: 6-8 × 8 OZ.	FRUITS: 2-4	VEGGIES: 3-5	WHOLE GRAIN SERVINGS: 6-11	PROTEIN: 4-6 OZ.	LIMIT FAT?	ALCOHOLIC BEVERAGES?	LIMIT "EMPTY" CARBS?
☐☐☐☐ ☐☐☐☐	☐☐ ☐☐	☐☐ ☐	☐☐☐ ☐☐☐ ☐☐☐ ☐☐	☐☐☐ ☐☐☐	Y N	Y N	Y N

WEATHER: SUN WIND RAIN CLOUDY SNOW TEMP: _____

- Distance: _____
- Time: _____
- Heart Rate: _____
- i-Rate (1-10) _____
- X-Training: _____
- Sleep Hours: _____
- Weight: _____
- Mood: ☺ ☺ ☹ Other

TUESDAY / Date: _____   Training notes: _____

Today's goal: _____

FUEL LOG

WATER: 6-8 × 8 OZ.	FRUITS: 2-4	VEGGIES: 3-5	WHOLE GRAIN SERVINGS: 6-11	PROTEIN: 4-6 OZ.	LIMIT FAT?	ALCOHOLIC BEVERAGES?	LIMIT "EMPTY" CARBS?
☐☐☐☐ ☐☐☐☐	☐☐ ☐☐	☐☐ ☐	☐☐☐ ☐☐☐ ☐☐☐ ☐☐	☐☐☐ ☐☐☐	Y N	Y N	Y N

WEATHER: SUN WIND RAIN CLOUDY SNOW TEMP: _____

- Distance: _____
- Time: _____
- Heart Rate: _____
- i-Rate (1-10) _____
- X-Training: _____
- Sleep Hours: _____
- Weight: _____
- Mood: ☺ ☺ ☹ Other

WEDNESDAY / Date: _____   Training notes: _____

Today's goal: _____

FUEL LOG

WATER: 6-8 × 8 OZ.	FRUITS: 2-4	VEGGIES: 3-5	WHOLE GRAIN SERVINGS: 6-11	PROTEIN: 4-6 OZ.	LIMIT FAT?	ALCOHOLIC BEVERAGES?	LIMIT "EMPTY" CARBS?
☐☐☐☐ ☐☐☐☐	☐☐ ☐☐	☐☐ ☐	☐☐☐ ☐☐☐ ☐☐☐ ☐☐	☐☐☐ ☐☐☐	Y N	Y N	Y N

WEATHER: SUN WIND RAIN CLOUDY SNOW TEMP: _____

- Distance: _____
- Time: _____
- Heart Rate: _____
- i-Rate (1-10) _____
- X-Training: _____
- Sleep Hours: _____
- Weight: _____
- Mood: ☺ ☺ ☹ Other

THURSDAY / Date: _____   Training notes: _____

Today's goal: _____

FUEL LOG

WATER: 6-8 × 8 OZ.	FRUITS: 2-4	VEGGIES: 3-5	WHOLE GRAIN SERVINGS: 6-11	PROTEIN: 4-6 OZ.	LIMIT FAT?	ALCOHOLIC BEVERAGES?	LIMIT "EMPTY" CARBS?
☐☐☐☐ ☐☐☐☐	☐☐ ☐☐	☐☐ ☐	☐☐☐ ☐☐☐ ☐☐☐ ☐☐	☐☐☐ ☐☐☐	Y N	Y N	Y N

WEATHER: SUN WIND RAIN CLOUDY SNOW TEMP: _____

- Distance: _____
- Time: _____
- Heart Rate: _____
- i-Rate (1-10) _____
- X-Training: _____
- Sleep Hours: _____
- Weight: _____
- Mood: ☺ ☺ ☹ Other

FRIDAY / Date:

Training notes:

Today's goal:

_____

_____

Distance:
Time:
Heart Rate:
i-Rate (1-10)
X-Training:
Sleep Hours:
Weight:
Mood: ☺ ☺ ☹ ☹ Other

FUEL LOG

WATER: 6-8 x 8 OZ.	FRUITS: 2-4	VEGGIES: 3-5	WHOLE GRAIN SERVINGS: 6-11	PROTEIN: 4-6 OZ.	LIMIT FAT?	ALCOHOLIC BEVERAGES?	LIMIT "EMPTY" CARBS?
☐☐☐☐ ☐☐☐☐	☐☐ ☐☐	☐☐☐ ☐☐	☐☐☐☐ ☐☐☐☐	☐☐☐ ☐☐	Y N	Y N	Y N

WEATHER:
SUN WIND
RAIN CLOUDY
SNOW
TEMP: _____

SATURDAY / Date:

Training notes:

Today's goal:

_____

_____

Distance:
Time:
Heart Rate:
i-Rate (1-10)
X-Training:
Sleep Hours:
Weight:
Mood: ☺ ☺ ☹ ☹ Other

FUEL LOG

WATER: 6-8 x 8 OZ.	FRUITS: 2-4	VEGGIES: 3-5	WHOLE GRAIN SERVINGS: 6-11	PROTEIN: 4-6 OZ.	LIMIT FAT?	ALCOHOLIC BEVERAGES?	LIMIT "EMPTY" CARBS?
☐☐☐☐ ☐☐☐☐	☐☐ ☐☐	☐☐☐ ☐☐	☐☐☐☐ ☐☐☐☐	☐☐☐ ☐☐	Y N	Y N	Y N

WEATHER:
SUN WIND
RAIN CLOUDY
SNOW
TEMP: _____

SUNDAY / Date:

Training notes:

Today's goal:

_____

_____

Distance:
Time:
Heart Rate:
i-Rate (1-10)
X-Training:
Sleep Hours:
Weight:
Mood: ☺ ☺ ☹ ☹ Other

FUEL LOG

WATER: 6-8 x 8 OZ.	FRUITS: 2-4	VEGGIES: 3-5	WHOLE GRAIN SERVINGS: 6-11	PROTEIN: 4-6 OZ.	LIMIT FAT?	ALCOHOLIC BEVERAGES?	LIMIT "EMPTY" CARBS?
☐☐☐☐ ☐☐☐☐	☐☐ ☐☐	☐☐☐ ☐☐	☐☐☐☐ ☐☐☐☐	☐☐☐ ☐☐	Y N	Y N	Y N

WEATHER:
SUN WIND
RAIN CLOUDY
SNOW
TEMP: _____

WEEK OF:

GOALS FOR WEEK:

WEEKLY TOTAL: _____

YEAR-TO-DATE TOTAL:

Becoming an athlete is almost that simple: You train, train, train. At first it's something you do. Eventually, it's something you are.

MONDAY / Date: _____ Training notes: _____

Today's goal: _____

Distance: _____
Time: _____
Heart Rate: _____
i-Rate (1-10): _____
X-Training: _____
Sleep Hours: _____
Weight: _____
Mood: ☺ ☺ ☹ ☹ Other

FUEL LOG

WATER: 6-8 × 8 OZ.	FRUITS: 2-4	VEGGIES: 3-5	WHOLE GRAIN SERVINGS: 6-11	PROTEIN: 4-6 OZ.	LIMIT FAT?	ALCOHOLIC BEVERAGES?	LIMIT "EMPTY" CARBS?
☐☐☐☐ ☐☐☐☐	☐☐ ☐☐	☐☐☐ ☐☐	☐☐☐☐ ☐☐☐☐ ☐	☐☐☐ ☐☐☐	Y N	Y N	Y N

WEATHER: SUN WIND RAIN CLOUDY SNOW TEMP: _____

TUESDAY / Date: _____ Training notes: _____

Today's goal: _____

Distance: _____
Time: _____
Heart Rate: _____
i-Rate (1-10): _____
X-Training: _____
Sleep Hours: _____
Weight: _____
Mood: ☺ ☺ ☹ ☹ Other

FUEL LOG

WATER: 6-8 × 8 OZ.	FRUITS: 2-4	VEGGIES: 3-5	WHOLE GRAIN SERVINGS: 6-11	PROTEIN: 4-6 OZ.	LIMIT FAT?	ALCOHOLIC BEVERAGES?	LIMIT "EMPTY" CARBS?
☐☐☐☐ ☐☐☐☐	☐☐ ☐☐	☐☐☐ ☐☐	☐☐☐☐ ☐☐☐☐ ☐	☐☐☐ ☐☐☐	Y N	Y N	Y N

WEATHER: SUN WIND RAIN CLOUDY SNOW TEMP: _____

WEDNESDAY / Date: _____ Training notes: _____

Today's goal: _____

Distance: _____
Time: _____
Heart Rate: _____
i-Rate (1-10): _____
X-Training: _____
Sleep Hours: _____
Weight: _____
Mood: ☺ ☺ ☹ ☹ Other

FUEL LOG

WATER: 6-8 × 8 OZ.	FRUITS: 2-4	VEGGIES: 3-5	WHOLE GRAIN SERVINGS: 6-11	PROTEIN: 4-6 OZ.	LIMIT FAT?	ALCOHOLIC BEVERAGES?	LIMIT "EMPTY" CARBS?
☐☐☐☐ ☐☐☐☐	☐☐ ☐☐	☐☐☐ ☐☐	☐☐☐☐ ☐☐☐☐ ☐	☐☐☐ ☐☐☐	Y N	Y N	Y N

WEATHER: SUN WIND RAIN CLOUDY SNOW TEMP: _____

THURSDAY / Date: _____ Training notes: _____

Today's goal: _____

Distance: _____
Time: _____
Heart Rate: _____
i-Rate (1-10): _____
X-Training: _____
Sleep Hours: _____
Weight: _____
Mood: ☺ ☺ ☹ ☹ Other

FUEL LOG

WATER: 6-8 × 8 OZ.	FRUITS: 2-4	VEGGIES: 3-5	WHOLE GRAIN SERVINGS: 6-11	PROTEIN: 4-6 OZ.	LIMIT FAT?	ALCOHOLIC BEVERAGES?	LIMIT "EMPTY" CARBS?
☐☐☐☐ ☐☐☐☐	☐☐ ☐☐	☐☐☐ ☐☐	☐☐☐☐ ☐☐☐☐ ☐	☐☐☐ ☐☐☐	Y N	Y N	Y N

WEATHER: SUN WIND RAIN CLOUDY SNOW TEMP: _____

FRIDAY / Date: _____   Training notes: _____

Today's goal: _____

FUEL LOG

WATER: 6-8 × 8 OZ.	FRUITS: 2-4	VEGGIES: 3-5	WHOLE GRAIN SERVINGS: 6-11	PROTEIN: 4-6 OZ.	LIMIT FAT?	ALCOHOLIC BEVERAGES?	LIMIT "EMPTY" CARBS?
☐☐☐☐ ☐☐☐☐	☐☐ ☐☐	☐☐ ☐☐	☐☐☐☐☐ ☐☐☐☐☐ ☐	☐☐☐ ☐☐☐ ☐☐	Y N	Y N	Y N

Distance: _____
Time: _____
Heart Rate: _____
i-Rate (1-10): _____
X-Training: _____
Sleep Hours: _____
Weight: _____
Mood: ☺ ☺ ☹   Other

WEATHER:
SUN   WIND
RAIN   CLOUDY
SNOW
TEMP: _____

SATURDAY / Date: _____   Training notes: _____

Today's goal: _____

FUEL LOG

WATER: 6-8 × 8 OZ.	FRUITS: 2-4	VEGGIES: 3-5	WHOLE GRAIN SERVINGS: 6-11	PROTEIN: 4-6 OZ.	LIMIT FAT?	ALCOHOLIC BEVERAGES?	LIMIT "EMPTY" CARBS?
☐☐☐☐ ☐☐☐☐	☐☐ ☐☐	☐☐ ☐☐	☐☐☐☐☐ ☐☐☐☐☐ ☐	☐☐☐ ☐☐☐ ☐☐	Y N	Y N	Y N

Distance: _____
Time: _____
Heart Rate: _____
i-Rate (1-10): _____
X-Training: _____
Sleep Hours: _____
Weight: _____
Mood: ☺ ☺ ☹   Other

WEATHER:
SUN   WIND
RAIN   CLOUDY
SNOW
TEMP: _____

SUNDAY / Date: _____   Training notes: _____

Today's goal: _____

FUEL LOG

WATER: 6-8 × 8 OZ.	FRUITS: 2-4	VEGGIES: 3-5	WHOLE GRAIN SERVINGS: 6-11	PROTEIN: 4-6 OZ.	LIMIT FAT?	ALCOHOLIC BEVERAGES?	LIMIT "EMPTY" CARBS?
☐☐☐☐ ☐☐☐☐	☐☐ ☐☐	☐☐ ☐☐	☐☐☐☐☐ ☐☐☐☐☐ ☐	☐☐☐ ☐☐☐ ☐☐	Y N	Y N	Y N

Distance: _____
Time: _____
Heart Rate: _____
i-Rate (1-10): _____
X-Training: _____
Sleep Hours: _____
Weight: _____
Mood: ☺ ☺ ☹   Other

WEATHER:
SUN   WIND
RAIN   CLOUDY
SNOW
TEMP: _____

WEEK OF: _____

GOALS FOR WEEK:

WEEKLY TOTAL: _____

YEAR-TO-DATE TOTAL: _____

Play is natural. The activity of running is not nearly as important as the fact that it is something that you enjoy doing.

MONDAY / Date:

Today's goal: _____

Training notes: _____

FUEL LOG

WATER: 6-8 x 8 OZ.	FRUITS: 2-4	VEGGIES: 3-5	WHOLE GRAIN SERVINGS: 6-11	PROTEIN: 4-6 OZ.	LIMIT FAT?	ALCOHOLIC BEVERAGES?	LIMIT "EMPTY" CARBS?
☐☐☐☐ ☐☐☐☐	☐☐ ☐☐	☐☐ ☐☐	☐☐☐☐☐☐ ☐☐☐☐☐	☐☐☐ ☐☐☐	Y N	Y N	Y N

WEATHER: SUN WIND RAIN CLOUDY SNOW   TEMP: _____

Distance: _____
Time: _____
Heart Rate: _____
i-Rate (1-10): _____
X-Training: _____
Sleep Hours: _____
Weight: _____
Mood: ☺ ☺ ☹ Other

TUESDAY / Date:

Today's goal: _____

Training notes: _____

FUEL LOG

WATER: 6-8 x 8 OZ.	FRUITS: 2-4	VEGGIES: 3-5	WHOLE GRAIN SERVINGS: 6-11	PROTEIN: 4-6 OZ.	LIMIT FAT?	ALCOHOLIC BEVERAGES?	LIMIT "EMPTY" CARBS?
☐☐☐☐ ☐☐☐☐	☐☐ ☐☐	☐☐ ☐☐	☐☐☐☐☐☐ ☐☐☐☐☐	☐☐☐ ☐☐☐	Y N	Y N	Y N

WEATHER: SUN WIND RAIN CLOUDY SNOW   TEMP: _____

Distance: _____
Time: _____
Heart Rate: _____
i-Rate (1-10): _____
X-Training: _____
Sleep Hours: _____
Weight: _____
Mood: ☺ ☺ ☹ Other

WEDNESDAY / Date:

Today's goal: _____

Training notes: _____

FUEL LOG

WATER: 6-8 x 8 OZ.	FRUITS: 2-4	VEGGIES: 3-5	WHOLE GRAIN SERVINGS: 6-11	PROTEIN: 4-6 OZ.	LIMIT FAT?	ALCOHOLIC BEVERAGES?	LIMIT "EMPTY" CARBS?
☐☐☐☐ ☐☐☐☐	☐☐ ☐☐	☐☐ ☐☐	☐☐☐☐☐☐ ☐☐☐☐☐	☐☐☐ ☐☐☐	Y N	Y N	Y N

WEATHER: SUN WIND RAIN CLOUDY SNOW   TEMP: _____

Distance: _____
Time: _____
Heart Rate: _____
i-Rate (1-10): _____
X-Training: _____
Sleep Hours: _____
Weight: _____
Mood: ☺ ☺ ☹ Other

THURSDAY / Date:

Today's goal: _____

Training notes: _____

FUEL LOG

WATER: 6-8 x 8 OZ.	FRUITS: 2-4	VEGGIES: 3-5	WHOLE GRAIN SERVINGS: 6-11	PROTEIN: 4-6 OZ.	LIMIT FAT?	ALCOHOLIC BEVERAGES?	LIMIT "EMPTY" CARBS?
☐☐☐☐ ☐☐☐☐	☐☐ ☐☐	☐☐ ☐☐	☐☐☐☐☐☐ ☐☐☐☐☐	☐☐☐ ☐☐☐	Y N	Y N	Y N

WEATHER: SUN WIND RAIN CLOUDY SNOW   TEMP: _____

Distance: _____
Time: _____
Heart Rate: _____
i-Rate (1-10): _____
X-Training: _____
Sleep Hours: _____
Weight: _____
Mood: ☺ ☺ ☹ Other

FRIDAY / Date:

Training notes:

Today's goal:

_____

Distance:
Time:
Heart Rate:
i-Rate (1-10)
X-Training:
Sleep Hours:
Weight:
Mood: ☺ ☺ ☹ Other

WEATHER:
SUN   WIND
RAIN CLOUDY
SNOW
TEMP: _____

FUEL LOG

WATER: 6-8 x 8 OZ.	FRUITS: 2-4	VEGGIES: 3-5	WHOLE GRAIN SERVINGS: 6-11	PROTEIN: 4-6 OZ.	LIMIT FAT?	ALCOHOLIC BEVERAGES?	LIMIT "EMPTY" CARBS?
☐☐☐☐ ☐☐☐☐	☐☐ ☐☐	☐☐ ☐☐	☐☐☐☐ ☐☐☐☐ ☐☐☐	☐☐☐ ☐☐☐	Y N	Y N	Y N

SATURDAY / Date:

Training notes:

Today's goal:

_____

Distance:
Time:
Heart Rate:
i-Rate (1-10)
X-Training:
Sleep Hours:
Weight:
Mood: ☺ ☺ ☹ Other

WEATHER:
SUN   WIND
RAIN CLOUDY
SNOW
TEMP: _____

FUEL LOG

WATER: 6-8 x 8 OZ.	FRUITS: 2-4	VEGGIES: 3-5	WHOLE GRAIN SERVINGS: 6-11	PROTEIN: 4-6 OZ.	LIMIT FAT?	ALCOHOLIC BEVERAGES?	LIMIT "EMPTY" CARBS?
☐☐☐☐ ☐☐☐☐	☐☐ ☐☐	☐☐ ☐☐	☐☐☐☐☐ ☐☐☐☐☐ ☐	☐☐☐ ☐☐☐	Y N	Y N	Y N

SUNDAY / Date:

Training notes:

Today's goal:

_____

Distance:
Time:
Heart Rate:
i-Rate (1-10)
X-Training:
Sleep Hours:
Weight:
Mood: ☺ ☺ ☹ Other

WEATHER:
SUN   WIND
RAIN CLOUDY
SNOW
TEMP: _____

FUEL LOG

WATER: 6-8 x 8 OZ.	FRUITS: 2-4	VEGGIES: 3-5	WHOLE GRAIN SERVINGS: 6-11	PROTEIN: 4-6 OZ.	LIMIT FAT?	ALCOHOLIC BEVERAGES?	LIMIT "EMPTY" CARBS?
☐☐☐☐ ☐☐☐☐	☐☐ ☐☐	☐☐ ☐☐	☐☐☐☐☐ ☐☐☐☐☐ ☐	☐☐☐ ☐☐☐	Y N	Y N	Y N

WEEK OF:

GOALS FOR WEEK:

WEEKLY TOTAL: _____

YEAR-TO-DATE TOTAL:

We must search for the limits of our body and demand that our spirit not give up on us.

MONDAY / Date:

Today's goal:

Training notes:

FUEL LOG

WATER: 6-8 x 8 OZ.	FRUITS: 2-4	VEGGIES: 3-5	WHOLE GRAIN SERVINGS: 6-11	PROTEIN: 4-6 OZ.	LIMIT FAT?	ALCOHOLIC BEVERAGES?	LIMIT "EMPTY" CARBS?
☐☐☐☐	☐☐	☐☐	☐☐☐☐☐	☐☐☐	Y N	Y N	Y N

WEATHER:
SUN WIND
RAIN CLOUDY
SNOW
TEMP: _____

Distance:
Time:
Heart Rate:
i-Rate (1-10)
X-Training:
Sleep Hours:
Weight:
Mood: ☺ ☺ ☹ Other

TUESDAY / Date:

Today's goal:

Training notes:

FUEL LOG

WATER: 6-8 x 8 OZ.	FRUITS: 2-4	VEGGIES: 3-5	WHOLE GRAIN SERVINGS: 6-11	PROTEIN: 4-6 OZ.	LIMIT FAT?	ALCOHOLIC BEVERAGES?	LIMIT "EMPTY" CARBS?
☐☐☐☐	☐☐	☐☐	☐☐☐☐☐	☐☐☐	Y N	Y N	Y N

WEATHER:
SUN WIND
RAIN CLOUDY
SNOW
TEMP: _____

Distance:
Time:
Heart Rate:
i-Rate (1-10)
X-Training:
Sleep Hours:
Weight:
Mood: ☺ ☺ ☹ Other

WEDNESDAY / Date:

Today's goal:

Training notes:

FUEL LOG

WATER: 6-8 x 8 OZ.	FRUITS: 2-4	VEGGIES: 3-5	WHOLE GRAIN SERVINGS: 6-11	PROTEIN: 4-6 OZ.	LIMIT FAT?	ALCOHOLIC BEVERAGES?	LIMIT "EMPTY" CARBS?
☐☐☐☐	☐☐	☐☐	☐☐☐☐☐	☐☐☐	Y N	Y N	Y N

WEATHER:
SUN WIND
RAIN CLOUDY
SNOW
TEMP: _____

Distance:
Time:
Heart Rate:
i-Rate (1-10)
X-Training:
Sleep Hours:
Weight:
Mood: ☺ ☺ ☹ Other

THURSDAY / Date:

Today's goal:

Training notes:

FUEL LOG

WATER: 6-8 x 8 OZ.	FRUITS: 2-4	VEGGIES: 3-5	WHOLE GRAIN SERVINGS: 6-11	PROTEIN: 4-6 OZ.	LIMIT FAT?	ALCOHOLIC BEVERAGES?	LIMIT "EMPTY" CARBS?
☐☐☐☐	☐☐	☐☐	☐☐☐☐☐	☐☐☐	Y N	Y N	Y N

WEATHER:
SUN WIND
RAIN CLOUDY
SNOW
TEMP: _____

Distance:
Time:
Heart Rate:
i-Rate (1-10)
X-Training:
Sleep Hours:
Weight:
Mood: ☺ ☺ ☹ Other

FRIDAY / Date:

Training notes:

Distance:
Time:
Heart Rate:
i-Rate (1-10)
X-Training:
Sleep Hours:
Weight:
Mood: ☺ ☺ ☹ Other

WEATHER:
SUN WIND
RAIN CLOUDY
SNOW
TEMP: _____

Today's goal:

FUEL LOG

WATER: 6-8 x 8 OZ.	FRUITS: 2-4	VEGGIES: 3-5	WHOLE GRAIN SERVINGS: 6-11	PROTEIN: 4-6 OZ.	LIMIT FAT?	ALCOHOLIC BEVERAGES?	LIMIT "EMPTY" CARBS?
☐☐☐☐ ☐☐☐☐	☐☐ ☐☐	☐☐☐ ☐☐	☐☐☐☐☐ ☐☐☐☐☐ ☐	☐☐☐ ☐☐	Y N	Y N	Y N

SATURDAY / Date:

Training notes:

Distance:
Time:
Heart Rate:
i-Rate (1-10)
X-Training:
Sleep Hours:
Weight:
Mood: ☺ ☺ ☹ Other

WEATHER:
SUN WIND
RAIN CLOUDY
SNOW
TEMP: _____

Today's goal:

FUEL LOG

WATER: 6-8 x 8 OZ.	FRUITS: 2-4	VEGGIES: 3-5	WHOLE GRAIN SERVINGS: 6-11	PROTEIN: 4-6 OZ.	LIMIT FAT?	ALCOHOLIC BEVERAGES?	LIMIT "EMPTY" CARBS?
☐☐☐☐ ☐☐☐☐	☐☐ ☐☐	☐☐☐ ☐☐	☐☐☐ ☐☐☐ ☐	☐☐☐ ☐☐	Y N	Y N	Y N

SUNDAY / Date:

Training notes:

Distance:
Time:
Heart Rate:
i-Rate (1-10)
X-Training:
Sleep Hours:
Weight:
Mood: ☺ ☺ ☹ Other

WEATHER:
SUN WIND
RAIN CLOUDY
SNOW
TEMP: _____

Today's goal:

FUEL LOG

WATER: 6-8 x 8 OZ.	FRUITS: 2-4	VEGGIES: 3-5	WHOLE GRAIN SERVINGS: 6-11	PROTEIN: 4-6 OZ.	LIMIT FAT?	ALCOHOLIC BEVERAGES?	LIMIT "EMPTY" CARBS?
☐☐☐☐ ☐☐☐☐	☐☐ ☐☐	☐☐☐ ☐☐	☐☐☐ ☐☐☐ ☐	☐☐☐ ☐☐	Y N	Y N	Y N

WEEK OF:

GOALS FOR WEEK:

Keep it real. No matter what you thought the training was going to be, it's been different. No matter what you thought being fit was going to be, I promise you it will be different.

WEEKLY TOTAL: _____

YEAR-TO-DATE TOTAL:

WORKING THE SHOVEL

Some of life's lessons I've only had to learn once; like not to put my tongue on a frozen flagpole no matter how funny my buddies think it will be. Some of life's lesson took me a little longer; like, when I'm given 16 weeks to do a project, I can't wait to start until the day before it's due. And some of life's lessons are absolutes. Thin is the only word to use in a sentence that contains the word hips.

But one of the most important lessons in my life happened in the blink of an eye when I least expected it. My teacher was someone I barely knew. And, the lesson came at a time when I was too young to truly understand the meaning of the lesson, and how it would come to define my life.

For six months, when I was twenty years old, I worked as a laborer in the Norfolk and Western train yard in Decatur, Illinois. I was a gandydancer. Our job was to replace broken rail and worn out ties. Most importantly, we had to look busy. In the yard, this wasn't difficult because there was almost always something to do. But on this day, our only task was to move a large pile of stone from where it was to where the foreman wanted it.

Shovel by shovel we began carrying rock from the big pile to a smaller pile about 100 feet down the track. The first shovel doesn't seem so bad. But, by the 10th, everything starts to hurt. But, with the foreman yelling, I was working as fast as I could, and in no time, I was exhausted. And then, just as I was ready to learn, the teacher appeared.

One of the older men on the crew came over, put his hand on my shoulder and said: "Ain't no man gonna break your back long as you working the shovel. Let that old man yell. You jest work at your pace" I looked at him and knew immediately what he meant. It wasn't the foreman that was wearing me out; it was my desire to please him.

It was me that controlled my effort. It was me controlled my fatigue. And, in the grandest sense, it was me that controlled my life. I had the choice. That day, and every other day, I could either work to my own limits or try to live up to the expectations of someone else.

My life as a runner began like my life as a laborer. I looked first outside of myself for guidance. I looked outside of myself for expectations. I tried to meet the goals that others set for me. I was overcome with 'shoulds'. And I was overcome with failure.

It wasn't until I began to work my own shovel, as a runner, that running became a nearly constant source of joy instead of a chronic source of frustration. It wasn't until I began to understand that ultimately my running matter only to me that I was free to run for myself.

Not that it was easy. Just like that day moving stone, it's hard to ignore the eyes and voices of those around me whose believe that I should live up to their expectations. It's hard to run with joy when all but one of the water tables has been taken away. It's hard to revel in the mystery of motion when you finish a race alone, and the chutes have been taken down, and the clock is sitting on a folding chair. But, I have. And I do.

And when I do, when I overcome my own need to please people I don't know, and who don't know me, I hear the voice of my teacher. I remind myself that my running, indeed my life is my shovel. And ain't no man gonna break my back, ain't no man gonna steal my joy, or rob me of my right to celebrate what I've accomplished, long as I'm working the shovel.

Waddle on, friends.

MONDAY / Date:

Today's goal:

Training notes:

Distance:
Time:
Heart Rate:
i-Rate (1-10)
X-Training:
Sleep Hours:
Weight:
Mood: ☺ 😐 ☹ Other

WEATHER:
SUN WIND
RAIN CLOUDY
SNOW
TEMP: ____

FUEL LOG

WATER: 6-8 × 8 OZ.	FRUITS: 2-4	VEGGIES: 3-5	WHOLE GRAIN SERVINGS: 6-11	PROTEIN: 4-6 OZ.	LIMIT FAT?	ALCOHOLIC BEVERAGES?	LIMIT "EMPTY" CARBS?
☐☐☐☐ ☐☐☐☐	☐☐ ☐☐	☐☐ ☐☐	☐☐☐☐☐☐ ☐☐☐☐☐	☐☐☐ ☐☐☐	Y N	Y N	Y N

TUESDAY / Date:

Today's goal:

Training notes:

Distance:
Time:
Heart Rate:
i-Rate (1-10)
X-Training:
Sleep Hours:
Weight:
Mood: ☺ 😐 ☹ Other

WEATHER:
SUN WIND
RAIN CLOUDY
SNOW
TEMP: ____

FUEL LOG

WATER: 6-8 × 8 OZ.	FRUITS: 2-4	VEGGIES: 3-5	WHOLE GRAIN SERVINGS: 6-11	PROTEIN: 4-6 OZ.	LIMIT FAT?	ALCOHOLIC BEVERAGES?	LIMIT "EMPTY" CARBS?
☐☐☐☐ ☐☐☐☐	☐☐ ☐☐	☐☐ ☐☐	☐☐☐☐☐☐ ☐☐☐☐☐	☐☐☐ ☐☐☐	Y N	Y N	Y N

WEDNESDAY / Date:

Today's goal:

Training notes:

Distance:
Time:
Heart Rate:
i-Rate (1-10)
X-Training:
Sleep Hours:
Weight:
Mood: ☺ 😐 ☹ Other

WEATHER:
SUN WIND
RAIN CLOUDY
SNOW
TEMP: ____

FUEL LOG

WATER: 6-8 × 8 OZ.	FRUITS: 2-4	VEGGIES: 3-5	WHOLE GRAIN SERVINGS: 6-11	PROTEIN: 4-6 OZ.	LIMIT FAT?	ALCOHOLIC BEVERAGES?	LIMIT "EMPTY" CARBS?
☐☐☐☐ ☐☐☐☐	☐☐ ☐☐	☐☐ ☐☐	☐☐☐☐☐☐ ☐☐☐☐☐	☐☐☐ ☐☐☐	Y N	Y N	Y N

THURSDAY / Date:

Today's goal:

Training notes:

Distance:
Time:
Heart Rate:
i-Rate (1-10)
X-Training:
Sleep Hours:
Weight:
Mood: ☺ 😐 ☹ Other

WEATHER:
SUN WIND
RAIN CLOUDY
SNOW
TEMP: ____

FUEL LOG

WATER: 6-8 × 8 OZ.	FRUITS: 2-4	VEGGIES: 3-5	WHOLE GRAIN SERVINGS: 6-11	PROTEIN: 4-6 OZ.	LIMIT FAT?	ALCOHOLIC BEVERAGES?	LIMIT "EMPTY" CARBS?
☐☐☐☐ ☐☐☐☐	☐☐ ☐☐	☐☐ ☐☐	☐☐☐☐☐☐ ☐☐☐☐☐	☐☐☐ ☐☐☐	Y N	Y N	Y N

FRIDAY / Date: _____

Training notes: _____

Today's goal: _____

Distance: _____
Time: _____
Heart Rate: _____
i-Rate (1-10): _____
X-Training: _____
Sleep Hours: _____
Weight: _____
Mood: ☺ ☺ ☹ Other

WEATHER:
SUN WIND
RAIN CLOUDY
SNOW
TEMP: _____

FUEL LOG

WATER: 6-8 x 8 OZ.	FRUITS: 2-4	VEGGIES: 3-5	WHOLE GRAIN SERVINGS: 6-11	PROTEIN: 4-6 OZ.	LIMIT FAT?	ALCOHOLIC BEVERAGES?	LIMIT "EMPTY" CARBS?
☐☐☐☐ ☐☐☐☐	☐☐ ☐☐	☐☐ ☐☐	☐☐☐☐ ☐☐☐☐	☐☐☐ ☐☐☐	Y N	Y N	Y N

SATURDAY / Date: _____

Training notes: _____

Today's goal: _____

Distance: _____
Time: _____
Heart Rate: _____
i-Rate (1-10): _____
X-Training: _____
Sleep Hours: _____
Weight: _____
Mood: ☺ ☺ ☹ Other

WEATHER:
SUN WIND
RAIN CLOUDY
SNOW
TEMP: _____

FUEL LOG

WATER: 6-8 x 8 OZ.	FRUITS: 2-4	VEGGIES: 3-5	WHOLE GRAIN SERVINGS: 6-11	PROTEIN: 4-6 OZ.	LIMIT FAT?	ALCOHOLIC BEVERAGES?	LIMIT "EMPTY" CARBS?
☐☐☐☐ ☐☐☐☐	☐☐ ☐☐	☐☐ ☐☐	☐☐☐ ☐☐☐	☐☐☐ ☐☐☐	Y N	Y N	Y N

SUNDAY / Date: _____

Training notes: _____

Today's goal: _____

Distance: _____
Time: _____
Heart Rate: _____
i-Rate (1-10): _____
X-Training: _____
Sleep Hours: _____
Weight: _____
Mood: ☺ ☺ ☹ Other

WEATHER:
SUN WIND
RAIN CLOUDY
SNOW
TEMP: _____

FUEL LOG

WATER: 6-8 x 8 OZ.	FRUITS: 2-4	VEGGIES: 3-5	WHOLE GRAIN SERVINGS: 6-11	PROTEIN: 4-6 OZ.	LIMIT FAT?	ALCOHOLIC BEVERAGES?	LIMIT "EMPTY" CARBS?
☐☐☐☐ ☐☐☐☐	☐☐ ☐☐	☐☐ ☐☐	☐☐☐ ☐☐☐	☐☐☐ ☐☐☐	Y N	Y N	Y N

WEEK OF: _____

GOALS FOR WEEK: _____

WEEKLY TOTAL: _____

YEAR-TO-DATE TOTAL: _____

What makes running a great sport is the untold acts of kindness performed by uncountable numbers of people, from race directors to sponsors to volunteers to the spectators.

MONDAY / Date:

Today's goal:

Training notes:

FUEL LOG

WATER: 6-8 × 8 OZ.	FRUITS: 2-4	VEGGIES: 3-5	WHOLE GRAIN SERVINGS: 6-11	PROTEIN: 4-6 OZ.	LIMIT FAT?	ALCOHOLIC BEVERAGES?	LIMIT "EMPTY" CARBS?
☐☐☐☐ ☐☐☐☐	☐☐ ☐☐	☐☐☐ ☐☐☐	☐☐☐ ☐☐☐ ☐	☐☐☐ ☐☐☐	Y N	Y N	Y N

Distance:
Time:
Heart Rate:
i-Rate (1-10)
X-Training:
Sleep Hours:
Weight:
Mood: ☺ ☺ ☺ ☹ Other

WEATHER: SUN WIND RAIN CLOUDY SNOW TEMP: ____

TUESDAY / Date:

Today's goal:

Training notes:

FUEL LOG

WATER: 6-8 × 8 OZ.	FRUITS: 2-4	VEGGIES: 3-5	WHOLE GRAIN SERVINGS: 6-11	PROTEIN: 4-6 OZ.	LIMIT FAT?	ALCOHOLIC BEVERAGES?	LIMIT "EMPTY" CARBS?
☐☐☐☐ ☐☐☐☐	☐☐ ☐☐	☐☐☐ ☐☐☐	☐☐☐ ☐☐☐ ☐	☐☐☐ ☐☐☐	Y N	Y N	Y N

Distance:
Time:
Heart Rate:
i-Rate (1-10)
X-Training:
Sleep Hours:
Weight:
Mood: ☺ ☺ ☺ ☹ Other

WEATHER: SUN WIND RAIN CLOUDY SNOW TEMP: ____

WEDNESDAY / Date:

Today's goal:

Training notes:

FUEL LOG

WATER: 6-8 × 8 OZ.	FRUITS: 2-4	VEGGIES: 3-5	WHOLE GRAIN SERVINGS: 6-11	PROTEIN: 4-6 OZ.	LIMIT FAT?	ALCOHOLIC BEVERAGES?	LIMIT "EMPTY" CARBS?
☐☐☐☐ ☐☐☐☐	☐☐ ☐☐	☐☐☐ ☐☐☐	☐☐☐ ☐☐☐ ☐	☐☐☐ ☐☐☐	Y N	Y N	Y N

Distance:
Time:
Heart Rate:
i-Rate (1-10)
X-Training:
Sleep Hours:
Weight:
Mood: ☺ ☺ ☺ ☹ Other

WEATHER: SUN WIND RAIN CLOUDY SNOW TEMP: ____

THURSDAY / Date:

Today's goal:

Training notes:

FUEL LOG

WATER: 6-8 × 8 OZ.	FRUITS: 2-4	VEGGIES: 3-5	WHOLE GRAIN SERVINGS: 6-11	PROTEIN: 4-6 OZ.	LIMIT FAT?	ALCOHOLIC BEVERAGES?	LIMIT "EMPTY" CARBS?
☐☐☐☐ ☐☐☐☐	☐☐ ☐☐	☐☐☐ ☐☐☐	☐☐☐ ☐☐☐ ☐	☐☐☐ ☐☐☐	Y N	Y N	Y N

Distance:
Time:
Heart Rate:
i-Rate (1-10)
X-Training:
Sleep Hours:
Weight:
Mood: ☺ ☺ ☺ ☹ Other

WEATHER: SUN WIND RAIN CLOUDY SNOW TEMP: ____

FRIDAY / Date:

Today's goal: _____

Training notes: _____

FUEL LOG

WATER: 6-8 x 8 OZ.	FRUITS: 2-4	VEGGIES: 3-5	WHOLE GRAIN SERVINGS: 6-11	PROTEIN: 4-6 OZ.	LIMIT FAT?	ALCOHOLIC BEVERAGES?	LIMIT "EMPTY" CARBS?
☐☐☐☐☐☐☐☐	☐☐☐☐	☐☐☐☐☐	☐☐☐☐☐☐☐☐☐☐☐	☐☐☐☐☐☐	Y N	Y N	Y N

Distance: _____
Time: _____
Heart Rate: _____
i-Rate (1-10) _____
X-Training: _____
Sleep Hours: _____
Weight: _____
Mood: ☺ ☺ ☹ Other ___

WEATHER: SUN WIND RAIN CLOUDY SNOW TEMP: ___

SATURDAY / Date:

Today's goal: _____

Training notes: _____

FUEL LOG

WATER: 6-8 x 8 OZ.	FRUITS: 2-4	VEGGIES: 3-5	WHOLE GRAIN SERVINGS: 6-11	PROTEIN: 4-6 OZ.	LIMIT FAT?	ALCOHOLIC BEVERAGES?	LIMIT "EMPTY" CARBS?
☐☐☐☐☐☐☐☐	☐☐☐☐	☐☐☐☐☐	☐☐☐☐☐☐☐☐☐☐☐	☐☐☐☐☐☐	Y N	Y N	Y N

Distance: _____
Time: _____
Heart Rate: _____
i-Rate (1-10) _____
X-Training: _____
Sleep Hours: _____
Weight: _____
Mood: ☺ ☺ ☹ Other ___

WEATHER: SUN WIND RAIN CLOUDY SNOW TEMP: ___

SUNDAY / Date:

Today's goal: _____

Training notes: _____

FUEL LOG

WATER: 6-8 x 8 OZ.	FRUITS: 2-4	VEGGIES: 3-5	WHOLE GRAIN SERVINGS: 6-11	PROTEIN: 4-6 OZ.	LIMIT FAT?	ALCOHOLIC BEVERAGES?	LIMIT "EMPTY" CARBS?
☐☐☐☐☐☐☐☐	☐☐☐☐	☐☐☐☐☐	☐☐☐☐☐☐☐☐☐☐☐	☐☐☐☐☐☐	Y N	Y N	Y N

Distance: _____
Time: _____
Heart Rate: _____
i-Rate (1-10) _____
X-Training: _____
Sleep Hours: _____
Weight: _____
Mood: ☺ ☺ ☹ Other ___

WEATHER: SUN WIND RAIN CLOUDY SNOW TEMP: ___

WEEK OF: _____

GOALS FOR WEEK: _____

WEEKLY TOTAL: _____

YEAR-TO-DATE TOTAL: _____

It isn't the socks, the shoes, or even the speed that makes me a runner. It's the running.

MONDAY / Date:

Today's goal:

Training notes:

FUEL LOG

WATER: 6-8 × 8 OZ.	FRUITS: 2-4	VEGGIES: 3-5	WHOLE GRAIN SERVINGS: 6-11	PROTEIN: 4-6 OZ.	LIMIT FAT?	ALCOHOLIC BEVERAGES?	LIMIT "EMPTY" CARBS?
☐☐☐☐ ☐☐☐☐	☐☐ ☐☐	☐☐☐ ☐☐	☐☐☐☐☐ ☐	☐☐☐ ☐☐☐	Y N	Y N	Y N

WEATHER: SUN WIND RAIN CLOUDY SNOW TEMP: _____

Distance:
Time:
Heart Rate:
i-Rate (1-10)
X-Training:
Sleep Hours:
Weight:
Mood: ☺ ☺ ☹ Other

TUESDAY / Date:

Today's goal:

Training notes:

FUEL LOG

WATER: 6-8 × 8 OZ.	FRUITS: 2-4	VEGGIES: 3-5	WHOLE GRAIN SERVINGS: 6-11	PROTEIN: 4-6 OZ.	LIMIT FAT?	ALCOHOLIC BEVERAGES?	LIMIT "EMPTY" CARBS?
☐☐☐☐ ☐☐☐☐	☐☐ ☐☐	☐☐☐ ☐☐	☐☐☐☐☐ ☐	☐☐☐ ☐☐☐	Y N	Y N	Y N

WEATHER: SUN WIND RAIN CLOUDY SNOW TEMP: _____

Distance:
Time:
Heart Rate:
i-Rate (1-10)
X-Training:
Sleep Hours:
Weight:
Mood: ☺ ☺ ☹ Other

WEDNESDAY / Date:

Today's goal:

Training notes:

FUEL LOG

WATER: 6-8 × 8 OZ.	FRUITS: 2-4	VEGGIES: 3-5	WHOLE GRAIN SERVINGS: 6-11	PROTEIN: 4-6 OZ.	LIMIT FAT?	ALCOHOLIC BEVERAGES?	LIMIT "EMPTY" CARBS?
☐☐☐☐ ☐☐☐☐	☐☐ ☐☐	☐☐☐ ☐☐	☐☐☐☐☐ ☐	☐☐☐ ☐☐☐	Y N	Y N	Y N

WEATHER: SUN WIND RAIN CLOUDY SNOW TEMP: _____

Distance:
Time:
Heart Rate:
i-Rate (1-10)
X-Training:
Sleep Hours:
Weight:
Mood: ☺ ☺ ☹ Other

THURSDAY / Date:

Today's goal:

Training notes:

FUEL LOG

WATER: 6-8 × 8 OZ.	FRUITS: 2-4	VEGGIES: 3-5	WHOLE GRAIN SERVINGS: 6-11	PROTEIN: 4-6 OZ.	LIMIT FAT?	ALCOHOLIC BEVERAGES?	LIMIT "EMPTY" CARBS?
☐☐☐☐ ☐☐☐☐	☐☐ ☐☐	☐☐☐ ☐☐	☐☐☐☐☐ ☐	☐☐☐ ☐☐☐	Y N	Y N	Y N

WEATHER: SUN WIND RAIN CLOUDY SNOW TEMP: _____

Distance:
Time:
Heart Rate:
i-Rate (1-10)
X-Training:
Sleep Hours:
Weight:
Mood: ☺ ☺ ☹ Other

FRIDAY / Date:

Training notes:

Today's goal:

Distance:
Time:
Heart Rate:
i-Rate (1-10)
X-Training:
Sleep Hours:
Weight:
Mood: ☺ ☺ ☹ Other

WEATHER:
SUN WIND
RAIN CLOUDY
SNOW
TEMP: _____

FUEL LOG

WATER: 6-8 x 8 OZ.	FRUITS: 2-4	VEGGIES: 3-5	WHOLE GRAIN SERVINGS: 6-11	PROTEIN: 4-6 OZ.	LIMIT FAT?	ALCOHOLIC BEVERAGES?	LIMIT "EMPTY" CARBS?
☐☐☐☐ ☐☐☐☐	☐☐ ☐☐	☐☐ ☐	☐☐☐ ☐☐☐	☐☐ ☐☐	Y N	Y N	Y N

SATURDAY / Date:

Training notes:

Today's goal:

Distance:
Time:
Heart Rate:
i-Rate (1-10)
X-Training:
Sleep Hours:
Weight:
Mood: ☺ ☺ ☹ Other

WEATHER:
SUN WIND
RAIN CLOUDY
SNOW
TEMP: _____

FUEL LOG

WATER: 6-8 x 8 OZ.	FRUITS: 2-4	VEGGIES: 3-5	WHOLE GRAIN SERVINGS: 6-11	PROTEIN: 4-6 OZ.	LIMIT FAT?	ALCOHOLIC BEVERAGES?	LIMIT "EMPTY" CARBS?
☐☐☐☐ ☐☐☐☐	☐☐ ☐☐	☐☐ ☐	☐☐☐ ☐☐☐	☐☐ ☐☐	Y N	Y N	Y N

SUNDAY / Date:

Training notes:

Today's goal:

Distance:
Time:
Heart Rate:
i-Rate (1-10)
X-Training:
Sleep Hours:
Weight:
Mood: ☺ ☺ ☹ Other

WEATHER:
SUN WIND
RAIN CLOUDY
SNOW
TEMP: _____

FUEL LOG

WATER: 6-8 x 8 OZ.	FRUITS: 2-4	VEGGIES: 3-5	WHOLE GRAIN SERVINGS: 6-11	PROTEIN: 4-6 OZ.	LIMIT FAT?	ALCOHOLIC BEVERAGES?	LIMIT "EMPTY" CARBS?
☐☐☐☐ ☐☐☐☐	☐☐ ☐☐	☐☐ ☐	☐☐☐ ☐☐☐	☐☐ ☐☐	Y N	Y N	Y N

WEEK OF:

GOALS FOR WEEK:

WEEKLY TOTAL: _____

YEAR-TO-DATE TOTAL:

Some of us started running because nothing else eased the pain of living.

MONDAY / Date:

Today's goal:

Training notes:

FUEL LOG

WATER: 6-8 x 8 oz.	FRUITS: 2-4	VEGGIES: 3-5	WHOLE GRAIN SERVINGS: 6-11	PROTEIN: 4-6 oz.	LIMIT FAT?	ALCOHOLIC BEVERAGES?	LIMIT "EMPTY" CARBS?
☐☐☐☐ ☐☐☐☐	☐☐ ☐☐	☐☐ ☐☐	☐☐☐ ☐☐☐	☐☐ ☐☐ ☐☐	Y N	Y N	Y N

WEATHER: SUN WIND RAIN CLOUDY SNOW
TEMP: _____

Distance:
Time:
Heart Rate:
i-Rate (1-10)
X-Training:
Sleep Hours:
Weight:
Mood: ☺ ☺ ☹ Other

TUESDAY / Date:

Today's goal:

Training notes:

FUEL LOG

WATER: 6-8 x 8 oz.	FRUITS: 2-4	VEGGIES: 3-5	WHOLE GRAIN SERVINGS: 6-11	PROTEIN: 4-6 oz.	LIMIT FAT?	ALCOHOLIC BEVERAGES?	LIMIT "EMPTY" CARBS?
☐☐☐☐ ☐☐☐☐	☐☐ ☐☐	☐☐ ☐☐	☐☐☐ ☐☐☐	☐☐ ☐☐ ☐☐	Y N	Y N	Y N

WEATHER: SUN WIND RAIN CLOUDY SNOW
TEMP: _____

Distance:
Time:
Heart Rate:
i-Rate (1-10)
X-Training:
Sleep Hours:
Weight:
Mood: ☺ ☺ ☹ Other

WEDNESDAY / Date:

Today's goal:

Training notes:

FUEL LOG

WATER: 6-8 x 8 oz.	FRUITS: 2-4	VEGGIES: 3-5	WHOLE GRAIN SERVINGS: 6-11	PROTEIN: 4-6 oz.	LIMIT FAT?	ALCOHOLIC BEVERAGES?	LIMIT "EMPTY" CARBS?
☐☐☐☐ ☐☐☐☐	☐☐ ☐☐	☐☐ ☐☐	☐☐☐ ☐☐☐	☐☐ ☐☐ ☐☐	Y N	Y N	Y N

WEATHER: SUN WIND RAIN CLOUDY SNOW
TEMP: _____

Distance:
Time:
Heart Rate:
i-Rate (1-10)
X-Training:
Sleep Hours:
Weight:
Mood: ☺ ☺ ☹ Other

THURSDAY / Date:

Today's goal:

Training notes:

FUEL LOG

WATER: 6-8 x 8 oz.	FRUITS: 2-4	VEGGIES: 3-5	WHOLE GRAIN SERVINGS: 6-11	PROTEIN: 4-6 oz.	LIMIT FAT?	ALCOHOLIC BEVERAGES?	LIMIT "EMPTY" CARBS?
☐☐☐☐ ☐☐☐☐	☐☐ ☐☐	☐☐ ☐☐	☐☐☐ ☐☐☐	☐☐ ☐☐ ☐☐	Y N	Y N	Y N

WEATHER: SUN WIND RAIN CLOUDY SNOW
TEMP: _____

Distance:
Time:
Heart Rate:
i-Rate (1-10)
X-Training:
Sleep Hours:
Weight:
Mood: ☺ ☺ ☹ Other

FRIDAY / Date:

Training notes:

Today's goal:

Distance:
Time:
Heart Rate:
i-Rate (1-10)
X-Training:
Sleep Hours:
Weight:
Mood: ☺ 😐 ☹ Other

WEATHER:
SUN WIND
RAIN CLOUDY
SNOW
TEMP: _____

FUEL LOG

WATER: 6-8 x 8 OZ.	FRUITS: 2-4	VEGGIES: 3-5	WHOLE GRAIN SERVINGS: 6-11	PROTEIN: 4-6 OZ.	LIMIT FAT?	ALCOHOLIC BEVERAGES?	LIMIT "EMPTY" CARBS?
☐☐☐☐ ☐☐☐☐	☐☐ ☐☐	☐☐☐ ☐☐☐	☐☐☐☐ ☐☐☐☐ ☐☐☐	☐☐☐ ☐☐☐	Y N	Y N	Y N

SATURDAY / Date:

Training notes:

Today's goal:

Distance:
Time:
Heart Rate:
i-Rate (1-10)
X-Training:
Sleep Hours:
Weight:
Mood: ☺ 😐 ☹ Other

WEATHER:
SUN WIND
RAIN CLOUDY
SNOW
TEMP: _____

FUEL LOG

WATER: 6-8 x 8 OZ.	FRUITS: 2-4	VEGGIES: 3-5	WHOLE GRAIN SERVINGS: 6-11	PROTEIN: 4-6 OZ.	LIMIT FAT?	ALCOHOLIC BEVERAGES?	LIMIT "EMPTY" CARBS?
☐☐☐☐ ☐☐☐☐	☐☐ ☐☐	☐☐☐ ☐☐☐	☐☐☐☐ ☐☐☐☐ ☐☐☐	☐☐☐ ☐☐☐	Y N	Y N	Y N

SUNDAY / Date:

Training notes:

Today's goal:

Distance:
Time:
Heart Rate:
i-Rate (1-10)
X-Training:
Sleep Hours:
Weight:
Mood: ☺ 😐 ☹ Other

WEATHER:
SUN WIND
RAIN CLOUDY
SNOW
TEMP: _____

FUEL LOG

WATER: 6-8 x 8 OZ.	FRUITS: 2-4	VEGGIES: 3-5	WHOLE GRAIN SERVINGS: 6-11	PROTEIN: 4-6 OZ.	LIMIT FAT?	ALCOHOLIC BEVERAGES?	LIMIT "EMPTY" CARBS?
☐☐☐☐ ☐☐☐☐	☐☐ ☐☐	☐☐☐ ☐☐☐	☐☐☐☐ ☐☐☐☐ ☐☐☐	☐☐☐ ☐☐☐	Y N	Y N	Y N

WEEK OF:

GOALS FOR WEEK:

WEEKLY TOTAL: _____

YEAR-TO-DATE TOTAL:

In the absence of talent, there is no substitute for preparation.

MONDAY / Date:

Today's goal:

Training notes:

FUEL LOG

WATER: 6-8 x 8 OZ.	FRUITS: 2-4	VEGGIES: 3-5	WHOLE GRAIN SERVINGS: 6-11	PROTEIN: 4-6 OZ.	LIMIT FAT?	ALCOHOLIC BEVERAGES?	LIMIT "EMPTY" CARBS?
☐☐☐☐☐☐☐☐	☐☐☐☐	☐☐☐☐	☐☐☐☐☐☐	☐☐☐☐☐☐	Y N	Y N	Y N

WEATHER: SUN WIND RAIN CLOUDY SNOW TEMP: _____

Distance:
Time:
Heart Rate:
i-Rate (1-10)
X-Training:
Sleep Hours:
Weight:
Mood: ☺ ☺ ☹ Other

TUESDAY / Date:

Today's goal:

Training notes:

FUEL LOG

WATER: 6-8 x 8 OZ.	FRUITS: 2-4	VEGGIES: 3-5	WHOLE GRAIN SERVINGS: 6-11	PROTEIN: 4-6 OZ.	LIMIT FAT?	ALCOHOLIC BEVERAGES?	LIMIT "EMPTY" CARBS?
☐☐☐☐☐☐☐☐	☐☐☐☐	☐☐☐☐	☐☐☐☐☐☐	☐☐☐☐☐☐	Y N	Y N	Y N

WEATHER: SUN WIND RAIN CLOUDY SNOW TEMP: _____

Distance:
Time:
Heart Rate:
i-Rate (1-10)
X-Training:
Sleep Hours:
Weight:
Mood: ☺ ☺ ☹ Other

WEDNESDAY / Date:

Today's goal:

Training notes:

FUEL LOG

WATER: 6-8 x 8 OZ.	FRUITS: 2-4	VEGGIES: 3-5	WHOLE GRAIN SERVINGS: 6-11	PROTEIN: 4-6 OZ.	LIMIT FAT?	ALCOHOLIC BEVERAGES?	LIMIT "EMPTY" CARBS?
☐☐☐☐☐☐☐☐	☐☐☐☐	☐☐☐☐	☐☐☐☐☐☐	☐☐☐☐☐☐	Y N	Y N	Y N

WEATHER: SUN WIND RAIN CLOUDY SNOW TEMP: _____

Distance:
Time:
Heart Rate:
i-Rate (1-10)
X-Training:
Sleep Hours:
Weight:
Mood: ☺ ☺ ☹ Other

THURSDAY / Date:

Today's goal:

Training notes:

FUEL LOG

WATER: 6-8 x 8 OZ.	FRUITS: 2-4	VEGGIES: 3-5	WHOLE GRAIN SERVINGS: 6-11	PROTEIN: 4-6 OZ.	LIMIT FAT?	ALCOHOLIC BEVERAGES?	LIMIT "EMPTY" CARBS?
☐☐☐☐☐☐☐☐	☐☐☐☐	☐☐☐☐	☐☐☐☐☐☐	☐☐☐☐☐☐	Y N	Y N	Y N

WEATHER: SUN WIND RAIN CLOUDY SNOW TEMP: _____

Distance:
Time:
Heart Rate:
i-Rate (1-10)
X-Training:
Sleep Hours:
Weight:
Mood: ☺ ☺ ☹ Other

FRIDAY / Date: _____

Training notes: _____

Today's goal: _____

FUEL LOG

WATER: 6-8 × 8 OZ.	FRUITS: 2-4	VEGGIES: 3-5	WHOLE GRAIN SERVINGS: 6-11	PROTEIN: 4-6 OZ.	LIMIT FAT?	ALCOHOLIC BEVERAGES?	LIMIT "EMPTY" CARBS?
☐☐☐☐ ☐☐☐☐	☐☐ ☐☐	☐☐☐ ☐☐	☐☐☐☐ ☐☐☐☐	☐☐☐ ☐☐☐	Y N	Y N	Y N

WEATHER: SUN WIND RAIN CLOUDY SNOW TEMP: _____

Distance: _____
Time: _____
Heart Rate: _____
i-Rate (1-10): _____
X-Training: _____
Sleep Hours: _____
Weight: _____
Mood: ☺ ☺ ☹ ☹ Other

SATURDAY / Date: _____

Training notes: _____

Today's goal: _____

FUEL LOG

WATER: 6-8 × 8 OZ.	FRUITS: 2-4	VEGGIES: 3-5	WHOLE GRAIN SERVINGS: 6-11	PROTEIN: 4-6 OZ.	LIMIT FAT?	ALCOHOLIC BEVERAGES?	LIMIT "EMPTY" CARBS?
☐☐☐☐ ☐☐☐☐	☐☐ ☐☐	☐☐☐ ☐☐	☐☐☐☐ ☐☐☐☐	☐☐☐ ☐☐☐	Y N	Y N	Y N

WEATHER: SUN WIND RAIN CLOUDY SNOW TEMP: _____

Distance: _____
Time: _____
Heart Rate: _____
i-Rate (1-10): _____
X-Training: _____
Sleep Hours: _____
Weight: _____
Mood: ☺ ☺ ☹ ☹ Other

SUNDAY / Date: _____

Training notes: _____

Today's goal: _____

FUEL LOG

WATER: 6-8 × 8 OZ.	FRUITS: 2-4	VEGGIES: 3-5	WHOLE GRAIN SERVINGS: 6-11	PROTEIN: 4-6 OZ.	LIMIT FAT?	ALCOHOLIC BEVERAGES?	LIMIT "EMPTY" CARBS?
☐☐☐☐ ☐☐☐☐	☐☐ ☐☐	☐☐☐ ☐☐	☐☐☐☐ ☐☐☐☐	☐☐☐ ☐☐☐	Y N	Y N	Y N

WEATHER: SUN WIND RAIN CLOUDY SNOW TEMP: _____

Distance: _____
Time: _____
Heart Rate: _____
i-Rate (1-10): _____
X-Training: _____
Sleep Hours: _____
Weight: _____
Mood: ☺ ☺ ☹ ☹ Other

WEEK OF:

GOALS FOR WEEK:

WEEKLY TOTAL: _____

YEAR-TO-DATE TOTAL:

Every day you are your own hero. Celebrate who you are.

MONDAY / Date:

Today's goal:

Training notes:

Distance:
Time:
Heart Rate:
i-Rate (1-10)
X-Training:
Sleep Hours:
Weight:
Mood: ☺ ☺ ☹ Other

FUEL LOG

WATER: 6-8 x 8 OZ.	FRUITS: 2-4	VEGGIES: 3-5	WHOLE GRAIN SERVINGS: 6-11	PROTEIN: 4-6 OZ.	LIMIT FAT?	ALCOHOLIC BEVERAGES?	LIMIT "EMPTY" CARBS?
☐☐☐☐ ☐☐☐☐	☐☐ ☐☐	☐☐ ☐☐	☐☐☐☐ ☐☐☐☐	☐☐☐ ☐☐	Y N	Y N	Y N

WEATHER:
SUN WIND RAIN CLOUDY SNOW
TEMP:

TUESDAY / Date:

Today's goal:

Training notes:

Distance:
Time:
Heart Rate:
i-Rate (1-10)
X-Training:
Sleep Hours:
Weight:
Mood: ☺ ☺ ☹ Other

FUEL LOG

WATER: 6-8 x 8 OZ.	FRUITS: 2-4	VEGGIES: 3-5	WHOLE GRAIN SERVINGS: 6-11	PROTEIN: 4-6 OZ.	LIMIT FAT?	ALCOHOLIC BEVERAGES?	LIMIT "EMPTY" CARBS?
☐☐☐☐ ☐☐☐☐	☐☐ ☐☐	☐☐ ☐☐	☐☐☐☐ ☐☐☐☐	☐☐☐ ☐☐	Y N	Y N	Y N

WEATHER:
SUN WIND RAIN CLOUDY SNOW
TEMP:

WEDNESDAY / Date:

Today's goal:

Training notes:

Distance:
Time:
Heart Rate:
i-Rate (1-10)
X-Training:
Sleep Hours:
Weight:
Mood: ☺ ☺ ☹ Other

FUEL LOG

WATER: 6-8 x 8 OZ.	FRUITS: 2-4	VEGGIES: 3-5	WHOLE GRAIN SERVINGS: 6-11	PROTEIN: 4-6 OZ.	LIMIT FAT?	ALCOHOLIC BEVERAGES?	LIMIT "EMPTY" CARBS?
☐☐☐☐ ☐☐☐☐	☐☐ ☐☐	☐☐ ☐☐	☐☐☐☐ ☐☐☐☐	☐☐☐ ☐☐	Y N	Y N	Y N

WEATHER:
SUN WIND RAIN CLOUDY SNOW
TEMP:

THURSDAY / Date:

Today's goal:

Training notes:

Distance:
Time:
Heart Rate:
i-Rate (1-10)
X-Training:
Sleep Hours:
Weight:
Mood: ☺ ☺ ☹ Other

FUEL LOG

WATER: 6-8 x 8 OZ.	FRUITS: 2-4	VEGGIES: 3-5	WHOLE GRAIN SERVINGS: 6-11	PROTEIN: 4-6 OZ.	LIMIT FAT?	ALCOHOLIC BEVERAGES?	LIMIT "EMPTY" CARBS?
☐☐☐☐ ☐☐☐☐	☐☐ ☐☐	☐☐ ☐☐	☐☐☐☐ ☐☐☐☐	☐☐☐ ☐☐	Y N	Y N	Y N

WEATHER:
SUN WIND RAIN CLOUDY SNOW
TEMP:

FRIDAY / Date: _____

Training notes: _____

Today's goal: _____

Distance: _____
Time: _____
Heart Rate: _____
i-Rate (1-10): _____
X-Training: _____
Sleep Hours: _____
Weight: _____
Mood: ☺ ☺ ☹ Other

WEATHER:
SUN WIND
RAIN CLOUDY
SNOW
TEMP: _____

FUEL LOG

WATER: 6-8 x 8 oz.	FRUITS: 2-4	VEGGIES: 3-5	WHOLE GRAIN SERVINGS: 6-11	PROTEIN: 4-6 oz.	LIMIT FAT?	ALCOHOLIC BEVERAGES?	LIMIT "EMPTY" CARBS?
☐☐☐☐ ☐☐☐☐	☐☐ ☐☐	☐☐ ☐☐	☐☐☐☐☐ ☐☐☐☐☐☐	☐☐ ☐☐	Y N	Y N	Y N

SATURDAY / Date: _____

Training notes: _____

Today's goal: _____

Distance: _____
Time: _____
Heart Rate: _____
i-Rate (1-10): _____
X-Training: _____
Sleep Hours: _____
Weight: _____
Mood: ☺ ☺ ☹ Other

WEATHER:
SUN WIND
RAIN CLOUDY
SNOW
TEMP: _____

FUEL LOG

WATER: 6-8 x 8 oz.	FRUITS: 2-4	VEGGIES: 3-5	WHOLE GRAIN SERVINGS: 6-11	PROTEIN: 4-6 oz.	LIMIT FAT?	ALCOHOLIC BEVERAGES?	LIMIT "EMPTY" CARBS?
☐☐☐☐ ☐☐☐☐	☐☐ ☐☐	☐☐ ☐☐	☐☐☐☐☐ ☐☐☐☐☐☐	☐☐ ☐☐	Y N	Y N	Y N

SUNDAY / Date: _____

Training notes: _____

Today's goal: _____

Distance: _____
Time: _____
Heart Rate: _____
i-Rate (1-10): _____
X-Training: _____
Sleep Hours: _____
Weight: _____
Mood: ☺ ☺ ☹ Other

WEATHER:
SUN WIND
RAIN CLOUDY
SNOW
TEMP: _____

FUEL LOG

WATER: 6-8 x 8 oz.	FRUITS: 2-4	VEGGIES: 3-5	WHOLE GRAIN SERVINGS: 6-11	PROTEIN: 4-6 oz.	LIMIT FAT?	ALCOHOLIC BEVERAGES?	LIMIT "EMPTY" CARBS?
☐☐☐☐ ☐☐☐☐	☐☐ ☐☐	☐☐ ☐☐	☐☐☐☐☐ ☐☐☐☐☐☐	☐☐ ☐☐	Y N	Y N	Y N

WEEK OF: _____

GOALS FOR WEEK: _____

WEEKLY TOTAL: _____

YEAR-TO-DATE TOTAL: _____

The miracle is that I had the courage to start.

NOTES, GOALS, TRENDS

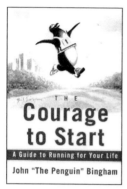

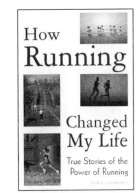
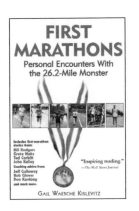

John "The Penguin" Bingham

He's been called the Pied Piper of the second running boom-and for good reason. Since his column, "The Chronicles," started in *Runner's World* magazine in 1996, John "The Penguin" Bingham has become one of the running community's most popular and recognized personalities.

Through his books and his *RW* column, now published in every English-language edition of *RW*, Bingham has inspired a generation of new runners to find joy in walking, running, and racing. His transformation from a life of "sedentary confinement" to marathoner has become a model for people of all ages and abilities.

Once an overweight couch potato, he looked midlife in the face—and got moving. Since then, he has participated in several dozen marathons and hundreds of 5K and 10K races. Bingham says, "Through running, I create myself as I have always wanted to be. Nothing in my experience was as powerful as crossing the finish line of my first race. With that single step, I overcame a lifetime of unkept promises to myself." In a self-effacing and humorous manner, Bingham delivers his message of hope and inspiration to people who've been running for a week or a lifetime.

Coach Jenny Hadfield

Jenny Hadfield is a fitness expert, coach, and co-owner of Chicago Endurance Sports. She is best known for empowering people to move outside their self-perceived limits and reach for higher ground. More than just a coach, Jenny has become a trusted guide, mentor, and good friend on the journey to the finish line. She is known for her personal and comprehensive approach to training. Jenny has been coaching for over 10 years, is a Boston-qualified marathon runner and three-time Eco-Challenge competitor (the world's toughest endurance race). Jenny is the co-author of *Marathoning for Mortals: A Regular Person's Guide to the Joy of Walk and Running a Half and Full Marathon.*